IN SEARCH OF OPERA

PRINCETON STUDIES IN OPERA

CAROLYN ABBATE AND ROGER PARKER
Series Editors

IN SEARCH OF OPERA

CAROLYN ABBATE

PRINCETON UNIVERSITY PRESS
Princeton and Oxford

Published by Princeton University Press,
41 William Street, Princeton, New Jersey 08540

In the United Kingdom: Princeton University Press,
3 Market Place, Woodstock, Oxfordshire OX20 1SY

Library of Congress Cataloging-in-Publication Data

Abbate, Carolyn.
    In search of opera / Carolyn Abbate.
        p.   cm.—(Princeton studies in opera)
    ISBN 0-691-09003-3 (alk. paper)
    1. Opera.   2. Music—Philosophy and aesthetics.   I. Title.   II. Series.

    ML3858 .A19   2001
    782.1—dc21   2001036271

British Library Cataloging-in-Publication Data is available

This book has been composed in 10.8/15 Dante
Printed on acid-free paper.

www.pup.princeton.edu

Printed in the United States of America

10 9 8 7 6 5 4 3 2 1

∞ CONTENTS

v

⚮ PREFACE

This book explores two extremes that may seem irreconcilable. At one extreme are a series of operatic moments that attempt something impossible: to represent music that, by the very terms of the fictions proposing it, remains beyond expression. Such music is so magical or fugitive that it escapes cages: we never hear it. At the other extreme, there are opera's "facts of life"—live performance, grounded and intensely material, with its laboring singers, breathing that becomes singing, staging, interpretation, and mortality. I have sought the connections between the two, the metaphysical flight and the fall to the earth. They come together as a paradoxical amalgam—one could even say, as a quintessentially operatic phenomenon. The notion that opera plays with representations of transcendence is not new. In earlier writings, I suggested that there are schisms in Romantic opera—especially the break between onstage songs and "everything else"—that reflect among other things a boundary between material and transcendent worlds, and ways to bridge the two.[1] This came to seem too simple and homogenous, encouraging too strongly a sense that "everything else" captures a transcendent object, when "everything else" is, rather, one aspect of representing a distinction. What began to interest me was something more radical, music that literally is not present in the work: a musical object to which, as I saw it, the listener is directed, without that object ever being revealed.

To write about music that is not present, rather implied, to see the music that is there as a pointer toward this other, may seem quite absurd, too aristocratic or abstract, futile, or may seem to embrace Romantic and Symbolist aesthetics, rather than dissect them as a historical curiosity.[2] And still, the gesture was insistent, so that refusing to question its presence appeared perverse. I wondered, for instance, whether the odd genius of Wagner's later music might not involve getting quite close to disclosing what is being concealed, or at least (of course) creating that impression. And perhaps the ineffability of music (or apparent ineffability)—the commonplace that music escapes philosophy, that musical works stand in oblique relationships to the force fields of culture or history, or to verbal description, and thus inspire many writers including myself to gnomic or paradoxical formulations—has been expressed within music by such gestures of concealment or flight. That imputes to music so much philosophy that, ironically, music trumps philosophy one more time. An inclination to praise the ineffable may be the high form of the banal impulse to rely on mystery. Mystery itself, however, has an ethical dimension, as Vladimir Jankélévitch points out in his critique of Enlightenment:

> There is the mystery and there is the secret. The thing that is secret, like the riddle of the Sphinx, is nothing more than a puzzle, whose entire problematic consists of convoluted terms: the baroque maze is the ideal type. In its negative form, as the arcane, "secret" is simply that which is refused to the profane and reserved for initiates, that which must not be spoken of, but which is already known to certain privileged individuals . . . and where the secret isolates, because it is a secret for someone in relation to someone else (or for one clan in relation to another, or one mystic in relation to another), the mystery, the self-contained secret—that is, universally, eternally and naturally mysterious, unknowable for all, no longer taboo or subject to interdiction—this mystery is a principle of fraternal sympathy, of shared humility.[3]

This goes beyond truisms that freedom for one subject creates slavery for another, or that enlightenment creates a class of the excluded, the - unenlightened. The ethical aspect, the issue of humility, should not be forgotten.

One might therefore say that contemplating the ineffability of music entails seeking out places where opera posits inaccessible music beyond what we can hear, as a specific sign for that general elusiveness. But it also means choosing to write about music in certain ways: no pins, no jagged edges. When musical works are required to represent pure structure or autonomous discourse, detached from the social conditions of their production and reception, something has been lost—no less, however, when they are fashioned into breathtakingly straightforward reflections of dramas, novels, class structures, nationalities, sexual politics, contemporary literary strategies or genres, into language (without words), or into something that has been waiting for the divining rod of post-structuralist knowledge. This is not because such arguments cannot or should not be made, nor because the possibility that musical works reflect social reality is foreclosed, nor because poetry, language, or stage action do not inflect the composition and interpretation of music, nor because music is not sometimes a beautiful ornament. The suffering and the loss devolve upon the sharp objects in the writing, and this is one reason why much academic discourse on music seems resistant to the very object it wishes to honor. The greatest exception I know is Jankélévitch himself, a philosopher whose luminous writing on an "unreal chimera" sees music as "engendering both metaphysical and moral problems." This is not just mystification: in that simple "both," there is so much to consider.[4]

When we write about music, what object are we honoring? This question is a catapult to my other extreme—opera as embodied, very far from being in any way metaphysical. To write about opera, to represent it in fiction, or as a metaphor in poetry, or as a figure in philosophy, is to add to the architecture of its necropolis. This is ironic, because the first and enduring bases for a passion about opera are not operatic works in the abstract, as intentional objects, but operas and their singers in performances. One could ask whether opera exists outside the performance that creates it in the only form of material being it can possess. The reason we put opera into video boxes or on film or inscribe it on LPs or CDs or other disks and cylinders is that we need to use "dead arts" to "rescue the ephemeral and perishing art as the only one alive."[5] A performance is "the only work that counts" and paradoxically is "not a work at all."[6]

By invoking the distinction between a work and its performance (between the transcendent and the material, in yet another form), I am referring to a longstanding debate on the ontology of music without citing philosophical pedigrees, or to the fine degrees to which a musical work-concept can be tuned. Lydia Goehr's *The Imaginary Museum of Musical Works* has already delved into nomenclature, pedigrees, alternate tunings, and most importantly what may be at stake ideologically in this debate.[7] Status plays a part in scholarly tastes for works as transcendent objects. The material forms of musical works (scores on the one hand, performances on the other) are embodiments, and that which is purely physical and/or ephemeral is conventionally dismissed in Western intellectual culture. Someone who dealt with a score as a physical object, rather than reading its notation as the trace of a work, might seem quite demented or radically unconcerned with the classic givens of scholarship. Someone who analyzes a specific operatic staging, performance, or recording appears to traffic in what is least important, even though many see such things as critical, as the only "music" worth worrying about. For, as Roman Ingarden and many others have argued, the real form of a musical work is the imagined form, marked with acoustic presence and unfolded in time, hence much more than the score and, unlike any performance, not dying away. This work is permanent, untied to material embodiments. Bad performances cannot mar it, and good performances do not enhance it. A temporal sense is immanent in every such work, which nonetheless has a "wholeness" that transcends linear time. Scores—as objects—are just doorstops. Performance is a spectacle of labor, marked by mortality: it sinks "into the past," from which it never returns.[8]

The idea of mortality, of course, with its undertone of mourning, tells us that anxieties about status alone cannot explain this affection for the virtual work. Opera in a curious way needs a defense against performance (including staging) and not just against bad performances, because in defending opera against performance, we defend it against the sense that something is being lost to us.

Musical performance has hardly been absent from academic writing on music, but the roles it plays have been delineated in precise ways. In philosophy, performance can be an object of subzero analytic scrutiny.[9] The history of classical music has been more a history of composers and compositions, and less a history of singers, instrumentalists, or the cultural contexts of performance. Criticism that focuses on great classical works or their reception may deal with performances as supplementary readings, which either affirm an enduring and immanent property or risk dismissal as illegible, or untrue. That musical works acquire alternative histories—identities constituted by licentious or excessive performances and (for opera) adaptations and stagings—is a threat many scholars regard with horror: one need only look at reactions to radical mises-en-scène. The threat seemed greater still after the advent of recording, since at that point an alternative history can attain permanent material status just like a score: one could begin to "mistake" such a history for better truths.[10] If there is a persistent intellectual tendency to think of classical music abstractly, there is thus a related tendency to regard performances as the faithful or unfaithful embodiments of a template, and to take critical interpretation of musical works—as far as it gives a nod to performance— as a guide to playing or singing those works.[11] Although musicologists may focus on performance as an activity, speculation within this domain about the ontological status of musical works remains unusual, as do doubts that musical works have a stable identity. Performers' duties are thus tacitly restricted to discovery of givens. This attitude is hardly new: its historical incarnations reach back to the eighteenth century. Pursuit of immanent structures or meanings in musical works, coupled with a belief that this creates pocket guides to good performances, can make scholarly studies of performance seem extra-planetary to professional performers. To me the related claim that "every interpretation [of a musical work] is . . . when written as analysis or criticism, construable as a [mere] set of 'instructions' for a performance" seems inscrutable.[12]

All the exceptions, all those who have escaped these limitations, deserve high praise, though I will cite only a very few individuals. Goehr herself has exposed a false distinction between the extra-musical and the musical by turning from "works" to performances as "expressive acts."[13] Franz Liszt—as performer-composer—has been a radioactive node in Jankélévitch's writings on verve, rhapsody, and virtuosity, in Charles Rosen's writings on Liszt's unstable compositions as captured improvisa- tions, and in Dana Gooley's history of the social meanings ascribed to Lisztian performances.[14] All three write against a certain grain, against prescription and proscription. Richard Leppert describes visual represen-

tations of musical performance with immense élan in his history of attitudes toward music making.[15] John Rosselli has investigated the careers of
opera singers, and operatic performance as a social phenomenon, joined
by Mary Ann Smart and Karen Henson, who have stressed the part singers
play in shaping operatic texts and their reception.[16] Performance becomes
central to criticism in other ways, through investigations of antique practices. Yet Richard Taruskin has deconstructed this institution by delving
systematically into the means by which contemporary performance styles
strive for legitimacy with fantastic appeals to historical authority.[17] The
debate on authenticity or faithfulness is likely to continue: legitimacy is a
powerful selling point in the marketplace, and the arguments about it
involve quasi-religious dilemmas.[18] Off in another corner entirely, Terry
Castle and Wayne Koestenbaum write as enthralled listeners: for them,
the imaginary work does not count for much. They use sensual praise of
operatic singers and their singing as an alienating gesture, to bring us up
short against our assumptions about what we should discuss when we talk
about music and how we write about it.[19] Their straightforward auto-
biographical fervor has nonetheless inspired dispiriting imitations by less
subtle writers.

I have chosen to mention only briefly specific singers or nights at the
opera. That elaborate rhapsodies to singers or to actual performances are
largely absent from this book may well seem a great irony, even a fatal
defect. But if one's impulse is to honor performance, to push thinking
about music toward the strange moment when music is realized, created,
and at that instant dies away, I think that this might also be served by other
means, and not surprisingly, my means are abstract. Performance is a phenomenon through which music attains life, and suddenly, in the eighteenth century, this seems to become a fraught idea. Images of musical
performance in fiction or film since that time, as well as philosophical
reflections on its nature, deal with issues such as the antagonism between
composers and performers but also move beyond this particular melodrama (chapter 1, on Orpheus). In the angry tango of diva and maestro,
the maestro is furious because musical power flows from performances,
and without them (and the diva), the "work" in some sense has no being.
If, as Goehr has suggested, the very concept of a transcendent work arises

at about this time, then what arises in tandem wants to undermine that concept, sometimes with violent force.

Performance—this was the crux of my belief—is so fundamental, so large and overpowering, so basic to a love of music, and can seem so threatening, that music turns to stare it in the face. Rather than accepting musical performances as ephemeral reflections of musical works, I toyed with a different idea. Perhaps it is the works that are the aftershocks, lingering shapes that give voice to an uncanny phenomenon. Acoustic images of performance press into musical works themselves; more specifically, opera takes into account the very means by which operatic works turn into sung reality.

These images assume various forms. There is something as ordinary as the self-conscious song on stage, an operatic commonplace and, for me, an enduring obsession. Less commonplace, however, are songs without any accompaniment, operatic moments at which everything except the human voice falls away. In opera, this is a phenomenon of the years after 1800 and might be seen as a form of hyperrealism, for shepherds in vernal landscapes seldom carry their orchestras with them. Since the singer has become the sole source of all musical sound, the gesture grounds music physically in a very intense way, creating an exemplary *corps sonore*, a resonant body on stage. However, in Wagner's hands (chapter 3, on *Tannhäuser* and *Parsifal*), this device also engenders a regression toward primal sound. Primal sound is a strange thing, at once transcendent and low, lying by nature and in its aggressive simplicity beyond representation. This was in fact one of the places where the incommensurable extremes come together.

The imprint of performance can take less obviously self-referential forms, reflecting instead a channel or network—the paths by which inscription becomes live sound, as well as what is lost or kept in that process. If musical works are phantoms inhabiting a network connecting composer, inscription, performer, interpretation, realization, and reproduction, relationships within this space are full of antagonism. Since singers can and often do improvise, composers seek ways to control them, hoping for the invaluable puppet who neither adds nor subtracts, and more than this, who is physically galvanized by a compositional utterance. The idea that a musical work or master voice physically animates and controls the performer's inert body is as rich in complications as it is macabre, and as Jankélévitch points out, is something few might wish to see: "a human being makes use of song, and does not want song to make use of him."[20] In opera, certain arias can convey a sense not that they are being sung, but that they instead are reaching out to give life to a moribund body, making it sing. One could go further still: perhaps it is the musical works that are alive, and we who are dead; perhaps musical pieces seek to manifest themselves repeatedly in the world and propel us into motion at their whim, whenever we are required for their purposes. They conspire. The sonatinas train children to become apt media, encouraged in this by sonatas, who will need large hands and strong bodies—the adults those children will become.

This hand-within-the-puppet effect, of course, raises the specter of mechanism, the performer as an automaton. Mechanical musical devices solve the problem of the capricious performer by collapsing an elaborate performance network into a singular technological artifact. Such devices seem to embody a kind of utopia: with them, a musical work reproduces itself without a human medium, resulting in what in principle should be a perfect facsimile of compositional thought. This utopia is false, and one can trace the arc in which a promise of perfection made in the mid–eighteenth century is both withdrawn (chapter 2, on *The Magic Flute*) and mined for all its ambivalence (chapter 5, on Ravel). Musical representations of mechanical music are representations of performance at its most disquieting. In Ravel's works, however, the musical gestures that reveal mechanism also conceal it, in acoustic double exposures, as entombed sound. In this way, now more tenuously, the materiality of performance (and with machines, it is material to the highest degree) once more collides with the unreal and transcendent, that which one cannot ever have.

There is, finally, the simple physical force of music in performance. Regretting the mortality of such sound, we preserve it imperfectly by inscribing it as a score, or in recordings: our scriptomania, so we suppose, was a first symptom of our phonophilia. Operatic works, however, reflect this sound and hopes for its preservation in ways that are fabulous and of course doomed to fail: they are dreams. Disembodied singing is another operatic cliché—all those voices from heaven, from hell, from the wings, from trapdoors and catwalks. Disembodiment conventionally conveys authority, loudness that is not physical. That is why dead fathers and prophets sing this way. Once a voice floats, however, it may also come to appear meaningless or dubious. Severing voice from its physical ground cuts a sign free of its signified, and the consequences can seem sublime, but not always (chapter 4, on *Pelléas*).

Yet to think in completely literal ways of detaching voice from body—the master symbol being Orpheus's decapitation—is to imagine infinite resonance, as if a performance were never ending. Opera's primal scene, Orfeo's big aria in Monteverdi's opera, represents sheer sonic force—performance as loud, powerful sound—and simultaneously proposes phantom singing that will never be known: the fall to earth and the flight, as one. Papageno's singing and his magic bell sounds, which come together to engender a chimerical half-man–half-instrument-performer, play out a similar collision between ground and transcendence.

Preambles have a responsibility to provide signposts, and signposts make me anxious because they can come to seem like the things whose design they resemble, pins and nails. Despite a tendency to excess, I have suppressed details in accounting for this book as a whole. But what I hope to convey is a fascination that in fact pays tribute to a small number of unforgettable live performances—mostly operas—at which I have been present over the past twenty-five years. These were not limited to highly polished interpretations by great singers or instrumentalists. Nor were they virtuoso displays, the type that foreground a specific performer and his or her personality and stage presence. These two kinds of experience represent the poles described by Goehr as "the perfect performance of music" and "the perfect musical performance." Goehr points out that one reflects an Apollonian ideal of knowledge, the other a Dionysian ideal of doing, openness, and spontaneity, and she sets out their claims to legitimacy.[21]

My performances are hard to fit into either category. What they had in common is difficult to grasp or elaborate. They conveyed the impression that a work was being created at that moment, "before one's eyes," never seeming to invite comparison between what was being heard and some lurking double, some transcendent work to which they had to measure up. In other words, they never produced the sinking feeling that one was in the presence of *Werktreue*, that "this is a good performance of that." Though they were performances of pieces I knew well, the template had been forgotten. Suggesting that what one heard was simultaneously being invented and fading away, they produced a strange undertone, inviting held breath as if that could arrest all loss. At the same time they were distinctly, exaggeratedly material, directing attention to the physical reality of the musicians and the sounds they create, and one's place as a listener or performer within that sound. There were acoustic irregularities or odd visual angles, all sorts of surplus allied to unique circumstances. Revisited in memory, they have often directed what I write about music. They raise an interesting question: how mortal is performance, if it can resonate this powerfully, this long?

IN SEARCH OF OPERA

1

∞

ORPHEUS.
ONE LAST
PERFORMANCE

Remember the death of Orpheus: attacked by crazy women, dismembered, he is finally decapitated, the worst indignity a singer could suffer. Crazy women throw his body parts in all directions. But his head, accompanied (in a new sense) by his lyre, floats down a river, its mouth still open in song. The journey by water ends at Lesbos, and as soon as the head washes up, a serpent approaches, wanting to bite the mouth and the eyes. Here Apollo steps in, freezes the snake into stone, and (in one source, Hygenius's *Astronomica*) makes a celestial happy end, placing the lyre but not the head among the constellations. Orpheus's death and dismemberment tell of poetry's survival and dispersal through nature: in the "Sonnets to Orpheus," Rilke contemplates the lamenting head as a miracle. Yet that dismemberment also entails a split between singing voice and human body in terms that suggest the work of those accustomed to butchery.[1] A terrible physical reality is precondition for the miracle—coexisting with the miracle, side by side. To be complacent about the head, to say it is just a metaphor, thus may reflect willed blindness to the awful aspects of Orpheus's fate, and to a symbolic force that is allied with horror, and not with poetry alone.[2]

Orpheus's life in opera began with classical Latin narratives, interpreted by Poliziano in his pastoral play (ca. 1480) and by Striggio for Monteverdi's opera, in 1607. These "two Orfeos" are heavy structural elements in accounts of opera's birth, said to prefigure operatic librettos on the one hand, and launch opera into history on the other.[3] Virgil and Ovid gave librettists three chances to catch Orpheus singing, and two were regularly adapted for operatic purposes. The first is Orpheus's appeal to the King of Hell during the rescue of Eurydice, a song tailormade for that occasion.[4] After he looks back and loses Eurydice, Orpheus retreats in mourning to the hills of Thrace, where he sings and plays. Trees of all kinds and then animals and birds come to hear his singing, and this concert became a common motif in European painting. He unfortunately also attracts the attention of the Bacchantes, who are thirsty for his death. His singing magically deflects their stones and spears, and the women can kill him in the end because they have sheer volume on their side, drowning out his voice with flutes and drums.

The third song is the one sung by the head, and everybody left it alone.[5]

Opera freely embraced the other acoustic image associated with Orpheus's death, the Dionysian symphony of the crazy women. Striggio included it in his 1607 libretto, in which act 5 closes with a long song for the Bacchantes.[6] Orpheus does not perish on the spot, yet the Bacchantes allude to his future: "flown from this avenging arm is our impious adversary, the Thracian Orpheus, despiser of our high worth. He will not escape." Monteverdi, of course, ended up writing music for another ending, in which the Bacchantes are nowhere to be found. Apollo appears and escorts his son into heaven, and surviving shepherds do a dance. In Haydn's *Orfeo ed Euridice* (also called *L'anima del filosofo*, composed in 1791), singing Bacchantes force Orpheus to drink poison; his life "ebbs away" rather languidly, and his corpse remains intact. The Bacchantes are punished when a storm disperses them: a fitting end for such women, we are given to understand. The women's singing and dancing provides librettists and composers with an ending that is satisfying as musical theater, even if dubious in conventional ethical terms.

Orpheus's death and his floating head did not become a common motif in European art until the end of the nineteenth century, when fin de siècle bards of exhaustion find his demise an apt metaphor for their condition.[7] By 1948, Stravinsky was ready to put his dismemberment on stage and give musical presence to its violence. Symbolist painters recalled his decapitation in many ways, in works that share one feature: the head is silent. Gustave Moreau's famous *Orphée* (1865) shows an unworried nymph gazing at Orpheus's extraordinarily peaceful head, which she has collected on his lyre (see fig. 1.1). Along with a convenient drapery, her hand hides any whipsawing tendons or severed arteries, and the closed mouth looks as if it never sang at all. But mouth and eyes are eloquent nonetheless, since, devoid of trauma, they lull the observer into a delusion. A dark shape floating off the bottom of the lyre is a rock that could be the torso and legs that are not there, a wish for wholeness in which the artist denies the torn body with a shadow, and the singing head with a silent one. Doubts arise only after one's eye goes further, encountering the Dionysians on the hill, and the flutes at their lips.

Moreau's reshuffling of Orpheus's fate acknowledges what librettists had realized for centuries: that postmortem song by the floating head is a frightful idea. As Herod says to Salome in Strauss's opera, "The head of a man that is cut from his body is a sickening sight." Sickening, but mesmerizing nonetheless. In Virgil, the head is rather eloquent, lamenting and calling out "Eurydice" with "its voice and icy tongue," and then repeating the name, which is echoed by the riverbank. Ovid's head is less energetic, less clearly musical: "a marvel! While they floated in midstream, the lyre gave forth some mournful notes, mournfully the lifeless tongue murmured, mournfully the banks replied."[8] One wonders how the head continues to sing. That is magic, but what sort? Anatomical magic, discharged organic electricity dying away as mindless babbling? Or is the head inspired from outside, breathed into, before it finally falls silent, like an aeolian harp? Those possibilities are separate, distantly related images of voice and authority in operatic singing.

The image is, then, not merely sickening, just as it is not merely allegorical. Orpheus's last song accesses a sense that is rare and peculiar yet familiar, the taste of something strange but instantly recognizable, the complex emotion experienced during a dream of the dead. The person is there, in the dream, smiling, perhaps speaking, and there is something

Figure 1.1. Moreau, *Orphée*.

joyful about the encounter. Yet even as we believe we are miraculously in the presence of the resurrected—of continued singing—we always know that he or she is dead still, that whatever the dead person is saying is being said by the dreamer, that a moment of dissolution will arrive.

What the head sings is also no less musical than what Orpheus otherwise sang; indeed, Ovid exclaims that the head and the lyre are a "marvel," and maybe he is suggesting that Orpheus's premortem performances belonged to a different category. If librettists and composers appear to turn a deaf ear to the singing head, however, the reasons are obvious. Brooding on this last gasp of one's prize doppelgänger—the founding father of the opera business—cannot be comfortable. Bodiless warbling heads are unsettling for professional reasons. Even in Poliziano's play, which ends with the head brought on in triumph after an offstage dismemberment, the body part is silent.[9] In the same way, Orpheus's last number, wished away by Moreau, was suppressed in the operatic versions of his myth. Nevertheless, the sound is a wholly operatic motif, one could even say *the* operatic motif in his myth.

Put bluntly: the singing head represents the uncanny aspects of musical performance, operatic performance in particular, precisely because one cannot say how it sings, who is in charge, who is the source of the utterance, and what is the nature of the medium through which musical ideas become physically present as sound. In this, Orpheus's head serves as a master symbol for the questions that are central to this book, and that arise not only with respect to opera, but in thinking about music in general. It summarizes the complications of the performance network: its instability, the deadness implicit in any object that has been animated by music, the living noise in the channels that run between compositional thought and the structures inscribed in a score, the creation of music by performers, and the sound that strikes the listener.

But if the head is a master symbol for performance, it also stands for several related phenomena whose significance is less global. The head represents singing that travels far from the body in which it originated, as a physical object that is cousin to a classic poetic image, the echo. Postmortem resonance suggests as well an immense original sonic force, so huge that it continues in a body part. Thus one could see the head as an expression of an opera singer's dream: sing at such volume, with such power, that the voice travels great distances and is heard everywhere. Listening ears are unable to escape. This dream unites mechanics (volume, resonance, and sound transmission) with the metaphysical (song's mythic capacity to "move" human thoughts and passions).[10] The juxtaposition of metaphysics with the material unleashes huge energies in certain librettists and opera composers.

As a minor symbol, Orpheus's postmortem singing summarizes the authority conventionally ascribed to disembodiment.[11] What is sung is, quite literally, music that "doesn't come from" the human body. Disembodied voice—seen less literally and brutally—is a voice originating from an unseen locus of energy and thought, and it has distinct powers, especially as represented in opera and film. If philosophical writings on voice have established a metaphysics of presence in Western thought, there is a powerful metaphysics of absence that runs alongside it, a tendency, at least before modernist disenchantment redefined the terms, to associate the voice with no visible point of origin with omniscience. Such voices are considered divine, or at least supernatural, free of ordinary encumbrances.

One might even see such music as cerebral, as merely hypothetical, or impossible, excluded from representation by virtue of its outrageous magic. Orpheus's singing head could stand for a musical work as a transcendent object, as opposed to that object's embodiment in any given performance.[12] Most importantly, opera itself could be regarded as a response to an outlandish question—how does the dead object continue to sing? Perhaps because Apollo plays it like some ghastly instrument. If so, it is a medium that, though dead, always has the capacity to be brought back to life: an instrument, or a performer. Or, the head sings because the sheer physical resonance of Orpheus's premortem songs endures. As a master symbol, one with several implications in its orbit, Orpheus's last performance reflects on the nature of musical execution in general, as well as the forms of musical power and how such power is construed.

I

Orpheus's head is a musical instrument, an object given life as long as a master plays it. This notion of the "instrument" can be broadened to include the performer, who might similarly be construed as a medium, channeling musical thoughts from elsewhere, "played" by an inscription, or by a musical work. Dead instrument and live performer might seem to be quite different, but collapsing them, in particular when the performer is female—hence assumed more amenable to manipulation, paralysis, or control—is a familiar Romantic cliché. E.T.A. Hoffmann's "Councillor Krespel," where a violin is linked to the body and fate of a human soprano, is one of many literary versions of the tale.[13]

While such narratives might seem historically limited to European Romanticism or the Gothic, the gesture that dismisses the (female) performer as mere instrument is in fact extraordinarily resilient. Joseph Mankiewicz's 1950 film *All About Eve* has a scene where actress Margo Channing (Bette Davis) gets into a fight with Lloyd Richards (Hugh Marlowe), the playwright who has written several works for her to star in. He dismisses her loudly as "nothing more than a voice and a body," thus cutting her up nicely into component parts. This salvo, getting rid of the actress as any kind of whole, is designed to expose just how fully *his* master voice animates *her* fragments and has always done so. Just to make sure she has gotten the point, his parting shot goes even further: "It is time for the piano to realize that it did not write the concerto!" His insult—she is not even the pianist, just the instrument—pushes her further back, making her the dead material medium of wood and strings. The irony, of course, is that the film never shows us one of Lloyd's plays, except as fragments, and that Margo Channing as embodied by Davis is so vivid, omnipresent, resonant, and whole that she might be said to be the film, in any scene in which she appears. Lloyd's parting shot is weak, yet it summarizes the persistence of a claim that while musical instruments are truly inanimate, and performers live human beings, the two can meet each other in any symbol that combines deadness and life.

Perhaps *All About Eve* does a playful take on Orpheus by alluding to the split between "a voice and a body," in Lloyd's intimation that performers are dead objects. But even if there is no direct reference, the terms by which the woman is made into the piano are a reminder that Orpheus's fate appears to involve a symbolic feminization. Indeed, taken as instrument-medium, Orpheus's head recalls another category of performer associated with Apollo, the priestesses of the oracle at Delphi, through whom Apollo announced his prophecies. As Giulia Sissa points out, these women were seen as "bodies in tune and capable, like a musical instrument, of a full and faithful rendition"; but once removed from their proximity to Apollo, the instrument-women remained "hermetically sealed, untouchable, and silent."[14] No one was playing them.

Such women have no voice of their own and are furthermore not capable of reading symbols and announcing their import. Rather, "a woman's body becomes a locus, a wall of glass, a blank page; speech does not find a symbolic order; it shines like a beacon."[15] Imagining that a transcendent voice speaks through female bodies and vocal cords means that certain protections, certain mental firewalls, must be in place, assuring listeners that the women are neither misinterpreting the message nor doing the unthinkable, inventing the message on their own. Sissa describes these firewalls in some detail, visual and literary fantasies that tended to erase the priestess. Such fantasies struggle to eliminate the threat of inauthenticity. By making the priestess's body invisible, they engineer a "double absence: of a subject who was not herself when words were uttered through her mouth, and of a female body that was not present when the god who inhabited it borrowed its voice."[16]

Still, no firewall can eliminate the fact that such media are not really dead and as the only source for Apollo's voice cannot be wholly erased. Thus Sissa, who prefers to recover the women's collaborative role, proposes a lunar metaphor and the concept of "living instruments." The priestess as moon alters and changes the light of the sun, so we can look at it without going blind. This lunar metaphor reenvisages the woman's voice as entwined with the transcendent voice in ways that entail neither mere repetition nor scandalous reinterpretation. She is not written upon passively, nor is she a distorting mirror: the sign that is created is the double work of god and priestess.[17]

By analogy, there are less polarized ways of understanding musical performance as well, and following Sissa, music criticism and especially feminist writings on opera might find some relief from the oppression of those extremes. Performers need not be either inert beings brought to life by a master plan, or illicit improvisers who invent music on their own when they should properly restrict themselves to their role as vessels for pedigreed texts. Such caricatures are familiar in literary representations of operatic singers, and refer more often than not to female characters: Trilby is the first, George Eliot's Armgart is the second, and they have many, many close relatives, since fictions about female singers recycled both types throughout the nineteenth and twentieth centuries.[18] What might it mean, however, to see the musical "sign" at once as something produced by the performer, and as implying "double work"? At the very least, it would entail moving beyond fictions about opera, and focusing on operatic performances. The import of Sissa's word "work"—meaning a labor of collaboration—can be reinterpreted as a sound-object. In *Pelléas et Mélisande,* for example, a "double work" comes into being between the text and its performance (see pages 176–77). And the signal this "double work" sends about gender is unconventional.

Yet one cannot simply assert that the move away from fiction, or from caricature, would create a critical utopia, save music's life, or insure that performers are not dishonored. This is because a fundamental problem—that musical performance is uncanny—cannot be suppressed. The performance network is not one thing, entailing one mood. Praising operatic voices as paradigmatic instances of presence and excess—or celebrating operatic works as an envoicing of women—can become a critical consequence of focusing on that network, one possible interpretation of its implications. There are, however, less euphoric conclusions to be drawn. One must not forget the obverse, the persistent vision of performers as dead matter, subject to mortification and reanimation. This vision is not just an outrageous fantasy, in which anxieties about performers' real power have given rise to unpleasant falsifications. Certain realities of performance lend credence to its assumptions about deadness and artificial life.

Apollo's priestesses were "mortified," made less than alive, through strict proscriptions on their behavior as well as fictions and fantasies about them, because they were women, but not for that reason alone. They were imagined to transmit sound that originated elsewhere, like faithful musicians playing an invisible score. Align Orpheus's head—as deadened as the priestess's body—with the instrument and the medium, and certain aspects of classical musical performance are immediately apparent:

suppose musicians are not gullible mesmerized women, but worse still, dead body parts making noise? Romantic aesthetics of musical performance in general imagine a text brought to life by an artist's careful interpretive genius. Invert the phenomenon, and the result is an inert performer that has been animated, taken over and made into a mechanism by something exterior.

In fact, being possessed by a musical work is something that happens all the time. I start playing a sonata. For a while, my mind drifts, then I come back into a consciousness of playing. Several minutes have passed; I am somewhere in the development section and have no idea how I got there or who or what was guiding my hands while my mind lingered elsewhere. Sometimes practicing is so boring that I put a novel on the music stand and occupy my mind, while something else plays through me. That something even knows to interrupt the piece to tell my hands to turn the novel's pages. Memorization, here manifest as pure body memory, is the process by which the motion required by the piece is imprinted physically on the performer, as a set of instructions that can move one's hands or mouth in the absence of consciousness or will.

From the audience's point of view, performance can engender an equally strong sense for a musical voice separate from the body executing its commands, the performer-piano that is dead or mechanical and clearly did not write the concerto. Parallels between performers and musical automata were articulated in fiction and theoretical writings beginning in the eighteenth century, paying tribute to this phenomenon.[19] These truly inanimate performers—the ones done in porcelain or wood—represent an endgame, a final comment on the dead-object problem, simultaneously utopian and grotesque.

II

But what is playing the instrument-performer? As Sissa does in assembling literary images of the Delphic priestesses, I want to juxtapose literary accounts of musical performance with operatic versions, starting with a story by Heinrich Kleist. My point is not simply to exclaim over misogyny, or a fully predictable narrative uneasiness about female performers' capacities. By beginning with Kleist I am beginning with an instance, like Orpheus, where it is men, male performers, who are in trouble. I want to untangle assumptions about the channels through which music travels on its way to realization. Those assumptions are variable, and no particular dogma emerges, since the performance network itself is not fixed. Performers are instruments, or embroiderers, or something related to both, in between. Musical works are texts, or ungraspable objects, or necessary delusions. There is a certain shared narrative realm, however, where Romantic ecstasy about music collides with the frankly horrendous. These incongruent moods are brought together under the sign of musical performance, undermining sentimental assumptions about classical music as the realm where great works, and great performances, invariably ennoble human spirits.

The title of Kleist's "Die heilige Cäcilie, oder die Gewalt der Musik" (1810) is usually given in English as "St. Cecilia or The Power of Music." "Violent force" would be a better translation of "Gewalt," since "power" implies controlled legitimacy, "Macht," what kings and cardinals have. Even before the story begins, Kleist hints that the saint and her female descendents are playing with lightning and not merely with kitchen fires. The story is set in the late sixteenth century and concerns a strange miracle that happens in a convent just outside Aachen. Four brothers, Protestant students inclined to iconoclasm, decide to attack the church attached to the convent on the feast of Corpus Christi. The Abbess and her nuns, who are talented instrumentalists, celebrate a musical mass as planned, even though Sister Antonia, the orchestral conductor, is sick in bed with a fever. As the four brothers lurk in the church, Antonia is found totally unconscious and the Abbess, hoping for a performance of "an extremely old Italian setting of the mass by an unknown master," orders the trembling nuns to play any "oratorio" they can manage. Suddenly, Sister Antonia appears, "a trifle pale," bearing the score and parts of the old Italian mass. The performance that is given is sublime:

> The music was played with supreme and splendid brilliance; during the whole performance not a breath stirred from where the congregation stood and sat; especially at the *Salve regine* and even more at the *Gloria in excelsis* it was as if the entire assembly in the church had been struck dead. In short, despite the four accursed brothers and their followers, not even a particle of dust on the floor was blown out of place.[20]

Here the narrator breaks off suddenly and adds simply that the convent thrived "until the end of the Thirty Years' War." But the words "struck dead" are hard to forget.

The tale is taken up six years later, when the mother of the four brothers arrives in Aachen, searching for her sons. She discovers that they have been in an insane asylum ever since their attempt to destroy the church. Visiting them, she is horror-struck to see how they sit silently, like phantoms, in long black robes, staring at a crucifix. The warder explains that the men "hardly sleep and hardly eat and never utter a word; only once, at midnight, they rise from their chairs and they then chant the *Gloria in excelsis* in voices fit to shatter the windows of the house." Determined to solve the mystery, the mother finally locates a witness who was at the church six years before. She learns that as soon as the music of the mass began, her sons were struck dumb and were later found "lying, with folded hands . . . as if they had been turned to stone." They are dragged from the church but behave like mute automata. Returned to their lodgings, they construct a crucifix, while their Protestant companions observe these "silent, spectral doings" in consternation. The witness goes on:

> Then, suddenly, it struck midnight; your four sons, after listening intently for a moment to the bells' dull tolling, suddenly rose with a simultaneous movement from their seats; and as we stared across at them, laying down our napkins and wondering anxiously what so strange and disconcerting an action might portend, they began, in voices that filled us with horror and dread, to intone the *Gloria in excelsis*. It was a sound something like that of leopards and wolves howling at the sky in icy winter; I assure you, the pillars of the house trembled, and the windows, smitten by the visible breath of their lungs, rattled and seemed to disintegrate, as if handfuls of heavy sand were being hurled against the panes.[21]

They sing this *Gloria* at midnight, every night of their lives, until they die in old age.

This concert represents the nadir of a peculiar trajectory, as the "very old Italian mass" by the "unknown master" burns its way through the story. First, the mass raises Sister Antonia from her sickbed and breathes "heavenly consolation" into the nuns. Their hands stop shaking and move with assurance upon their instruments. But if this ancient text gives life and physical animation to female performers, their performance of the mass immobilizes listeners, whose bodies are deadened into stillness. Most of the audience is released once the concert is over. But hints that music takes possession are realized in the four brothers. For them, the sounds the nuns played take over their bodies and voices and turn them into spectral machines that scream like wolves and leopards. Somehow, these living corpses sing the same *Gloria in excelsis* that the nuns had played, but Kleist's point is that music's meaning, as well as its power to move listeners, is entirely predicated upon the way music is performed, and by whom. The same notes, yet how different the effect.

All that is left at the nadir is this "violent force" of musical performance in its most brute and physical sense, with the brothers' "ghastly ululation" reimagined as various material phenomena, as breath that hits windowpanes like sand. Yet at the same time that he foregrounds the vast differences between two performances of the *Gloria,* Kleist also imagines a descending spiral, with the unknown master and his musical text—a score preserved in Sister Antonia's library—at the top. While the realization of that text during the Corpus Christi mass is marvelous, there has already been a fall from transcendence at the hands of the nuns. The fate of the four brothers is presented straightforwardly as a consequence of divine justice. But their grotesque performance is also a next logical step, suggesting how any performance of music already constitutes a form of disintegration. Music has started on the path toward mechanical horror at the very moment—during the nun's concert—it seems most sublime. The spiral, which places an unknown at the highest point, is reproduced within the narrative, in which the brothers' singing is never witnessed by the mother or the narrator, only by others, whose accounts are cited at second- and thirdhand.

There is considerable ambivalence about musical performance implicit in Kleist's ontology of music, and the nuns, presented as trembling ladies, are at the same time gatekeepers for powers ascribed to the Italian mass. Thus the mother, still playing the detective, finally visits the convent and is given an audience by the Abbess. During her audience, she is confronted by a series of mysteries. She catches sight of the score of the Italian mass, now kept by the Abbess, and stares at its "unknown magical signs . . . she thought that mere sight of the notes would make her fall senseless." There is almost a fatal short circuit, as the inscription itself, the hieroglyph at the highest point in the spiral, seems ready to strike another person down. But the inscription cannot do what the performance did: the mother survives. The Abbess then recounts a great miracle: Sister Antonia, who had seemed to conduct the mass, had in fact been paralyzed in bed the whole time, and no one knows who led the orchestra that night by taking Antonia's earthly form.

This miracle is explained by archbishopric decree as the intervention of St. Cecilia herself, an enigma that seems to match the enigma of the score and its present impotence. The mother puts the score to her lips when she feels its threat. This is a strange gesture, which the narrator suggests we understand as piety and submission, but which simultaneously represents the woman's ascendancy over the mysterious work. By placing notation near her mouth, she recreates herself in sign language both as someone who sings the mass and someone with the power to absorb it, eat it up.

Kleist's tale thus postulates three sorts of musical performance. In the first, the nuns play a mass to incredible effect; in the second, their performance is positioned downwind of a transcendent work, far away from the four brothers' clockwork howls but of the same order of materiality. So far the attitudes are familiar. In the third, however, the work, the "very old" text and the unknown master disappear. Suddenly, women are not gatekeepers but what is behind the gate, and their music making stands at the head of all spirals. We know this when the narrator, late in his tale, at last gives a description of the Abbess. A "noble lady of serene and regal appearance," she is "seated on an armchair with a footstool resting on dragon's claws." When we look down, we see the sign: the claws under her human feet, showing that she is the master of the screaming leopards, as she is their distant relative.

"Die heilige Cäcilie" as a story about women and power has been cited in feminist critiques for this progressive element.[22] Yet the gender of the superior surviving characters is not the most radical aspect of the story, which calls into question several fundamental assumptions about music. The performance network as represented in the story is unnerving at every stop along the line. The very existence of a work or master text is uncertain; there is no indication that the mass as a text—as opposed to one unique performance by the nuns—should be construed as the real source of music's violent force. Turning the story back to reflect upon Orpheus's head suggests a new possibility: that the head is not being "played" by a master hand or voice after all. Violent physical resonance, the aftershocks of a performance, may account for its singing.

III

An iconic reminder of the performance network, its master symbol, Orpheus's head also has other, lesser implications. Among them is the enduring quality of live sound. "Die heilige Cäcilie" represents the four brothers as quiescent organic matter that, having been struck by music, resonates with aftershocks for quite a long time. The four brothers, like the body part, sing on the verge of dying, and thus their singing is also an acoustic decay that parallels the gradual dying out of neural energy. Such songs are echoes, bound to fade away. In Stephen King's novella "The Breathing Method," performance is presented more obviously in this light, though with complications in the modes of transmission.[23]

In "The Breathing Method" we encounter a bodiless head like Orpheus's, but this time the corpse is female. Miss Stansfield is an unwed pregnant woman whose quiet determination is much admired by the doctor who cares for her. He has developed a method for controlled breathing during childbirth and schools her in its details. On her way to the hospital in labor, however, she is decapitated in a freakish accident. Her head rolls away into a gutter, but the body, breathing postmortem, continues to give birth. Sly classical references abound: Miss Stansfield's whistling severed larynx becomes a set of panpipes, a "crude reed" that "no longer had a mouth to shape their sounds." After the child is saved, and right before the infernal panting body collapses, the head finally speaks, "breathed into" by the body's lungs. But the sound that emerges is that of an aeolian harp, strings stirred by wind:

> Her lips parted. They mouthed four words: *Thank you, Dr. McCarron.* And I *heard* them, gentlemen, but not from her mouth. They came from twenty feet away. From her vocal cords. And because her tongue and lips and teeth,

all of which we use to shape our words, were here, they came out only in unformed modulations of sound. But there were seven of them, seven distinct sounds, just as there are seven syllables in that phrase, *Thank you, Dr, McCarron.* "You're welcome Miss Stansfield," I said. "It's a boy." Her lips moved again, and from behind me, thin, ghostly, came the sound *boyyyyyy*—[24]

Her final sigh, a whisper of delight, lies miraculously on the border between articulate speech and music, typifying the "dark and unarticulated discourse" that is the signified of language.[25] Miss Stansfield's speech is music, however, for a physical reason that is made plain enough: because she was decapitated right below her chin, and the vibrating "reed" left in the neck lacks the physical apparatus that turns tones into words. Orpheus's head, it appears, got cut off at the collarbone, and was left with the vocal cords necessary to give music to the word formed by his lips, *Euryyyyyydice.*[26] By nature a male voice is sensible, and the means of articulation are never separated from the pipes that produce musical notes. With women, on the other hand, speech is naturally (conventionally) imagined as merely musical, pretty sound. So decapitation exposes an essential difference, putting female vocal cords twenty feet away from what is needed for clear speech. How perfectly, and how grimly, Miss Stansfield mirrors a Romantic representation of the Mother, circa 1800, as a figure whose language "acquires a vibratory nature, which has separated it from the visual sign and made it more nearly proximate to the note in music."[27]

A man or a woman: the difference matters not simply because Miss Stansfield is a humbler and female version of Orpheus, an allusion to Orpheus saddled with childbearing and contained by popular fiction. She falls silent without any legacy other than the survival of her child. If Orpheus's postmortem vocalizations are like Miss Stansfield's, the remnant of mechanical force, mystical aftershocks in a dying organism, the hope for Orpheus as a male poet is that his singing nonetheless escapes her dead end. Thus when Rainer Maria Rilke confronts the head, he fully acknowledges its singing as an echo. What separates Orpheus from Miss Stansfield, however, is that this echo does the impossible and never decays:

Keine war da, daß sie Haupt dir und Leier zerstör.
Wie sie auch rangen und rasten, und alle die scharfen

Steine, die sie nach deinem Herzen warfen,
wurden zu Sanftem an dir und begabt mir Gehör.
Schließlich zerschlugen sie dich, von der Rache gehetzt,
während dein Klang noch in Löwen und Felsen verweilte
und in den Bäumen und Vögeln. Dort singst du noch jetzt.

[Not one of them could shatter your head or your lyre, / struggle and rage
as they could; / and all the sharp stones, which they cast at your heart, /
became gentle when they touched you, able to hear. / Finally, they murdered you, fevered by vengeance, / Yet your sound lingered in lions and
cliffs, / and in the trees and the birds. You are singing there still.][28]

The voice, disembodied at the moment of death, disperses and finds
other objects to strike, stones and plants and animals. Orpheus *intacto* was
a great bell, and now that bell no longer rings, but the force of its last
sound set a thousand lesser bells—including one floating head and one
lyre—vibrating through all history: "you are singing there still." Before is
a voice that is mine, that originates in me and finds a way out past my
larynx and my throat and my tongue. After is defined as the dispersing
remnants of that voice.

In none of these literary fantasies, however, neither in Kleist's story,
nor King's variation on the Orpheus myth, nor even in Rilke's, does
Orpheus emerge with his authority as composer—as the ultimate source
of thought and sound—wholly unscathed. Rilke's art is highest, and his
view of performance, shimmering behind the sonnets, is most anxious for
Orpheus's singular immortal force, even as his voice is fragmented. Kleist
and King undo the master voice, which dies away or is dispersed, or split,
travestied, or denied, assigned to women. King's retelling makes things
clearest, but even the classical sources suggest disbelief in Orpheus's
autonomy, and Ovid hints at his feminization with a floating head that
"murmurs" pure sound. Orpheus's denouement might be seen to separate the great Apollonian voice from the hapless corporeal medium in
grotesquely clear fashion, reflecting back on Orpheus's life, raising the
possibility that he has always been just a larynx and some hands, animated
by a transcendent god.

This is, finally, no less true of operatic Orpheuses than of their literary ancestors and siblings. In Monteverdi's opera, the apotheosis—the
duet for Apollo and Orfeo—gives musical form to the son's lesser and

mechanical status. And the organ-grinder quality in "Che farò senza Eury-dice," Orfeo's aria to lost Eurydice in Gluck's 1762 opera, may similarly expose an Orpheus who is manipulated. The aria's happy C-major mood famously strains our aesthetic prejudices: this is a lament?[29] But if Orpheus is strung to the hand above, the aria suits absolutely. This Orpheus is ready at any moment to tumble down Kleist's spiral, reverting to the automaton. In other words, Orpheus was already just an opera *singer* centuries before opera was invented.

IV

A work passes through channels, into performers' bodies, performers who are in a chimerical state between aliveness and deadness, singers who produce sound that has violent force. Asking how opera refl-ects these images means seeking their acoustic traces in operatic music, since what opera does, what fiction cannot, is both self-evident and worth remembering. Opera in performance is an embodiment, which makes the force of music palpable. At the same time, the work that is present as a performance, the "double work" that is a collaboration between per-formers and a master voice, creates representations of that force in the form of sound. Rilke's poetic vision of permanent resonance—his scien-tifically impossible echo—is the sort of trick that opera can put right up on the stage, or in the orchestra pit.

Every operatic Orpheus, for instance, eventually descends to hell, where he must get Eurydice back by singing, working an ill-disposed audience, in an environment choked with smoke, sulfur, and other air-borne substances that interfere with vocal production. Monteverdi's ver-sion of Orpheus's song—"Possente spirto"—has acquired such mythic status that there may seem to be little aria left to contemplate. The aria, which begins with several strophes in virtuoso coloratura, is tra-ditionally seen as achieving its effect only when Orfeo abandons orna-mental singing in the later strophes and adopts natural declamation.[30] Equating natural declamation and suppression of coloratura with oper-atic efficacy has a distinct Wagnerian ring, as if Monteverdi's opera were merely the geological substratum below Calzabigi and Gluck, or *Das Rheingold*.

If the aria creates an effect, however, who has been affected besides all the post-Wagnerian listeners? Orfeo's audience within the opera is never clearly identified. In Ovid, Orpheus comes "through the unsubstantial throngs and the ghosts who had received burial" to stand before "Persephone and him who rules those unlovely realms, lord of the shades." Then, "singing to the music of his lyre," he begins his plea, addressing Pluto and Proserpina directly as they sit before him.[31] Orfeo in 1607 is not yet in hell when he sings, and in act 3 confronts the boatman Charon, demanding to be ferried over. A theatrical non sequitur splits this confrontation in act 3 from act 4, which opens with Pluto and Proserpina discussing Orfeo's songs, in the past tense. This gap has seemed troubling to modern listeners, inspiring a lot of hermeneutic stitching—as if by gluing the acts to one another the classical confrontation could be recovered. You do this by asserting that the singing Proserpina describes in act 4 is the same singing Charon yawns over in act 3, and that she overheard the aria though she was not present in the scene.[32]

But this is a contrivance in the reading, an attempt to erase the non sequitur, responding to anxieties about theatrical logic that are historically conditioned, troubling to post-Wagnerian habits of libretto appreciation. Perhaps the uncontrived, literal assumption is inherently preferable, as less strained: Proserpina heard some other song, one neither Charon nor the theater audience has witnessed. But this reversion to the uncontrived, ironically, opens up the possibility for several strange elaborations. The first is that "Possente spirto" is a red herring: Orpheus's most important song is being excluded quite carefully from any actual onstage manifestation. Just as the song by the floating head was suppressed, so the mythic song before Pluto is suppressed, once more in response to dismay, since no opera can discover the song that brings back the dead, and any attempt to create it fails before a note has been written or sung. An ultimate operatic noumenon can be kept safe (along with one's compositional self-respect) by being shown indirectly, or not at all. Thus the netherworld performance in the opera is not the primal operatic scene at all, but a prelude.

Without knowing Striggio's libretto, Calzabigi practiced the same exclusion in his libretto for Gluck: Orfeo in 1762 also sings in front of gatekeepers; the "groaning portal" is opened for him when he finishes, and again the performance for Pluto happens elsewhere. But Orfeo in 1607, unlike Gluck's Orfeo, is notoriously unsuccessful with his onstage audience. Charon comments that he is unmoved and will not let Orfeo on the boat, and then he gets put to sleep by Orfeo's further laments, an unintended result that Orfeo exploits to cross the river. The listener is without proper feelings. The narcotic sand in the boatman's eyes was accidental.[33]

Still, even as he sings to the boatman visibly present, Orfeo seems to understand that his voice must reach other ears. He sings into the void beyond Charon with promiscuous desperation, addressing Eurydice, himself in the third person, the gods of Hades, and a host of invisible characters that he believes are within range. This may be a way of representing his singing as magical: as Jules Combarieu pointed out, composers imply this not by means of any particular musical device, but simply by postulating a single invisible listener who is excluded from the real space in which the song is performed.[34] After the non sequitur, in act 4, Proserpina confesses she was so moved by Orfeo's voice that she must plead with Pluto for Eurydice's release. But what song did she hear?

Orfeo's "Possente spirto"—and this is a final elaboration—contains and conceals this other song, a mythic performance that exists only by implication. Phantom singing is hidden within present singing, centered in the famous instrumental echo effects within the virtuoso strophes, in which paired instruments fill in time between Orfeo's laments. Thus the prelude or preamble, the song heard by Charon and the theater audience, harbors the primal song without ever allowing it to be heard.

These echoes create a sonic image of voice sent forth through a void. Klaus Theweleit notes that each instrument "quietly repeats from 'behind' what the instrument 'up front' played loudly, thus bringing *the beyond*, which Orpheus seeks to enter, as a presence into the ear of the listener: as if he were already over there, since the tones already are."[35] This is a blueprint for musical power, in the form of space that is collapsed by sound. At the same time, however, the echoes are also a residue or remnant, something left behind. The instruments that echo one another over three verses—the violins, cornets, and harp—do not mirror the Orfeo-

Example 1.1. Monteverdi, *Orfeo* act 3

I

voice that is present and singing. Instead, in each verse there is a strange set of threefold repetitions. Orfeo sings, and an instrument repeats the gesture, opening its "mouth" to "sing" in turn yet not singing his melody; then another instrument behind both of them opens its mouth to repeat what the first instrument had sung (see music ex. 1.1).

The instruments, strings and brass alike, are all being passionately vocal: they imitate expulsions of coloratura, pauses for breath, and repeated floods of singing, doing so hard on the heels of Orfeo, as if they *were* his voice, and still, not imitating exactly *what* he sings. Thus the instru-

Example 1.1. (*continued*)

II

ments seem to hear an Orpheus voice that is not present. But they suggest its presence without ever suggesting that their melodies provide exact copies of its unimaginable music. This "brings the beyond" into orbit, not as a distant physical space, but as a transcendent object. Only the much maligned coloratura strophes point toward this object, which is no longer even indirectly accessible once Orfeo begins to declaim in a more natural style, so perhaps it is time to acknowledge that coloratura, as Adorno claimed, "is no mere outward form of expression, but precisely in it the idea of opera emerges most purely, as an extreme."[36] Those post-Wagnerian

Example 1.1. (*continued*)

III

readings that went for the unornamented singing in the later verses may betray a taste for forms of nature that are contrived and controlled.

Echoes were a persistent presence in music before 1607, which is no reason to suppose that the echoes in "Possente spirto" should be dismissed as a stylistic tic; echo effects endured in opera, but few are so unscientific or suggestive. In *Abduction from the Seraglio*, Konstanze's "Traurigkeit" aria inverts the traditional image of singing as wind, as a declaration traveling toward a beloved. In both poem and music, breathing is instead turned back upon the speaker, like a sudden back draft into her throat, stopping her voice. The music pauses, as if to wait for an echo, but the echo of course never breaks this silence. There has been no transmission. Not surprisingly, Wagner's echoes behave in improbable ways; *The Flying Dutchman* is a study in the distinction between proper bourgeois echoes and interesting impossible ones.

But strictly scientific instrumental echoes appear in Gluck's *Orfeo ed Eurydice.* In act 1, Orfeo sings a strophic aria about throwing his voice, "Chiamo il mio ben così." He mourns the loss of Eurydice by calling her name to the cliffs and rocks and rivers. At the end of each verse comes a conclusion, "non mi risponde," "l'eco risponde," "il rio mi risponde" (she does not respond, only the echo responds, the river responds). Responding straightforwardly to the classic echo setup, Gluck places a second orchestra at a distance from the stage and has that orchestra imitate Orfeo's voice directly and without significant variation (see music ex. 1.2). While the echoes are unsurprising, the aria represents a rare operatic allusion to Orpheus's postmortem vocalizations: the "river" that answers back refers obliquely to the riverbank that calls "Eurydice" back to the lamenting head, as in Virgil. Orpheus, alive, plays out a scene that part of him will replay in the future, once he is dead. The musical echoes, then, refer equally indirectly to future echoes, the ones that will record an unusual sound. When echo reflects something we have not heard (as in "Possente spirto" or in Wagner), the escape from laws of nature invariably ushers in the otherworldly.

This operatic device is saluted in Walt Disney's *Snow White* (1938), in Snow White's wishing-well song. Snow White sings about her desires, leaning over a well whose natural sounding chamber gives back each phrase: "I'm wishing . . . *I'm wishing* . . . for the one I love to find me . . . *to find me* . . . today . . . *today.*" When she goes into Bellini-esque roulades right before the reprise, the echo voice suddenly decides to play Adalgisa to her Norma and sings with Snow White, a third below. It is a very strange moment. Not that there is somebody in the well after all, but there is an instant premonition of magic, which turns out to be accurate: the Prince appears out of nowhere, as if conjured up by the impos-

Example 1.2. Gluck, *Orfeo ed Eurydice* act 1

I

Example 1.2. (*continued*)

II

sible duet. By singing a final *"today"* back to the real Snow White, he ends the vertiginous play of female voices with a firm masculine hand.

If Monteverdi's instruments are an Adalgisa who does not wait until the last minute to announce her presence, they are also the ur-form of a fundamental operatic gesture, as music that is present but that points toward music that is absent, and that can never be captured. Instrumental echoes trace this impossible object within an aria that declares that such singing exists and is heard, but not by us, never by us. In alluding to a transcendent song, the gesture reminds the theater audience, finally, that divine ears are different, and that the frequencies they detect are out of human range. Perhaps in 1607, while a Mantuan audience listened to early baroque coloratura, unseen immortals could hear *Götterdämmer-*

ung. What, then, do unseen immortals hear when *L'Orfeo* is performed nowadays?

Avoiding Orpheus's song was a dilemma faced by every other operatic composer who set the Orpheus plot, a foundational challenge presented by opera. Suppressing Orpheus's primal song seems to distinguish great Orpheus operas from silly ones. Lesser composers put Orpheus directly in front of Pluto and are diminished by their hubris. In 1647, Luigi Rossi wrote a song for Orfeo that is strophic and remorselessly banal. Pluto and Proserpina's giddy responses ("O dolcissimi accenti! O note omnipotenti!"), far lovelier that anything Orfeo just sang, suggest quite straightforwardly that they heard something the theater audience did not. This absurdity may signal Orpheus's descent in the later seventeenth century, when his mythic image was debased in broad comedy, as if the subject were easily exhausted or too serious to bear repetition.[37]

V

Echoes, however, also have a more strictly mechanical implication. They can "bring the beyond" downstage. Monteverdi's echo effects allude to noumenal singing but are also a representation of high volume, and a wholly different kind of magic in the form of a voice that travels through great distances. Echo represents transmission and as such is a symbolic correlative to the very idea of monumental vocal power.

In reality, an echo is a sound that bounces back, transformed, to its point of origin, that ricochets with diminished force until it dies away. Yet speaking unscientifically and subjectively from one's own point of listening, echo could just as well be the sound of one's voice passed on, sent afar. If I am a singer listening to my echoes, I might dream that my voice is diminished not because of acoustic decay, but because my song, loud as ever, is simply going away, and that far away someone is hearing that song, as loud as when I sang each note. Musical power as affective power becomes musical power as mechanical force, in an operatic singer's dream of a voice thrown undiminished across great distances. The dream predates by centuries the technology of the microphone or the loudspeaker.

Postulating echo as a pretechnology of reproduction is by no means new. In act 5 of Striggio and Monteverdi's opera, Orfeo sings a lament that

Echo (the nymph herself) repeats in little fragments, quite accurately. As Theweleit says, librettist and composer invented "Ms. Echo" "because they do not have the apparatus that *would in fact do* what they have in mind."[38] These echoes dream of recording: "you may laugh, but . . . Orpheus is asking for Edison."[39] He has a passionate need for permanence, as a frustrated gramophonomaniac without the machine that could preserve his sounds on a recording medium.

But postulating echo as a pretechnology of transmission is somewhat more fraught. As long as echo is understood as a proto-loudspeaker or amplifier or telephone line, the dream of unbroken transmission refers to a nightmare, to Orpheus's dismemberment, though that fate is never openly invoked in Striggio and Monteverdi's opera, nor in Calzabigi and Gluck's. How do you engineer musical sound detached from the body and sent away, as loud elsewhere as when it left the body? With the poetic resources of 1607, you can imply it with an echo; centuries later you can do it with a loudspeaker relay and lots of copper wire. You can also do it with literal detachment and a butcher's knife, when you dismember Orpheus and toss his singing head into a river. The crazy women are dreaming too.

VI

Understanding Orpheus's head as a minor symbol for mechanical force implies two different readings of the symbolic object, suggesting in turn two closely related kinds of musical power. There is Rilke's idea of a very big sound and its permanent aftershocks that affect objects in their path, and there is the idea of pretechnological sound transmission, the head and the lyre as long-distance carriers. Both images raise a related question about the means by which Orpheus's voice persuades and raises the dead. His voice in fact commands the intervention of a god who does the actual job of resurrecting. Thus in most Orpheus operas there is simply a point at which somebody gives an order, and Eurydice strolls out. Sometimes she was not previously on stage, as in Calzabigi and Gluck's opera: no Before and After. And though there is a rich and well-documented medieval Christian tradition that associated Orpheus with Christ raising Lazarus, the mechanism by which the dead one returns is clearly very different in these two cases. Orpheus needs to recruit a divine collaborator. Christ need only speak. Pagans and Christians alike seem to agree that mortal singing does not really resurrect anyone, and a question posed by Aeschylus in *Agamemnon* remains a rhetorical plaint to which no hopeful answer could be given: "once a man has reddened the earth with his blood, what song can recall him to life?"[40]

Operatic singing, if it cannot raise the dead, has nonetheless seemed miraculous in two distinct senses. Singing moves the passions—that is a familiar claim. Operatic voices however, apart from what they sing, can fill large spaces without amplification. While it is entirely proper to admire music for its capacity to stir emotion, admiring sheer volume has not seemed so elegant. Such taste is imagined to be the sole province of melomanes, or worse, of audiophiles, for whom timbre and power is more important than the musical content of what is being sung. Infinite volume and miraculous transmission is thus the mechanical analogue not merely for persuasiveness, but for what is beyond rational analysis, and thus a little bit of a scandal.

Yet the collision between phenomenal, physical force and metaphysical flight—the flight implicit in unrepresentable music—recurs in opera as a ground zero, seeming to cut through historical mutations in operatic style, and the geographical customhouses of distinct local traditions. For instance, Catherine Kinzler argues that in French opera of the Enlightenment, a Cartesian image of mechanical vibration and its effect on the body is replayed in operatic recitatives, in which the music produces sympathetic material responses that are fundamentally inscrutable to the mind. As she indicates, the audience nonetheless responds to the music of the recitative in ways that are not merely physical. In this paradox lies a phenomenon that is beyond philosophy.[41]

The poet par excellence of impossible mechanics, however, the master of undisclosed music, was Wagner himself. While a more elaborate reflection on Wagner is reserved for a later chapter, allusions to Wagner are unavoidable whenever overwhelming sound comes into play, especially with any intersection of noise and transcendence. This intersection is right on the surface in act 1 of *Lohengrin* (1848), when Elsa tells the assembled Brabantians how she produced a very loud sound:

Da drang aus meinem Stöhnen ein Laut so klagevoll,
der zu gewalt'gen Tönen weit in die Lüfte schwoll:
Ich hört' ihn fern hin hallen, bis kaum mein Ohr er traf;
mein Aug' ist zugefallen; ich sank in süssen Schlaf.

[Then out of my groans emerged a sound full of lament, / It swelled into mighty tones, into the whole atmosphere. / I heard it resonate far away, until it barely reached my ear; / My eyes closed, and I sank into sweet sleep.]

This passage and the narrative that follows obsessed Adorno, who saw it as a phantasmagoric episode, a dream in which Elsa summons a tiny silver-plated knight, accompanied by miniaturized and acoustically deracinated music.[42] For Friedrich Kittler,

Elsa's closed eyes hallucinate this knight, which is why he will soon appear on stage, just like Senta's Dutchman. And yet his presence—which, of course, coincides with the dramatic interaction as a whole—is the product of an acoustic hallucination. Elsa's pleas, laments, and moans have successfully commanded Lohengrin to appear from a distance of four hundred miles, the distance between her Duchy, Brabant, and his holy mountain, Montsalvat . . . Elsa passes over the contents of her laments, pleas, moans—to mention only the fact of these sounds.[43]

Wagner's ambition, Kittler indicates, constructs an imaginary sound technology without benefit of electricity or wiring. Orfeo may ask for Edison, but Elsa has stolen a march on Alexander Graham Bell.[44]

Wagner's amplifier, his musical response to Elsa's loud emission, is all but preordained: as she chants, "It swelled into mighty tones, into the whole atmosphere," the orchestra gets louder. The sound wave recedes for "I heard it resonate far away" (see music ex. 1.3). This direct translation of Elsa's "sound" into an instrumental swell, turning up the volume on the orchestra, reflects an absence that Elsa herself has acknowledged. She needed no words, no "content," to create her imaginary telephone line, just volume as a direct thunderbolt from her inarticulate heart. Her reference to unformed vocal noise also entails regression to a more primal music in both voice and orchestra. The vocal line becomes a series of repeated high E-flats, less a melody than pure intonation, ending with an arpeggio in C-flat major. The orchestra reverts to vibrating chords in the strings and single pitches held by winds and brass, humming vocal cords, crude reeds and pipes. As Elsa sings her E-flats, distinct individual instruments also sound single pitches. But unlike her, they do not seem to pause for breath or put effort into loudness. Each instrument sustains its note longer and louder than any instrument powered by human lungs can plausibly blow, and each passing second adds brush strokes to a portrait of instruments and lungs "not of this world." This is accomplished technically with smoke and mirrors: what sounds like one horn or one flute is actually two or three of each instrument, often playing in overlapping relays, with the acoustic join between the entrances—the place where the baton is passed—concealed from the ear.

Such techniques creating the acoustic impression of a supernatural instrument did not originate with Wagner. He learned them from operas like Carl Maria von Weber's *Der Freischütz* (1822), where in act 2, in the "Wolf's Glen" scene, some ghostly hunters fly across the sky and sing typical hunter yo-hos, with a sinister twist. The hunting horns that accompany them play horn calls, but not on the usual consonant open fifth: they play a diminished fourth, the dissonant interval $A\flat$ to $D\natural$. But no real hunting horn could do this, since hunting horns, which are valveless horns, play the overtone series above the fundamental note physically natural to their particular size and tuning. Such a horn built in $A\flat$ can play the fifth from $A\flat$ to $E\flat$, but not the interval from $A\flat$ to D. Weber thus had to construct a horn call that implies an imaginary horn, by using two sets of horns in tight formation, $A\flat$ horns playing the $A\flat$ alternating rapidly with D horns playing $D\natural$. This allows listeners to hear the single horn that is not of this world.

Weber's ambitions remained modest, while Wagner's desire to usher in the impossible grew immense. His accomplishment was to create a much bigger illusion, that a last gate would open, and that sound from a transcendent unknown would simply stream forth: what ended as *Parsifal* began with minutiae of orchestration, with Weber's bag of tricks. Wagnerians, of course, tend to make Wagner the first, or the worst (or best). Yet Wagner's techniques might simply be seen as extremes, not innovations. According to Kittler, for instance, Wagner imagines media technologies designed to produce the illusion of infinite resonance. But that

Example 1.3. Wagner, *Lohengrin* act 1

I

Example 1.3. (*continued*)

Example 1.3. (*continued*)

Example 1.3. (*continued*)

IV

was not new. What may be different is that Wagner's technology, unlike earlier operatic technologies, seems less innocent, having lost that quality from the moment Adorno likened Wagner's timbral effects to a deluding magic lantern show. Or, as Kittler puts it, "Amplifiers put philosophy out of commission."[45] This too is not just a Wagner problem. One might as well put it more bluntly: opera puts philosophy out of commission, and perhaps this is why the relationship between the two has been so tense. The musical technologies that decommission rationality are an operatic commonplace.

Their strictly theoretical pedigrees also predate Wagner by several hundred years, appearing for example in Enlightenment writings on acoustics, above all in the most famous acoustical fantasy of the modern era, the *Phonurgia nova* (1673) of Athanasius Kircher.[46] Kircher's direct and explicit comparison of mechanical force with suasion is testimony to commonplaces in Enlightenment theories of music and the senses, and follows from a discussion of musical miracles in his *Musurgia universalis* (1650).[47] The synapse between brute acoustics and metaphysics had nonetheless already been composed as opera, and would continue to be reinterpreted within opera well into the twentieth century.

Still, *Phonurgia nova* can stand for a large body of related theoretical fantasies, treatises about musical power, Neoplatonist or Cartesian retakes on musical affect, on mimesis as sympathetic vibration. Such fantasies appear as a collage, in the frontispiece to the treatise (see fig. 1.2). Putting Orpheus together with St. Cecilia, the illustration sneaks in a decapitation and illustrates the long spiral that connects music to wind and screams, anticipating the vastness of a Wagnerian orchestra. In a pictorial cornucopia devoted to sound transmission, every imaginable horn, trumpet, cornet, panpipe, and other brass or woodwind instrument vies to be heard. Many vignettes illustrate arguments from the treatise: the hunters and army on the right side allude to a disquisition on hunting-horn calls and field signals. Kircher (like Kleist) recognized two kinds of musical force at work in the woods and the battlefield. There is the semiotic system understood by hunters and soldiers (they decode commands associated with this or that fanfare), and this system conspires with the sheer hortatory impact of volume to create a realm in which music has imme-

Figure 1.2. Frontispiece, *Phonurgia nova*.

diate power and an instant effect. Content versus volume: the symbiosis between meaning communicated by musical content, and physical power consequent upon mechanics and acoustics, is a recurring theme in both the treatise and its symbolic frontispiece.

Kircher appears as the reclining figure on the lower right, listening to an echo that bounces off the pedestal on which a female figure with Apollo's laurels, rather than singing to the lyre, blows on one horn, while a second, upturned, is collecting cherubic breath in its mouth. Wind is everywhere. Fabled musicians populate the landscape: St. Cecilia with wings appears at her organ, right below the divine triangle. The nine muses give a concert on the hill below the wind-tossed trees. But the observer's attention is caught, precisely because of all the noise, breathing, wind, and blowing, by some quiet detritus. Below the satyrs and the figure of Silenus on his donkey (lower left) lie three abandoned objects: a lute, a set of panpipes, and a face with open mouth and hollow eye sockets.

This face, so bizarre, so unlike anything else in the visual field, is the mask of tragedy poised on the edge of an allusion to the head of Orpheus, abstract, resting in a dry and abstract riverbed next to an instrument, beneath the Dionysians associated with his dismemberment. The artist depicts Kircher's dreams of loud sounds, sounds that travel, reverberate, get the army moving, transmitted by angelic megaphone, bounced off the rocks. But he does not forget a nightmare in which voice travels only by means of a rolling head. Orpheus appears, in this form alone, among the instruments.[48]

An allusion to Orpheus's head invokes both infinite volume and persuasive power, also brought together (though independent of Orpheus) in Kircher's discussions of acoustics. There is another iconographic reference, however, which one senses whenever trumpets are blown from heaven. Behind this celebration of living sound is a last sound. Thus in the final paragraphs of a treatise that imagines loudspeakers, acoustic lenses, magical speaking tubes, whispering chambers, aeolian harps, and every imaginable device for amplifying and transmitting music, Kircher acknowledges that he has merely dreamed of earthly forms for the trumpets of the apocalypse, the loudest instrument of all:

Therefore, let everything that exists and that I have herein described be offered in honor of His holy name, and let my ears be opened by the breath and tuning of His holy spirit, so that they might HEAR. Otherwise, nothing remains to be said, except that our souls, turned to a noble heaven, may be worthy, after this vain and earthly existence, to be admitted to the sweet and loving chorus of heavenly angels; there can be no higher wish than the wish to be of their number. And this can happen, when we serve God in true love and fear, without failing, and in contemplation of those fearful divine trumpets of the Apocalypse, when this shall be sounded: Surgite Mortui, venite ad Judicium.[49]

Kircher's *Phonurgia* begins with an iconic allusion to Orpheus among instruments but ends with the instrument alone.

In other words: Orpheus works by persuasion, by enlisting a more powerful voice. But the trumpet needs no mediums; it commands, and the dead rise up. Dead souls are sleeping: a body part or dry bone needs to hear and respond, so the brute noise of the unimaginable instrument speaks directly to brute inert fragments and rattles the body back into wholeness and animation.[50] There is no correct fanfare, no semiotic code, no score or particular melody that must be present for the trick to work. Like Elsa's loud noise, the sound without verbal content or musical differentiation, the instrument summons the dead without regard to the notes it blows, and in the very end, the performer-instrument wins out over content or text.

VII

Kircher's acoustic dreams take shape as nonexistent machines and imaginary architectural spaces, devices that symbolize massive vocal power. No aria, no matter how loud, can really resurrect a dead man. But by the seventeenth century, anatomists (including Kircher) knew that recently dead ears still reacted to sounds, that the mechanism of hearing—tympanum, small bones, and fluids—was still moved by vibration after death.[51] This knowledge cast sentimental notions about the power of music into disquieting anatomical terms. Music, if it could not call back the dead hero, could nonetheless travel from the cup of his outer ear to a place within his skull. "What song can bring him back to life": this impinges upon ideological issues connected to performance and gender in music, now in perhaps more theoretical terms.

This question about resurrection through music can be posed in alternative forms, each differing a bit from Aeschylus's "what voice can recall him to life" or "what sound can recall him to life." In another form, this distinction between song and voice is the one that Kleist's "Die heilige Cäcilie" proposes as a question about the force of music, and its ascription to the configurations preserved in the score, or to the performance.

Saying that a song holds the secret is to say that music's force resides in a particular composition, an arrangement of notes, melody, and rhythm; to say that a voice or a sound is at work suggests that it is a particular singer, only one, or a certain instrument or timbre, that can breathe life into the body. Then it does not matter (or it matters little) which composition is being sung or played. In one view, power is in a work per se, in another, in its execution. Power may reside in the transcendent aspect of music that rests above its own precipitation into live performance. Or it may reside in the performer, who produces the immanent matter of the moment. As a master symbol for the performance network, Orpheus's postmortem singing reflects the former, suggesting an Orpheus-puppet moved by Apollo, who speaks through heads and lyres as well as through women and men. As a minor symbol of musical power, however, it can also imply an Orpheus who is the source of all sound, a body part that sings through residual energy.

On paper, we have a distinct appetite for "the song." As Lydia Goehr puts it, "one prominent thesis" about music "determines that most, if not all, value should be placed in the permanently existing works and not in their transitory and fleeting performances" and that "performances *qua* copies of works are regarded as necessarily imperfect." Modernist composers in particular were fond of this position, which dreams of erasing performers entirely. Goehr cites broadsides by Stravinsky and Hindemith, which articulate a sense that performers are "imperfect pointers toward the transcendent" whose duty consists in attaining invisibility.[52] Such attitudes arrived at their inevitable dead-end in two self-consciously scandalous essays by Hans Heinz Stuckenschmidt, "Die Mechanisierung der Musik" (1925) and "Mechanische Musik" (1926), written as manifestos, hyperbolic. The first ends by saying "the role of the performer belongs to the past," and the second predicts "the end of the era of musical inter-

preters" in the wake of machines that mechanically—and perfectly—
reproduce musical works.[53] But such claims are not clinical and rational,
not just happy statements of progress.

Richard Taruskin was first in identifying the real emotion: it is rage,
"the rage against flux and impermanence, the same refuge in fixity and
necessity, the same fear of melting into air."[54] Igor Stravinsky's poetics of
music, the attack on performers' volition and autonomy, are thus born of
impotence, wrought by anxieties that the work is created in performance
after all. What seems surprising—given all the anger repackaged as glee—
is that Arnold Schoenberg, though notoriously vigilant in controlling the
execution of his works, was resistant to the siren song of the single, true,
and objective realization. In his opinion performers must struggle to "discover from the score what is true and eternally constant." Yet since the
minds and ears of performers and listeners are contingent upon and
shaped by their culture and historical era, performances of a given work,
to convey that "constant," naturally and rightly change over time, a possibility precluded by the specter of a single mechanically engendered,
eternally inscribed and perfect interpretation. Thus "insofar as the mech-
anization of music . . . states as its main aim the establishment, by composers, of a definitive interpretation, I should see no advantage in it, but
rather a loss, since the composer's interpretation can by no means remain
the finally valid one."[55]

From the school of Schoenberg nonetheless comes a fabulous vision
that goes far beyond wistful thinking about obedient pianists. René Leibowitz's *Le compositeur et son double*—the title nods to Artaud's *Le théâtre
et son double*—begins by restating several basic musical-ontological
precepts:

> Recent scholarship has taught us that the musical work is not only situated
> outside time and space, but also *outside of the real,* outside of existence. . . .
> In addition, the performance of the work, which is itself situated in time
> and space, is nothing more than the *analogon* of the work per se. We can
> add to this that the musical work *does not exist for anyone* except in being
> performed, and that a performance alone causes it to exist, as much for the
> listener as for the interpreter. If we accept this point of departure we can
> try to define the role of the performer, as well as the notion of an "authen-
> tic" performance.[56]

So far, this is well-mapped territory. But after going on to define the transcendent work as something imaginary, Leibowitz plays with a series of paradoxical inversions. The "performer unveils the work not only because that work has unveiled itself to him, but because, conversely, the work unveils the performer." And, "it would be possible to say that, just as the performance is the *analogon* of the work, the performer is the *analogon* of the composer." Through a series of conflations, the performer's penetration of the "sense" of the work enables him to become the precise "double" of the composer. This, however, is Leibowitz's terminal point:

> Thus in the end, it is the composer and the musical work that have *created* the performance and the performer. . . . [The performer] seizes and realizes [the musical structures of the work] at the moment when, delivered up to his score, he is as if possessed by it, at the very moment he possesses it. . . . The performer has no life except through the score that he brings alive, and it may be possible to say that such a communion is based in a rapport that one might call the *eros* that exists between the performer and the musical work. Merleau-Ponty (in *Phenomenology of Perception*) has spoken of the body as an en-sexed being, drawing our attention to the fact that our bodies are nothing but inert and will-less things, but that, in certain circumstances, even our bodies are capable of a certain intentionality. In the same way, for the true performer, the musical work is not some inert and fixed object, but it is—insofar as the performer is capable of grasping it, of imagining it—a true *provocation*.[57]

More is at stake than reverent performances of great works. Since the performer is styled a double, he or she is made less visible, made compliant. And then he or she becomes an organic machine switched on by the work, a figment. The work exacts vengeance for its lack of reality by creating the performer, thus becoming an erotic partner, which in being brought to sensual life also brings the performer to life. How neatly the tables have been turned, and how fully Leibowitz, with no apparent nose for the uncanny, has proposed a strange reversal of terms in which human beings are dead material, forced into motion by something operating from behind or beyond their bodies.

This reversal had been articulated before Leibowitz, notoriously by Wagner in *Opera and Drama* (1850), and in his later essays on performance, particularly "On Actors and Singers" (1872).[58] Wagner argues that performers must erase themselves (this comes as no surprise), thus making their bodies and throats into vessels for another voice: his. This regime was written into the very fabric of his music, as into the architectural innovation of the hidden orchestra. In the essay, a survey of European theatrical practices, one thing meets with unequivocal praise. This is a marionette theater performance that Wagner had once stumbled upon in the streets, in which "poor dolls" are animated by the puppet master.[59] The remark is typical in one respect, as approval lavished on a natural, unforced art that has arisen as if from the bedrock of folk inspiration. As master figure for a particular philosophy of performance, however, the rhapsody about the puppets is almost too much. The fearful autocrat of Bayreuth is easily, artlessly betrayed, and the target is too broad to be worth an arrow.

Later along the same lines, that autocrat has become less obvious, for instance in his sly identification of castrati as the "expressly adjusted human instruments" among all the other (less carefully altered) human instruments played by operatic works and their composers.[60] And finally, though he denies that he hopes to "fetter the life" of performers by the "mechanical minutiae" of his notation and expressive instructions, fetters and mechanism were right there on the surface, as the puppet theater that draws so much praise.[61] Still, Wagner (again) was not the first. Hegel in his *Aesthetics* endorses a similar logic, speaking of performers as matter given life by works (see pages 197–98). Not, however, with such complete relish, such elaborate detail.

Leibowitz's reversal—like Wagner's essay, or Hegel's treatise—rewrites the conundrum posed by Orpheus's head, now by way of philosophy. His description, however, brings to mind one specific operatic moment, Violetta's "Addio del passato" in act 3 of *La traviata*. Violetta is, of course, an almost dead lady at this point, notoriously so, since her singing seems incompatible with her tubercular agonies and imminent demise. But perhaps this objection, with its vulgar requirement of simple verisimilitude, misses the point.

"Addio del passato" is an aria in couplets, two repeated musical strophes, in which Violetta sings of her past life, takes her leave of it, and pleads for compassion. The couplet form is a reference to her Parisian

Example 1.4. Verdi, *La traviata* act 3

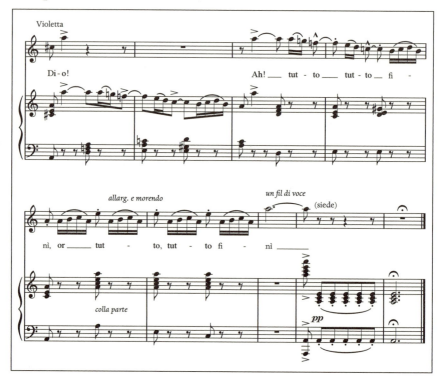

identity, a formal borrowing from French opera. If, however, the couplets are a sign for history and culture, their various kinds of repetition are much more. There is a weary and forced quality to the verses, a quality enhanced by a slow tempo and by the minimal orchestral accompaniment and harmony. The final cadence to each couplet is a fourfold vocal repetition of one monotonous triadic pattern, seeming to recapitulate in miniature the strophic repetition within the aria. Even further—the pattern is repeated "too many times," as if a winding-down Violetta were caught somewhere in her descending arc (see music ex. 1.4). There are few ways that this could be finished off, and the orchestra's cadential blare is so sharp as to suggest something strangled instantly when the blade descends. This is not a dying woman improbably managing to sing a final aria, but an aria that reaches its hand out to animate a moribund body, forcing it to sing, and then sing the same thing again.

Any performer like Maria Callas who omits the second verse has therefore left out something important, a pity not because the "original text" has been tampered with, but because the grotesque effect Leibowitz describes in his "reversal" has been erased. A taste for that reversal, ironically, flourishes among those who prefer Callas as Violetta. Such preferences entail more than just ghoulish tastes for precarious voices, more than the fantasy that Violetta's physical affliction has been precipitated into the singer's body, creating a gratifying fusion of the two. These tastes fuel the perennially resurrected "Callas-Tebaldi" debate, which centers on their Violettas, and whether a technically gifted singer with a perfect voice, fully in control of the musical demands of the part, is at a disadvantage by seeming too untroubled. Verdi's original Violetta, Fanny Salvini Donatelli, was a singer of this type, praised for her "indescribable skill and perfection" in singing, but reproached for her girth and good health.[62]

Callas, seeming to lose control, struggling so openly with the sheer musical and physical demands of the role, embodies quite vividly the spectacle of a performer taken over by a work. Her vocal flaws seem thus to mark a strange somatic resistance to the whole procedure, as if the body were rebelling after all. Error and breakdowns are byproducts, exposing the dead-object problem, an aspect of the performance network that few wish to see. This is one reason why performances that go wrong—where someone forgets, or where the music making threatens to fumble or stop—do not simply create frustration or disapproval in the audience. The emotions are more complicated. There is a sense of fear, of anxiety or even panic. And not only from sympathetic identification with those on stage: the spectacle has shown its other face, as a moribund collective that has somehow gotten derailed from the commands that have supplied it with temporary, harmonious life.

La traviata, however, sits on both sides of Leibowitz's seesaw. Violetta's act 1 aria, with its coloratura, illustrates the other extreme. Requiring immense vocal control, and soliciting improvisation in the cabaletta, it would seem to create a vocal presence that has little to do with Violetta and much to do with the performer's virtuosity and autonomy. Convention would see this as a thin place in the work, where the female singer's capacity to transcend the text constitutes an offense that must be framed or suppressed, either by plot or by a musical corrective.

VIII

Bringing up Violetta brings up gender in opera, and the way in which operatic representations of women may seem radically different, depending on whether one focuses on the performance or on the virtual work. Within the performance network, the leveling of gender distinctions is inevitable. The euphoric view that performed arts destabilize authority, hence the very idea of a transcendent work, decouples the master/puppet regime between work and interpreter and places music making at the top of the spiral. Then all performers, women and men, occupy a powerful position. Recalling the dead-object problem, with its grim prognosis for performers' autonomy, means admitting that men— Orpheus or the four brothers—are manipulated and possessed. And while Gothic and Romantic fictions on the whole favor women in the mesmerized object role, and while this is a cultural phenomenon whose implications must not be trivialized, there is nothing about performance that assigns either gender to any kind of extreme. That Orpheus initially symbolizes a performer as a creator but is revealed to be a passive medium, and finally a dead and dismembered medium, means that his fate is not inseparable from that of the women whose relation to Apollo resembles his, the Delphic priestesses. He is "just a voice and a body," and, finally, just a piano, a head, or a lyre.

For Theweleit, that fate—the conversion into instrument or device— is strictly reserved for another woman in Orpheus's orbit, for Eurydice. In Monteverdi's opera, as he remarks, Eurydice is a minor role, and when Orpheus drags her back to the upper world, she is strikingly quiet. Theweleit sees her second death, after Orpheus looks back, as the consequence of a composer's irrepressible anxieties about impermanence. Is there an audience to look at me? Is there an ear to hear what I am saying? Is my voice leaving traces? I have to see.[63] Once she is gone, Orpheus's fantasy instantly seeks her and reconstructs her in the form of two material media, as "the instrument in his arm" and as Echo, the devices on which Orpheus seeks to imprint his laments:

In the space reserved for the most adequate hearing and the preservation of their music, they place—this is a fact—the ear of this dead person, to whom *Heaven generously granted all its gifts*. In other words, the place of the best possible reception of their music and of a hoped-for *transmission* is *encoded* with a woman's soul. To describe the relationship to this (vanished) "soul" as "love" is a translation of the physiological functions of the eardrum. Thus they translate the quality of Eurydice's wonderful ear into a quality of her "soul."[64]

What Theweleit leaves unsaid, however, is that Monteverdi's opera ends with Orpheus himself transmuted into an eardrum. In Orfeo's final duet with Apollo, the poetic text might well suggest male triumphalism, as father and son ascend, singing, into heaven. But in every paired vocal entrance, Apollo leads and Orfeo mimics, as his "lunar surface" transmits the voice that turns everyone into echo, into a head that sings. As Joseph Kerman points out, theatrical representations of Orpheus, even those ending happily, imply the tragic end, the real end that contradicts the terminal celebration.[65]

Given Theweleit's emphasis on Eurydice as proto-gramophone, a receptive medium that is no longer even a performer, it is instructive to consider the alternative version of the scene in Calzabigi and Gluck's opera, in which Orfeo leads Eurydice to the upper world. This Eurydice is far from silent: she talks about herself, she berates Orfeo, she reproaches his odd behavior, solicits declarations of affection, and, finally, begs for his gaze, within three long accompanied recitatives that lead into and out of a duet as well as an aria (for her, not him). Indeed, she says so much that Orfeo constantly tells her to "be quiet" and stop singing.

This is no simple domestic quarrel: Eurydice in 1762 has come to resemble Orfeo in 1607, sharing his narcissistic anxiety about listeners and audiences and his need for the mirror, or the wax cylinder. Calzabigi's Eurydice asks how she got here, what she looks like, whether her eye is unclouded and her cheeks "still rosy." She even expresses a desire to return to the underworld, as the place she likes best. Calzabigi invents a woman whose volubility reflects her independence, and at the same time, a woman so distressing that she is only indirectly present. This Eurydice is the one Rilke saw in his long poem "Orpheus. Eurydice. Hermes," a

Eurydice who walks "terribly slowly," her foot "entangled by her shroud," full of her "great death." Rilke's gray, decomposing Eurydice comes last, a last truth after Orpheus's impatient speed and Hermes' fluttering wings. By 1762, the external prohibition against looking back had become the mask for an internal prohibition: a premonition of what might be seen or heard after turning around. Only the woman full of death is eager to have a mirror put before her face.

Gluck's musically realized Eurydice is no echo, in keeping with her forceful character and her self-positioning as a performer (Look at me!). In the duet with Orfeo, she constantly refuses his melodic ideas, singing her own in ways that suggest how impossible it will be for him to lead her, a forceful person, like Orfeo in 1607. Any hints about her uncorrected morbidity thus reflect back on that Orfeo as well. The unscientific echoes that bounce between the two operas suggest again that Orpheus's death and dismemberment, his fall into silence, left some traces in 1607. In an opera that will not represent that death on stage, his fate is reflected nonetheless.

Rilke's image of Eurydice is a morbid nadir that seems indirectly to mirror Leibowitz's bizarre vision of performers as dead bodies roused to life by impatient works. The real corpse, the one in "The Breathing Method," was a pulp-fiction variation on this theme. For this reason, it is darkly appropriate that Miss Stansfield, the pregnant heroine, works as a perfume saleslady: "In a department store," she replies, when her doctor asks where she is employed. "I sell perfume to fat ladies." Her supervisor's office is "littered with perfume samples," a place where glass bottles with atomizers are natural surroundings. Miss Stansfield squeezes the atomizers to give samples of the perfumes, prefiguring her end, when her head "breathes into" her body and forces it to give birth.

Atomizers are strange objects. They look like lungs, of course, and suggest how puffing breath can produce an alluring substance (poetry, perfume). On the other hand, they also resemble a bellows giving the semblance of life to inert material. And atomizers themselves are motionless until a hand reaches out to grasp them. Breath and wind, ancient metaphors for being made to speak from outside the self, are crystallized as kitsch, as an expensive boudoir accessory. But the reference to classical antiquity in King's story is once again clear. Apollo's priestesses were "breathed into" from below, in a process kept quite separate (firewall!) from another, similar action of the wind: that by which poets are inspired, from above.[66]

"The Breathing Method" thus imagines that an Apollonian master voice blows into singers, and that they perform his instructions. The work concept implied by this fantasy appears elsewhere in the novella. The tale about Miss Stansfield is framed within an outer narrative about a club where old men gather and spook each other with horror stories. One of the stories they tell is hers. Their motto is engraved above a fireplace: "It is the Tale, not he who tells it." The overarching motto rewrites Miss Stansfield's miraculous death, suggesting that "in the end" it was the doctor's "breathing method"—the script, the "tale"—and not Miss Stansfield's superhuman will that inspired the headless body to postmortem effort. Or, it is the Opera, not she who sings it, and "she" is deliberate. Composing opera and singing opera are separate activities historically restricted by gender, the first being all but exclusively male. Throughout operatic history, it would seem that men have been squeezing, while women have been atomizers and bottles and puffs of air.

Yet the fictions that struggle to assign fixed differences to men and women in the performance network turn out to be historically limited, and by the later eighteenth century, these assignments were challenged. While this destabilization is inherent in performance itself—real performance rather than its representations—literary fictions like Kleist's story, responded sympathetically to ambiguities about the meaning of musical execution and the source of music's power. Performed arts themselves, including film as a captured or imaginary performance, have still greater means to give expression to those ambiguities: plot, poetic language, what is seen, motion on stage, musical gesture, sounds, acoustic life, the presence of instrumentalists and singers, the very fact of noisiness and temporality. The message can be sent several times, in several different phenomenal registers. By the 1930s, with the advent of sound, film could join opera in deflating the great clichés. Josef von Sternberg's film *Dishonored* (1931) lets the air out of several old assumptions. In the movie, a pianist-spy (Marlene Dietrich) is at once a composer, performer, and human gramophone, yet it is her performer's "dishonor" and excess, presented as an unwillingness to follow scores or scripts, that comes to represent a high form of heroism.

Like Salome, this pianist-spy in von Sternberg's movie is good at occupying spaces once reserved for men, and that turns out to be fatal for her as well. My point, however, is not to rehearse once more the truism that female performers invested with creative power create anxieties that are resolved when framing devices are mustered to constrict their force and silence their voice. Death is an excellent frame. But the frame is not simply predicated on gender resentment. There is another emotion, which Taruskin added to rage: "fear." It is not just fear of the performer's caprice, however, not just of the ephemeral, but of the nature of music itself. As a live art that shows how one's own voice is taken over by another (and that goes both ways between authors and executants), music is made to be lost, as a vanishing surplus beyond a "work" that is an idea, but not music. Despite musicology's devotion to critical editions and sanctioned texts, such things are only pretexts for a phenomenon that depends on the dishonored: on performers, on their excess.

An uncompromising text-oriented stance toward the performed arts, a position that would seem unusual in ethnomusicology and is rare in work on popular and avant-garde music, is conventional in music-critical dealings with high-art Classical repertory: the focus is usually on the intentional object. And while good postmodernists acknowledge that a musical work's meaning is unstable or variable, constructed by the listener, as shaky as the self constituted by one's interaction with that work, most are certain that it is a musical work, and not a performance, that should be taken as the limit value from which to begin thinking and writing. The musical work is thus both an object of desire—since choosing a transcendent object over some temporary noises demonstrates academic sobriety—and pepper in the postmodernist eye, since discussing musical "works" rather than performances could be mocked as the lingering remnant of certainty, revealing a secret admiration for authorial genius.

Mockery, however, strikes a harsh note. The cults that surround famous singers—the fans who may worship wardrobes as passionately as they do musical virtuosity—self-evidently give expression to emotions that ensue from what listeners have heard. The apparatus surrounding musical masterpieces—as well as the scholarly industry focusing on virtual works—has a similar meaning. Summoning the fiction of a work, like the interpretation assigned to such fictions, gives expression to what was experienced in a moment of hearing or playing or singing. Although several performances were my own limit value, they make no overt appearances onstage, and the operatic works go on in their place. What, then, are operatic "works"; what is "Parsifal," or "The Magic Flute"; what role do works play in discourse about opera? One answer is that the works are *souvenirs*. Not a postcard or a piece of porcelain, nor a program book with color pictures and a cast list: they are not tangible, and you cannot put them in a drawer. Yet perhaps musical works, imagined objects, are mementos nonetheless, a reminder (though, unlike porcelain, not evident to the senses) that can stand for an embodiment, and what was once experienced in present time. Those performances (as my limit value) had a significant effect: shaping an impulse to weave between opera and performance, between listener, author, and noisemaker, to return to performance as a phenomenon, to contemplate the possibility of a "double work." The irony, of course, is that in writing about music there is a chimerical middle ground, impossible to reach, and worth seeking again and again.

This ontological question, finally, is important to feminist approaches to musical interpretation. Arguing that instrumental works or operas are encoded narratives about gender conflict or sexuality, or about how men envisage women, is one common feminist strategy: Susan McClary's writings on the classical repertory are a paradigmatic instance, and many follow this lead. Laudable for its interpretive hubris, for a belief in music as social fact finder, this strategy backfires on certain other counts. Music's capacity for narration becomes straightforward or self-evident. The text, the authority of a male composer, and the strangleholds of objectification and representation, are ultimate objects of celebration, and in a peculiar sense the music—the realization of that text, and those responsible for it—has begun to vanish. Thus Suzanne Cusick argues that "the music itself"—that is, the very idea of an imaginary work, a disembodied "representation of [musical] sound"—must be interrogated as "the ultimate feminist issue."[67]

Avoiding interpretation of performance, some feminists would argue, is a habit that reflects larger problems, the devaluation of physical or ephemeral phenomena in intellectual culture, as well as that culture's reservations about immediacy and pleasure. The opposition of disembodiment and embodiment, or hermeneutic culture and presence culture, is important in contemporary feminist theory, which is fretting about which to embrace. One stance resists assigning value to decorporealization and insists on the truth or worth of the physical, as Christine Battersby has argued in *The Phenomenal Woman*.[68] Is the embrace of embodiment an essentialist end run? Or is the irony even greater: is this embrace a sister under the skin to claims for an unmediated or pure experience of art, something used in the past to dismiss certain styles of interpretation, often the feminist ones?[69] It is at least a move to peel away bad associations from the idea of voice as physically grounded, and from the corporeal in general, habitually dismissed as essentially female, weak, merely sensual, hence unworthy. In this respect, it is significant that many operatic examples of disembodied authority are male voices.[70]

One can sketch out a traditional antiessentialist response. For instance, it is not that women have embodied voices. Rather, it is that having an embodied voice makes you a woman and ordinary, whether you are a woman or a man. As Carol Clover argues in her analysis of slasher movies—it is not that women cower and scream, it is that cowering and screaming, even if your genotype and its expressions are male, constructs you as female.[71] I would rather ask why grounding in the physical (or screaming) should belong to the feminine alone. What is at stake when this is so loudly proclaimed? The analogous assumption would postulate that mesmerized performing bodies are always female, or that performance, as far as it enslaves, produces a metaphorical feminization of those singing or playing. That is there, of course, in Kleist or King, and yet one could also protest the idea that enslavement is equivalent to feminization.

More still, one could challenge the idea that the performance network inevitably produces mortified bodies as a final result: that challenge is there in Kleist and even King, too. Recognizing the role that women play in musical reality means understanding how performed arts break down the Apollonian master voice, questioning that voice's existence by their very nature. They continually reset the magnetic points in a spiral that goes from a transcendent "work" to Nina Stemme's performance as Senta in New York, on 20 November 2000. Opera's unsettling rhapsodies to the power of performers, acoustic images of sound channels, echoes, transmissions, disembodiment, improvisation, all appear in a double light: as warnings and as memento mori, but also as a salute.

IX

Music has violent force. Thus one common metaphor for referring to a commanding voice is to say it is an instrument. When God speaks in the apocalypse of St. John, his voice is "like a great trumpet." And when the castrato Farinelli sang, his voice, so powerful and sustained that it was perceived as supernatural, was compared to a silver trumpet. The same is said centuries later of Wagnerian clarion Birgit Nilsson. Countless baroque arias pit instruments against singers.

Was Orpheus not a lyre, but a trumpet? He is a man who is an instrument even as he clutches an instrument in his hands. There was a strange reciprocal economy between the man and the instrument, a zero-sum game played out from Enlightenment to fin de siècle. Orpheus hardly exists in nineteenth-century opera; there is a single parody of the legend (Offenbach's 1858 *Orphée en enfers*). He appeared in two new forms. Opera after 1800 replaces him with fictive singers, all those Undines, Trovatores, Carmens, Tannhäusers, Walthers. These are the satellites, still forceful singing voices. In fiction and fact, he continues in the person of the divas, capricious virtuosi of Romantic literature, female singers who exercise their musical capacities to stun listeners into silence. But what voice can recall the dead to life? Can it possibly be a woman's voice? Can it be heard?

The other Orpheus metamorphosed; by gradual stages he changed into an instrument. As he dies out as an operatic subject, he is gradually replaced by curved tubes of brass and silver, as well as strings that twang on their own. By the nineteenth century, composers of requiems wrestled with a sound as fugitive to their representational clasp as Orpheus's singing: the trumpets of the Apocalypse. Orpheus's vocal authority, his power to command obedience, raising the dead, all these gifts, settled down into the brass section of the orchestra. In the requiems of the nineteenth century, as in Monteverdi's *L'Orfeo,* the magic sound appears in phantom forms.

But before Orpheus settled into this trumpety place, the intermediate stages of his metamorphosis took strange shapes. Late eighteenth-century German opera displayed a sudden fondness for magic zithers, violins, flutes, and bells, the self-starting instruments whose mechanics were investigated contemporaneously by the great automaton makers of the Enlightenment. These autonomous instruments in opera were associated with Orphic power, and the greatest work in this tradition is Mozart's *The Magic Flute,* whose animal-charming scene, in which Tamino plays the flute and attracts the beasts of the forest, refers directly to Orpheus's legend. But Tamino is not Orpheus: instead, Orpheus is present in the form of a flute that enchants, represented metonymically as he is in the constellations, by an instrument.

Such magic instruments do not need Orpheus's fingers on their strings, because they stand for his unviolated body and commanding voice, undivided. But while this is marvelous, the nightmare is never far away. The autonomous instrument may well represent *Orfeo intacto.* Inevitably, however, it also refers to the lyre that played on its own, sailing down the river next to the head. The singing head and the uncanny instrument were partners; and so they continued in opera. Indeed, one might think of opera as the shore that received these pieces of flotsam, the head, the lyre, collecting them, contemplating them like Moreau's inscrutable nymph in both their ecstatic and nightmarish forms. They are singing there still.

2

MAGIC FLUTE, NOCTURNAL SUN

For those who love perversity, here are some unorthodox interpretations of *The Magic Flute,* followed by an appalling fairy tale. The first is Melanie and Rudolf Heinz's *Silberglöckchen, Zauberflöten* (1992)—a collaborative book by a philosopher and a radical feminist theater artist who is also an opera singer.[1] Never mind that the two armored men in the act 2 finale are homosexuals in love with Tamino who decide to feminize their singing, desperately imitating the genuine female sounds that have just caught Tamino's ear.[2] "Yes, yes," they exclaim brightly, "that is Pamina's voice!" Or that the Monostatos menacing Pamina in act 1 is really Sarastro in a black mask. He has put on the Queen's darkness to attract her lost child, and sings with feigned voice, as if he were Siegfried in *Götterdämmerung* act 1. The book's most elaborate arguments are centered on Papageno, as a "male mother" who rocks infant-women to sleep, a virile "animal-music machine" whose potency is attacked by Tamino, with those lessons in neatness and obedience.[3] The magic bells that ensnare Papageno are the silver-plated corpses of the same live birds he has delivered to the Queen, and he should be suspicious of them: "one cannot eat sounds."[4] Hence Papageno's Glockenspiel aria in act 2 belongs to the realm of the dead, to technology: it is "music box music" full of "Rococo automatism," as far from anything natural as one could imagine.[5] The aria represents

> an anxious dream . . . not that all the bells in the entire world might start to ring, but rather, that everything in the world might begin to ring like a bell: Mozart, playing the Glockenspiel in the orchestra, without ever stopping again. Thus Papageno, in a gesture that assuages culture, is himself made into the musical instrument: the body wrapped in a bag, in short, a head, windbag, noise box.[6]

The conversion of nature into technology becomes the province of the Queen of the Night, but is also deemed characteristic of the Enlightenment per se. This technophilic Queen of the Night is thus sinister in an entirely new way, in a counter-Enlightenment reading of the opera's text that sees industry as a symbolic form of hyper-rationality.[7] As Industrial Goddess, the Queen lurks in vaults beneath the Temple of Wisdom, preferring chthonic landscapes, as if she were Alberich *avant la lettre.* Her taste for the subterranean, and the location of her throne inside a mountain, reflect her association with the mythic figure Cybele, the mother-goddess of mines and metallurgy, a connection routinely cited in literary accounts of the Queen's character.[8]

But *Silberglöckchen, Zauberflöten* is not the first interpretation along such lines. Igor Stravinsky heard similar hints of morbidity in *Magic Flute,* declaring that "the intentional meaning of the opera, the triumph of life over Death, is reversed at times in the depths of the music." He referred to the orchestral March accompanying the Fire and Water Trials in act 2 as a "funeral march."[9] In fact, viewing this piece as mortuary art is an interpretive swerve that predates even Stravinsky by a century or so. In a survey of Mozart's operas written in the 1840s, Aleksandr Ulybyshev had harsh words for the March, describing a cruel affective disjunction that separates its automatism from the ecstatic vocal quartet that preceded it.[10] Mozart, he wrote, completed his "mystery" in music—the quartet—just at the point where Schikaneder brings on *his* mystery—the ritual of the Trials. Thus for Ulybyshev the March "has suddenly sunk to a level of complete meaninglessness, as if merely obeying the whistling of the puppeteer."[11]

In this view, the March is authorless music, dancing helplessly in red shoes and switched on by a tune not its own, with the marionette theater right on the surface when what appears to be improvisation, a sign of live human agency, is revealed as mechanical repetition. According to the stage directions, Tamino plays his flute, and "muffled drums accompany him at intervals underneath." The flute melody in the March sounds as if Tamino were inventing music on the spot, rhythmically free, with missing phrases and displaced entrances and ornaments, seeming to have all the time in the world. This very unpredictability, however, the quality of being improvised, is immediately kidnapped by pure repetition: the "improvisation" is repeated *da capo* for the second round, captured and replayed. Was it not, then, a reproduction the first time round as well, the nth repetition of something that is switched on, and off again as needed?

Suspicion about Papageno's magic bells as something inhuman and mechanical, finally, arose long before the postmodernist interpretive flight of *Silberglöckchen, Zauberflöten*. Ernst Bloch's essay "Magic Rattle, Human Harp" (from the 1930s) harbors a certain antipathy toward the instrument and its sounds.[12] Bloch argues that all such stage instruments are far from charming, seeing in them the metamorphoses of human singing, a phenomenon that is no longer magical. With instruments, musical notes have "surmounted" the instrument-bodies as music disembodied and disassociated from the object that engendered it.[13] Bloch prefers the human singing voice, as a paradigmatic instance of presence, to all such flights or substitutions. Human singing—the "human harp"—is the only timbre that still works like a shamanist instrument in a disenchanted world, in large part by referring faultlessly to the creature-object that produces the sound, to its (to his, or her) essence. Papageno's bells "no longer qualify as vestigial proofs of ancient magic instruments": that role is reserved for singers, who are the "remnant which shows the most life."[14] Opera's utopian spirit transforms instrumental sounds into human singing voices; the opposite is an occasion for despair.

All four unorthodox interpretations write a counternarrative to the conventional reception history of *Magic Flute*, in particular to Kierkegaardian rhapsodies to Papageno as "natural man," or to triumphalist readings that see a day-night problem ironed out for good when Sarastro defeats the Queen of the Night. Winding back through history to 1791 is a thread that ensnares even Bloch, a philosopher notoriously free of pessimistic responses to music, as to history itself. Those who attend to the music rather than reading for the plot, swimming "in the depths of the music," are the ones most deeply afflicted by doubt.

Then there is the strangest reading of all, a set of engravings from 1912 to 1918, Max Slevogt's *Die Zauberflöte: Randzeichnungen zu Mozarts Handschrift*, which are marginal drawings around musical fragments reproduced from Mozart's autograph score for *The Magic Flute*. Here, no one seems to have listened to the music, since in any sense other than a purely optical one, music migrated to the margins of the project. Slevogt made collages, cutting pieces from a printed *Magic Flute* score, pasting them on drawing paper, and surrounding them with extraordinary sketches. These illustrations are not merely depictions of "what is going on" during this or that musical passage, but complicated allusive embroideries. For the final engraved versions, photographic facsimiles were made of the autograph. Slevogt sliced the photographs and selected certain passages—now both musical excerpts and images of Mozart's handwriting—that were etched into copper plates, going on to make new drawings around impresses from those plates. The last stage was to etch a final version of the drawings in their turn back into the same plates. At every point, music has to be there—to draw the illustrations alone was inadequate. This is such an imperative that an expensive musical object was blithely ruined in the initial creative process. Yet despite music's presence, Slevogt's drawings are exegeses of the libretto, and seem not to refer directly to the musical text whose material trace has been so poorly served. Seeing Slevogt's *Randzeichnungen* and his sketches for them, one sees what is not there, the score with the missing rectangles, the fluttering remnants of photographs that captured musical notation. One sees *Magic Flute* as characters, actions, and stage props that have been made alive, but music that falls silent through dismemberment.

Slevogt's gift, however, was to imagine that *Magic Flute* is not subject to weary binarisms regularly rediscovered and acclaimed in accounts of the opera, the dyads masculine/feminine, light/darkness, reason/superstition, and all the rest. His most disquieting figure is Papageno, seen as a Satanic Don Giovanni. His drawing for the chorus in the act 2 Trial scene, "Triumph! Triumph, du edles Paar" imagines dissolute priests blowing

Figure 2.1. Slevogt, "Triumph du edles Paar."

swordlike trumpets as Sarastro, transfixed by the light of an artificial sun-chandelier, seems both to extend his hands in blessing and stop his ears in horror at the cacophony (see fig. 2.1). This is a "meridinal mystery" in which the "sun has become nocturnal."[15]

A similar vision shapes the penultimate illustration, "die Strahlen der Sonne vertreiben die Nacht" (see fig. 2.2). The observer's eye is placed at a stairway to the underworld in the right foreground, as if he or she were a reception committee for those thrown out by Priests of Wisdom. But the women are not wholly "banished," for even as they seem to sink slowly toward the earth, they have also spread their arms like winged creatures: they are cast down, but they are also flying away. To see this, one must look at the direction of their movement. Right is the path into the earth; left is the path into the air. Only Monostatos is destined for the abyss, for the fall to the right. The Queen looks at him, but hers is a gaze of abandonment; she is going another way, to the left, escaping in a corridor that is open between two rays of the sun. At any moment, the Queen will turn her head in that direction. Next to her one Lady is unmasking, shedding her helmet in anticipation of some unimaginable transformation, while another, about to soar upward, has premonitions of flight written on her transfigured face. Meanwhile in the background Sarastro has become Titurel, a corpse propped up by Tamino and Pamina that sings impossibly through a closed mouth.

In this extraordinary vignette, Slevogt taps into a series of images: the avian, the escape from plotted closure, the mortuary telos of perfected order. The Queen and her Ladies, alone among all the characters, are the ones flying away from death. In the collection as a whole, there is in fact a resemblance between good and evil. For Slevogt, Papageno's Glockenspiel aria, once more, is no longer just a work of sublime childishness, or a representation of natural song, but has as many undertones as the Queen's aria in act 2.

To mention the childish is to invoke an aspect of *Magic Flute* music that has been highly prized, that is associated with Papageno's music generally but also with the simplicity of "O Isis und Osiris," or the music for Tamino's animal-taming scene in the act 1 finale. This is the strain easily seen as a reflection of Mozart's character as the miraculous adult infant,

Figure 2.2. Slevogt, "Die Strahlen der Sonne vertreiben die Nacht."

as a prodigy who, never spoiled by maturity, simply got bigger. He ends as an old child, unconsciously wise and oddly feminine. In the course of the twentieth century, a new biographical staple arose, and Mozart became an adult and masculine artistic personality, facing severe musical forebears like Bach in a struggle with and against paternal authority. This mortal combat finds its flower in the fugues and elaborate contrapuntal ideas in works like the *Jupiter Symphony* finale, the chorale prelude in *Magic Flute,* or the *Requiem.*[16] To say that each image fulfils certain requirements, articulates certain assumptions about high artistry typical of a historical time, is to state a commonplace. But it would be no small matter to investigate the very presence of that extreme, the dyad of unlike terms. Like good and evil in *Magic Flute,* the biographical images of Mozart, as well as the music understood as their echo, define an irreconcilable pair. Imitating Slevogt's gesture, one would seek the resemblance between extremes and ask whether they bear some common mark.

I

And now, the appalling fairy tale, Louis Chevalier de Mailly's "Le roi magicien" ("The Wizard King"), first published in 1698.[17] The story has never been cited in connection with *The Magic Flute.* Yet it shares with Slevogt's penultimate engraving a sense that the nocturnal endures, in the form of a last avian escape. What it shares with *Magic Flute* are several curious affinities, even specific narrative moments. As a source the story is merely suggestive, but as a provocation it is much more, creating a passage into the underground space where *Magic Flute* is suspended like a nocturnal sun, with many, many perverse objects in its orbit.

Les illustres Fées, the anonymous collection in which "Le roi magicien" first appeared, is now attributed to Mailly because so many of its tales bear witness to an obsession that recurs in his known literary works: metempsychosis and metamorphosis as the means of penetrating forbidden enclosures. In "Le roi magicien," a Wizard King, after a promiscuous youth, marries a beautiful Queen who bears him a son. Secretly—fearing her husband's disapproval—this Queen takes the infant to visit a good fairy, who blesses him with beauty and wit. Soon afterward, the Queen dies. The Wizard King spends years mourning his loss while his son grows to adulthood. In order to escape his sorrows, the Wizard King undertakes a journey with some of his courtiers, but he often slips away from them and by changing himself into an eagle ranges over vast distances.

As an eagle, the Wizard King one day catches sight of a wonderful garden, in which beautiful women are boating on artificial canals. Among them are the Queen of the realm and her daughter, a Princess whose beauty surpasses all others. Seeing her, the Wizard King is all but blinded and unmanned, "he was so enchanted by this beautiful sight that he lost the use of his wings, and found himself transfixed by a power which it was not possible to resist. He came to rest in the top branches of a large orange tree." This moment of physical impotence, of being incapacitated by emotion, is a first hint of the Wizard King's fate; the gesture will be replayed several times in the tale, always at a higher volume, until a final disaster ensues.

Resolving to have the Princess, the Wizard King waits until she separates from her entourage and then grabs her and flies away with her. She cries and begs; he assures her of his devotion and "respectful sentiments," demanding "a thousand pardons" for the violence he has practiced. He installs her in a magic castle, reappears in his human form, and converses gallantly with her over several months. She remains unmoved. Fearing that she may somehow hear of his son's great attractions, the King sends the Prince on a journey abroad.

And while abroad, the Prince encounters the kidnapped Princess's grieving mother, who tells him of the abduction. Upon seeing a picture of the Princess, he falls instantly in love and resolves to find her; the Queen gives him a miniature portrait of her daughter so that he may recognize her. In order to discover where she is kept, he appeals to the fairy that had blessed him in infancy. This fairy not only reveals that the princess has been abducted by his own father but also devises a plan for her rescue: she will transform the prince into a comical talking parrot, and he will take the place of a real one that the princess keeps by her side. Avian metamorphosis thus becomes a matter of genealogy: the giant raptor bird is father to the tiny parrot. Mailly also had a particular fondness for changing his men into birds and domestic animals, so that they might penetrate protected feminine interiors, displacing the notion of seduction onto a room or chamber whose physical defenses, locks, and labyrinths are thus easily conquered.

Here the story departs from stock devices of French fairy tales and swerves into violent terrain. Locating the princess, the parrot-Prince begins to chatter fluently, telling her "a thousand beautiful things" to beguile her distress. At last he takes the miniature portrait out from under his wing, revealing that he has come to rescue her. The princess is convinced of his benign purpose; he appears in human form, and she falls in love. With the fairy's help, they flee through the air in a chariot drawn by eagles. But the Wizard King discovers their flight.

Suddenly, he is transformed. He had been a polite suitor, a sad widower, and (we are told several times) he is revered by his people. All that falls away: he changes into a Harpy, the avian chimera of myth with its slashing claws and woman's face. "Possessed by rage," this being can now countenance the worst of transgressions, and it vows to catch and eat its own child. The Prince and Princess escape only through the fairy's cunning. They arrive at the palace of her mother, and suddenly another King appears, the princess's father, absent from the tale up to this point. He is conjured up as if the Wizard King's transformation into a female monster had left a paternal void to be filled at all costs. The prince and princess are quickly wed, and just afterward the Wizard King arrives in Harpy form.

Unmanned by metamorphosis into a female creature, the king is feminized again in a metaphorical unmanning, one that recalls the odd fainting spell that had occurred when he first saw the princess. The Harpy looks down from the air, now driven mad, "troubled in mind," and, unable to control its own physical state, is helpless to prevent a shift back into human form as it falls from the air. Landing with a vial in his hand, the Wizard King tries to throw a black poison on the couple, but the fairy turns the liquid back in midair and it splashes the Wizard King, who falls down unconscious. His body is picked up and thrown into prison. The Prince, feeling pity for his father, pleads for his release. The door of the prison is opened, and "no sooner had it been opened, than they saw the Wizard King fly into the air, in the form of a bird no one knew, and he said in parting only that he would never forgive his son, nor the fairy, for the cruel affront they had done to him." The tale closes with a few sentences about the fairy, rewarded with riches, and the Prince and Princess, happily ever after. But a skull remains in the garden, the unknown bird that flew off singing of revenge. Something escaped.

There is a cornucopia of anxiety expressed in Mailly's tale, centered in the first instance in the Oedipal tension between a father and son who vie for the same bride. Certainly most modern and post-Freudian readings focus on the agon of father and son, or on the incestuous longing implied by an older man's passion for a younger woman. "Le roi magicien" has thus been associated with a far more famous tale by Perrault—"Peau d'âne"—in which a father falls in love with his own daughter.[18] The two stories are unusual among French baroque *contes des fées* in exploring this theme. Obvious and pedigreed fears, the safe fears that concern parent-child relationships, nonetheless themselves serve as masks.

What is that raptor bird with fainting spells, the being "troubled in mind," the conversationalist whose voice turns to shrieking, the human male whose body becomes an avian female? The Wizard King—as a bizarre and central enigma—dominates the tale not least because he is transsexual. He begins distinguished by his self-control and fluent command of courtly language. Once he becomes the female Harpy, his mind changes accordingly. His hysteria, his uncontrolled body—shifting without volition from form to form—the loss of words as his human voice drops out of the story, can all be seen as byproducts of his feminization.

But what is most troubling is that this fearful end product has been anticipated long before the jealous rage that seems to precipitate it. Even when the Wizard King's masculinity had seemed secure, there were those slips and swoons. He changes into birds: a magical attribute represented as a product of will, as a means to conquer. Yet perhaps it is also an esoteric symptom of the opposite, indicating how masculinity is always in peril, maintained through effort against the threat of metamorphosis.

Put this way, the primal anxiety about transsexuality in "Le roi magicien" can be understood as typical of a culture whose understanding of sexuality and attendant anatomical fantasies are now fabulously antique.[19] If biological gender is not a secure and permanent physical given but subject to inflection by evil humors, if maleness and femaleness are not absolute opposites but extremes cast out from the hermaphroditic center to which they might revert, then the Wizard King's fate warns against failed vigilance.

II

But I have paraphrased "Le roi magicien" in a way calculated to fortify its resemblance to *Magic Flute,* with which it shares both a mood and several narrative turns.

The question of intent, whether Schikaneder or Mozart read or recalled the story when work on the opera began, is unanswerable. Translated into German as "Der Zauberkönig," it appeared in the most important German anthology of French tales published in the eighteenth century, Immanuel Bierling's *Das Cabinett der Feen* (1761–65), a collection that launched the German vogue for *Märchen.* "Le roi magicien" was republished in French in 1787 as part of *Le Cabinet des fées,* an exhaustive anthology that famously served Christian Martin Wieland as one source for *Dchinnistan.* Though none of Mailly's stories were directly translated or adopted in *Dchinnistan,* there are odd threads that connect his work to Wieland's collection.[20] One can only say that the story circulated somewhere in the same economy—translations from the French and anthologies of fabulous stories—that includes familiar literary sources for *Magic Flute.*

There are coincidences between story and libretto, especially interesting because flirting with a hypothesis that "Le roi magicien" was echoed in *Magic Flute* seems to account for certain famous disjunctions in its libretto. One leaps to the eye, the courtship scene between the parrot-Prince and the Princess, with miniature portrait as starring prop. In act 1 scene 14 of *Magic Flute,* Papageno finds his way to kidnapped Pamina and they have a long private conversation, by far the longest stretch of spoken dialogue in the opera. He has the miniature portrait that the Queen's ladies had given earlier to Tamino. Even Papageno's own explanation suggests an enharmonic comma. Pamina examines the portrait, asking how he obtained it. "To tell you would take too much time. It was passed from hand to hand." Then, strangely: "I caught it." Evading an answer, he tells her instead about Tamino, that her mother gave *Tamino* the portrait, and that *Tamino* fell in love with it. Seconds later, he is rushing headlong down this path, explicitly conflating Tamino with himself: "This great love for you was the lash that set our steps in motion, and now we are here, to say a thousand beautiful things to you, to take you in our arms, and if possible just as swiftly if not more, to hurry back to your mother's palace."

Low-comic Papageno is suddenly envoiced by a courtly doppelgänger whose "mille jolies choses à dire"—the standard Gallic formula is unmistakable—represents lovemaking as verbal excess. For a moment there are two men present, the one who is there and the double behind him, and what follows is "Bei Männern welche Liebe fühlen," the love duet that Pamina and Tamino themselves never sing.

All of this—the mysteriously transferred portrait, the erotic charge, the love duet sung by the "wrong" pair—has engendered uneasiness in accounts of *Magic Flute*.[21] As often as not, these things are ascribed to Schikaneder's casual illogic, evident as well elsewhere in the libretto, or to an impulse to write himself into a good long scene. But maybe the pair is not wrong, and the erotic charge thus transparently apropos. It is certainly transparent: the duet's close musical relative in the Mozart canon is "Là ci darem la mano," which has the same measured slow pace, the same sensual back-and-forth between two voices, and the same baritone-soprano pair. What remains in the dialogue as in the musical number suggests the withdrawn shadow of a fairy-tale figure, a parrot-Prince-lover, whose unseen presence is graven into a duet celebrating the discovery of true pairs, into these conjoined voices and no others.

Then there is the Wizard *King* and the *Queen* of the Night, the Queen of the Night and all the critical energy she has inspired as a pivot around which so much seems to turn. To point out that she appears in the opera in two different forms—in act 1 benign, in act 2 monstrous—and to claim that the first is a deception, is to recapitulate a now widely-disseminated view. In this interpretation, she is sinister from the outset, displaying the passions of maternal grief when her true aim is to usurp power. Most stagings of *Magic Flute* now strive to make this obvious, requiring the Queen in act 1 to overact, or to sneak sly glances at Tamino to check the effect of her performance, as in Ingmar Bergman's 1975 film version. The second Queen, the one in act 2, has simply taken all her masks off.

Belief in the Queen's deceptiveness has come to predetermine musical analyses of her aria in act 1, which is seen to bear musical signs of trouble now and trouble to come. In Rose Subotnik's reading, "sensuousness" is evident in the syncopated pulse of the orchestral prelude, and there are many "occasions to question the authenticity of her emotion," intrusions of high baroque style that speak of artifice.[22] A similar claim is repeated by Christina Zech.[23] This raises an irritating question: if little baroque flourishes prove bad faith, what is signified by the same kind of flourish when it appears in connection with the Speaker's voice, or Sarastro's? Seeing the Queen in act 1 as false has also entailed some soul-searching about her ability to outfit the heroes with various useful objects like the magic flute, and to invoke the Three Spirits, but there are ways of setting aside these objections. Irreconcilable differences can be attributed to the libretto's production in bricolage, or to the whimsy of a work that must not be subjected to judgments about consistency.

In the reception history of the opera, the reading of the Queen as consistently dubious has replaced a discredited theory that arose in the earlier nineteenth century, which accounted for the second Queen as pentimento. Mozart and Schikaneder were said to have originally planned to follow the conventional rescue plot, in which the mother-Queen is truly benign and the sorcerer-abductor evil. But under pressure for various reasons, they "changed their minds" after getting to the middle of the first act and after that point reversed the valences in the plot.[24]

That such theories arise at all is testimony to the obvious fact that the presence of two different Queens is hermeneutically radioactive, very, very hot. And still both explanations, the epistemological earthquake and the change of course, seem equally hollow. One mirrors too readily the concept of "Weibertücke," the inherent deceptiveness of women, so often cited by Sarastro and the Priests of Wisdom. The other, presenting itself as a history of the work's genesis, has no factual basis. What might seem less hollow— less void of possibilities for wonderment, and more frightening by far— would be to suppose that the Queen is as she appears: both the kind regent, and the monster ready to eat up its child. There is no initial deceptiveness, no revelation of a hidden truth, but simply a great change. She is prone to metamorphosis, to mutation in body and mind: that is her symptom.

Two transformed beings—the Harpy of "Le roi magicien" and the second Queen in *Magic Flute*—thus appear as sisters in affliction. One started as a man and one as a woman, but they both end up vengeful, uncontrolled, violently opposite to a previous benign incarnation, ready to kill their children and their rivals. *Magic Flute*'s first Queen originated in a fairy-tale cliché, the sad mother who sends the hero on his quest. Models for this figure are found in the opera's most direct literary sources, such as *Lulu, oder die Zauberflöte*. From what fragments was the second Queen assembled? From a tradition of furious women, the "rasende Weiber" of eighteenth-century theater, from previous operatic characters and their rage arias.[25] From misogynistic anxieties concerning female power: all these, to be sure. And none of these can in the end account for the second Queen's incarnation as musical voice, as a chimerical being, one whose avian features are written into the transformation of her voice into piping and trills.

In "Le roi magicien" the immediate cause of the King's transformation is spelled out and in *The Magic Flute* metamorphosis is simply there, yet the former suggests an understanding of the latter. The Wizard King's transsexual conversion into a Harpy happens in full view of the reader, explained by jealousy. At the same time, it is both prefigured and echoed in the other transformations, other reversions to impotence as a symbolic condition of the feminine. Thus, his metamorphosis becomes something more than a logical consequence. It is a recurring motion, a gesture approaching the condition of music: a leitmotif. Once more a curious aspect of the opera's libretto—in this case the two Queens—might be understood as a trace, laid down by a hidden fable about a terribly changed King.

Yet the entire question of intention in the relationship between fairy tale and libretto is irrelevant, though imagining the Queen of the Night to have been modeled on a man is hugely attractive precisely because it is so beautifully ironic. One need not understand the Queen's shift from benign to monstrous as based on the Wizard King's, to understand that the fairy tale has intimated how her transformation might be understood: as a descending arabesque, a habitual fall toward the earth.

And one need not assume conscious borrowing on Schikaneder's part to reflect upon one particular observation in "Le roi magicien" and upon its significance for *Magic Flute* as occupants of a shared cultural territory. The fairy tale, mirroring a contemporary science of biological gender, intimates that metamorphosis and metempsychosis are magical powers but also symptoms that point to instability in sexual identity. They are both the cause and the consequence of crossing a certain forbidden line and are thus the betraying mark of feminized men and masculine women.

While the avian superstratum in what the Queen sings seems self-evident, what might connect her music in the opera not just with a chimera—the human who becomes the bird—but with her symptom, metamorphosis?

III

Contemplating that music in terms of contemporary philosophies concerning both musical voice and female speech means acknowledging its ambiguous nature. The Queen's coloratura represents pure music as a transcendent utterance, but a form of transcendence that at any moment can revert to irrational shrieks, soulless birdsong. By now it is utterly commonplace to understand coloratura—indeed any kind of wordless singing—as symbolic and suspect, being a representation of voice without the anchor of logos. As Mladen Dolar summarizes it, this is a trope that

> will recur throughout history with astonishing obstinacy . . . music, in particular the voice, shouldn't stray away from words, which endow it with sense; as soon as it departs from this textual anchorage, the voice becomes senseless and threatening, all the more so because of its seductive and intoxicating powers. Furthermore, the voice beyond sense is self-evidently equated with femininity, whereas the text, the instance of signification, is in this simple paradigmatic opposition on the side of masculinity . . . the voice beyond words is a senseless play of sensuality, it is a dangerous attractive force, although in itself empty and frivolous.[26]

And still: musical voice without words—incarnate as "pure instrumental music"—is also the other extreme: the transcendent.

Moreover, music suffering from an absence of logos is not, *pace* Dolar, simply equivalent to music lacking a vocal part with words. In the forms of musical aesthetics that circulated during the Enlightenment, music's representational capacity is another "instance of signification" whose absence was deplorable, again by creating senseless or merely sensual sound. In the "Querelle des Bouffons," in the famous debates on the relative merits of French or Italian music, this criterion—possessing or lacking the instance of signification—was exploited by both sides. Thus for Rousseau, French music suffered from an excess of harmonic complexity, from a penchant for sheer sonorities, which are empty because, unlike melody as a trace of human passions, they are not a sign.

For proponents of the opposite side, Italian music with opera as its chief representative tended toward emptiness in another way, the one identified by Dolar.[27] Vocal melody in Italian opera seria is broken and stripped of mimetic capacity by becoming sheer virtuosity, coloratura singing. It is not just the degradation of sensible language into vowel sounds that creates the "voice beyond sense," but also the degradation of melodic line, which has the capacity to represent passion, into that which should have remained supplementary: into the ornament. But not all the philosophers in the world can deprive this empty and sensual music of its power. Railing against it is like railing against beauty itself; the doggedness of the antagonism is testimony to the futility of the enterprise. The earthquake of 1800, the upheaval in musical aesthetics during the decline of mimetic theories of music, might thus be seen as an attempt to cope with a residue that should have been defeated by argument yet refused to go away. Musical beauty, freed from the imperative to imitate the world and from the guilt of failing to do so, is reconstrued as fallout from the noumenal. The path to Schopenhauer becomes self-evident.

But of course there are ways of condemning the musical voice without words—without the instance of signification—as something profoundly degraded. The most powerful way is to restyle it metaphorically as the voice of a woman. How easy it is to align that voice without words as senseless and feminine, with familiar eighteenth-century images of female speech as void of meaning and purely sonorous, whether in the worst sense, or the best.[28] The priests in *Magic Flute* are eloquent on the subject, especially the Speaker in the act 1 finale. If Schikaneder's immediate inspiration was the Abbé Terrasson's novel *Sethos,* in which Queen

Daluca is demonized for her constant chattering, parallel judgments resounded in contemporary misogynist discourse.[29]

By act 2 Tamino has learned to be equally dismissive, but his revoicing of this sentiment adds a new and interesting note. In the Quintet, he tells Papageno that the admonitions of the three Ladies are "idle chatter, repeated by women, but thought up by blasphemers!" Here, women's talk is no longer just senseless noise, but something more disquieting still: a mechanical repetition of sounds that are a priori. In this single line, Tamino does away with the possibility that female speech might be an incomprehensible and silly language understood by other aliens, much as birds might understand one another. Women instead have been made into acoustic marionettes and sound reproduction devices.

Tamino's brief remark makes the connection developed at length as a savage image of chattering women as talking machines in Jean Paul's satiric essay on Wolfgang von Kempelen (1788). Jean Paul envisages a *Damengericht,* an imaginary law court of women whose judgments are capricious and pronouncements formulaic. The peril to women represented by Kempelen's invention of a "speaking machine" is that they will be deprived of their livelihood: machines can clack as routinely and thoughtlessly as they can. In a bizarre final vision, women conversing in salons are seen as doubles for lifeless machines that emit sounds at one another. As the narrator puts it:

> We have no wish that the misery, which Herr von Kempele has inflicted upon us through his speaking machines, should in turn visit him upon his deathbed and make him break out in a sweat. In truth, we require nothing worse than that he, perhaps even while still in the flower of life, should perchance go by a salon full of talking machines and clearly hear them talking, and be plagued by this recurring thought. "Alas, alas, here in this commodious chamber, every armchair could have been occupied by a talking lady, and even more could have been sitting on the sofa, holding forth in their usual, I believe, court of judgement, and all in all satisfy one another frightfully well, had I only withstood Satan. But now twelve highly deadly machines are chattering in there in quite lively fashion, and are listening neither to themselves nor to one another."[30]

The sardonic point being, the two populations recumbent on the furniture are easily interchangeable. One might even say that in Jean Paul's alchemy, these women's voices reveal their vulnerability to metamorphosis of another sort entirely. Rather than changing into birds, or shifting along a spectrum of femininity and masculinity, they are subject to what was by 1788 becoming the most uncanny mutation of all: they were changing into automata. Blasphemers are capable of thought, while female machines that reproduce sound have no mind, no capacity to know whether what they emit is benign or evil, good music or bad. Doubts about sexuality have become doubts about subjectivity. Jean Paul's essay bears witness to profound fears about the chimera as something arrested between two states. Our monsters are all of this order: the bird with a woman's face, the man with a woman's body, the human voice that sounds like a flute, the natural bird that is also a machine.

IV

Jean-Paul's essay also serves to remind us obliquely that the avian was by the latter part of the eighteenth century by no means simply a trope for unspoiled nature, just as birdsong was not straightforwardly symbolic of natural music.[31] In the same way, "Le roi magicien" reminds us how men (like Papageno) who have avian features are not just charming rustic creatures straight out of Rousseau. In one Victorian illustration for the story, the King, courting his sulky Princess, has resumed human form (see fig. 2.3). However, he has cloth feathers on his cape, as if bird forms were marking his body but leaving his head unscathed, anticipating the future Harpy. And that snake on the cape is eating a baby's head.

Those cloth feathers recall quite powerfully, if coincidentally, the *Urbild* for Papageno, the famous Alberti engraving of Schikaneder with his birdcage, first published in the original 1791 libretto, a visual model for dozens of subsequent Papagenos (see fig. 2.4). This echo may be allowed some legitimacy merely as a goad toward thinking about human beings that take on bird forms. In this mutation, they play out over time what the Harpy freezes into a simultaneous physical combination, into a grotesque corporeal melange. One could say therefore that men who are half bird represent at once the essence and the worst of the chimerical.[32]

But in certain eighteenth-century intellectual cultures, you do not even need a chimera: the bird per se already invokes at once the natural

Figure 2.3. Illustration for "The Wizard King."

Figure 2.4. From the original *Magic Flute* libretto.

creature and the automaton bird. As such, the bird is a famous figure in eighteenth-century mechanist philosophy, since the perfected reproduction of birdsong by automata and "bird-organs" made them into highly resonant objects in eighteenth-century philosophical discourse.[33] Meditations on birds and automaton birds appear frequently in such writings, as in La Mettrie's *L'homme machine* (1748), in which one broad stroke aligns men, animals, and birds with their artificial simulacra:

> We can see that there is only one substance in the universe, and that man is its most perfect one. He is to the ape and the cleverest animals what Huygens's planetary clock is to one of Julien Leroy's watches. If it took more instruments, more cogs, more springs to show the movement of the planets than to show or tell time, if it took Vaucanson more artistry to make his flautist than his duck, he would have needed even more to make a speaking machine, which can no longer be considered impossible, particularly at the hands of a new Prometheus.[34]

This argument by gleeful juxtaposition, the claim that automaton forms (cited here specifically as Vaucanson's automaton duck and flute player) are no other than human or animal forms, found its most famous expression in Diderot's *Entretien entre d'Alembert et Diderot* (1769). This was, of course, a work whose radical atheism precluded its open circulation during Diderot's lifetime. Musical instrument, man, bird, and automaton bird: these are the four creatures that inhabit Diderot's discourse, and they are constantly and easily elided. In a passage that echoes La Mettrie, Diderot writes: "That leaves only one substance in the universe, in man, in animals. The bird-organ is made of wood; man is made of flesh. A canary is flesh, a musician is flesh differently organized, but they have one and the same origin, formation, functions, and end."[35] Diderot does not postulate a metamorphosis that transforms one into the other, nor does he invent little narratives about men mutating into birds, or musical instruments into men.

Instead, the equivalence and interchangeability of the four objects is precipitated into the argument itself. After comparing philosophers to clavichords and the fibers of human organs to vibrating strings, Diderot asks why one should not imagine that clavichords have memories and thus know and replay the melodies that are performed on them. They mate with female clavichords, who give birth to "little clavichords, alive and resonant." This thoughtful, mobile, and self-playing instrument is just what "a finch is, or a nightingale, or a musician, or a man."[36] Mechanist analogies make them one and the same:

> The bird emerges, walks, flies, feels pain, runs away, comes back again, complains, suffers, loves, desires, enjoys, it experiences all your affections and does all the things you do. And will you maintain, with Descartes, that it is an imitating machine pure and simple? Why, even little children will laugh at you, and philosophers will answer that if it is a machine you are one too![37]

Such delight at the mechanical status of man is characteristic of an innocent moment in the history of automata, a moment at which they are still fine philosophical toys without an underside. This moment was extraordinarily brief. Anxieties about the human simulacrum and its ability to take over human tasks surfaced by the 1780s, as Jean Paul's essay suggests.

The King who becomes a Harpy has suffered metamorphosis as the sign of his dangerously fluid sexual identity. Yet in the philosophical discourse concerning men and birds, the Harpy-King, like Jean Paul's chattering women, came to summarize the mechanist chimera, the slide between human being and machine.

V

What kind of music does a chimera make? One can create a chimera-voice easily now through computer generation, as a colloidal suspension of human and machine timbre: a cyborg voice, where one hears both at once. With the musical resources of 1791, the means are different.

Papageno appears as a "natural" character, and he even refers to himself as a "Naturmensch." This is not to say that he is merely rustic or comic. There is an equally strong interpretive tradition, based in Kierkegaard's famous discussion in *Either/Or,* which views him as derived from antique archetypes, as Dionysus. Adding Mozart's music for Papageno's numbers into this brew seems not to inflect these images in the least. How easily this music has been at once admired and set aside as expressing happy simplicity, the cyclic force of elemental nature and natural reason, or as a representation of lower-class music making.[38] Other

aspects of his musical persona seem analogous. As the only male character who reverts to singing without words—in the act 1 quintet when his
mouth is locked shut, and in the act 2 finale, stammering "Pa-pa-pa"—he
can exemplify a prelinguistic creature from some lost Arcadia. In the duet
with Papageno, this creature along with its bride is caught at a mythic
moment, acquiring language as the audience looks on.

The magic bell sounds, however, combine with Papageno's singing to
produce unnatural effects. Where his panpipes seem self-evident as a natural instrument, the bells are in every sense the opposite. Their sounds
suggest artifice at high volume, and their entanglement with Papageno's
voice creates the chimerical sound-object.

Papageno gets his bells from the Queen's ladies during the act 1 quintet, when the First Lady says, "Here, take this little thing, it is yours."
Papageno's response is "Oh ho! What might be in there?" This implies
that the prop hides something. After the ladies reply, "From inside you
will hear little bells ringing," he asks an interesting question. Can he play
these bells as well? The object handed to Papageno is thus said to produce musical sound with or without a human performer to operate the
instrument.

This object, what it might mean that it is hidden, what it looks like,
what it was in October 1791, why it remains mysterious and must remain
so: these have been largely unasked questions, for two hundred years. The
Neue-Mozart-Ausgabe refers to the prop generically as a "Glockenspiel."
But the prop handed to Papageno in 1791 had two given names. The original libretto called it "eine Maschine wie ein hölzernes Gelächter"—literally "a machine like wooden laughter"—and the stage directions in the
autograph score say that the First Lady gives him "ein stählnes
Gelächter," laughter in steel. "Hölzernes Gelächter" is an archaic Viennese dialect term for a rustic wooden xylophone, but the phrase also had
a connotation of "empty" or "hollow laughter," a definition metaphorically connected with the sound of the instrument, the rattle made of
bones.[39] Grimms' dictionary cites one seventeenth-century source that
refers to its timbre as "sounding happy, but without content."[40] The
instrument has lost the capacity to suggest human discourse, while keeping the outward forms of human noise.

Of course, the instrument that actually produced the bell sounds was in the wings; Mozart himself played it at the performance of 8 October 1791, as we know from one of his most famous letters. The autograph calls it "Istromento d'acciaio" ("instrument of steel"), a new keyboard instrument with at least a three-octave range, in which hammers struck metal bars. Not literally a Glockenspiel (since there were not literally bells), this thing was an addition to the instrumentarium of the eighteenth century. Its later descendent, the celesta, was to take over responsibility for realizing Papageno's bells by the mid-nineteenth century. The magic bell music is written "for the keyboard" with rapid arpeggios and chords that lie under both hands over more than two octaves.

Thus the disjunction between sight and sound implicit in the prop itself, as a box that hides what is inside, reflects another disjunction. The music conjures up the keyboard instrument and the flashing pianist hands, but those sounds are associated on stage with the little prop that Papageno strikes. The physical gesture of Papageno's hand on the object is radically separate from what one hears. To reunite gesture and sound, to perfect the illusion that music comes from the prop, one must assume that Papageno possesses a music machine of unknown morphology, "a machine like wooden laughter": from inside, music plays. Yet the bell music connects directly and without fault or omission to another part of Papageno's body, to his *throat:* with a single exception, Papageno's voice falls silent the instant he engages the bells.

Why? The bells are not a woodwind instrument, like the panpipes and the magic flute. Flutes and pipes, played with the mouth, entail an absolute suppression of voice. They are wind instruments that substitute for singing, with breath and melody but no words. With the panpipes, the singer cast as Papageno actually stops singing to blow on them. With the flute, Tamino sometimes "plays" between his sung lines, and the singer must mime accordingly. The magic bells are in a box and are played with hands alone, yet Papageno is nonetheless unable to sing with them. This is striking because in general all stage instruments held in the lap, or on the arm, in the hand, away from the mouth, have the opposite effect. You play them, and you sing at the same time, whether you are holding a percussion instrument (Carmen and her castanets), or pressing keys or plucking strings. Stringed instruments especially seem to cry out for serenading—as in Don Giovanni's "Deh, vieni alla finestra" with its mandolin, or Pedrillo's song in *Abduction from the Seraglio* (or Beckmesser, or Orfeo and his lyre).

When the magic bells ring in between Papageno's singing, and only then, it is as if they too were a wind instrument, as if their music were a product of Papageno's lungs, or they were something that makes him mute. In the act 2 "Glockenspiel" aria, shifts between voice and bells often occur at breathless half-measure intervals (see music ex. 2.1). During the final part of each verse, the bells repeatedly cut off the rising melodic figure and fragment the text ["doch küsst mich . . . ein weibli- . . . cher Mund"]. Like a glottal stop, the bell sounds clap down over a portal that emits the Papageno voice, rise up to allow that voice passage, then slam shut to silence it again. With the technological resources of 1791, one cannot generate a cyborg voice, a chimerical voice that combines mechanistic and natural human sound. But the chimera may arise magically within the alteration of bells and voice, as if, in the rapid oscillation between one and the other, the blur might represent a metamorphic timbre that cannot otherwise exist.

This absolute separation of voice and bells is an extraordinary phenomenon, concealed in plain sight. Panpipes and flutes encourage an acceptance of "play-sing-play-sing" as nothing more than the way these things are done, the hand waved to distract the eye from a grotesque sight: a mouth that has been shut by strange musical sounds.

When Papageno thus falls silent, his enforced muteness echoes a comic moment from act 1, his locked mouth in the Quintet. The same gesture turns up in another form, however, when Monostatos and his slaves hear the magic bell sounds in the act 1 finale. They are not exactly struck mute, since they are singing away, "That sounds so wonderful, that sounds so beautiful, I have never heard or seen anything like it." Yet as autonomous beings, they make no noise at all: the bell sounds have kidnapped their bodies and forced new voices into their throats. When the mechanical figures march stiffly across the stage and speak stilted marionette speech, metamorphosis takes place in plain sight, as an automaton collective that comes into being out of raw human material. Those danc-

Example 2.1. The Glockenspiel aria

ing slaves even recall a typical ornament on automata of the eighteenth century, little moreschi with striped costumes and bells.

The music for this episode is simple in form and melody, transparent to the ear. What exactly separates it from the other music that sounds much like it, Papageno's songs, those rhapsodies from the *Naturmensch* himself? In such music, the natural and the unnatural have come together

Example 2.1. (*continued*)

II

as a form of musical discourse that is chimerical and deceptive, one that is in between. During the nineteenth century, this scene from *The Magic Flute* became a typical "number" for music boxes, as if musical automata were claiming their own from within the opera. That music boxes should play this music seems logical but is not necessarily innocent and charming, and can give rise to grim fantasies, as in Jonathan Demme's film *The Silence of the Lambs* (1991). In the movie, a music box playing this "number" is found in a dead-end space: in an abandoned room belonging to a girl who has been killed, murdered so her skin can be put to the sewing machine. A girl, in other words, converted into industrial raw material.

When Papageno at last sings with the bells (in the final seconds before Papagena's appearance in the act 2 finale), there is thus a miraculous escape from all machines, from their grip and their needle. He is using the bells, at the suggestion of the Three Spirits, to conjure up his lost beloved, and the passage begins with the bells, as usual, replacing his voice in typical statement-echo patterns. But in the final measures his voice suddenly sings over the bells, drowning them out (see music ex. 2.2, mm. 21–24). The threat of metamorphosis—the mutation of human voice into "laughter in steel"—is laid to rest in the instant that the bells are reduced to accompaniment, something that has no power to replace or arrest human singing. The chimerical half-man half-instrument is split in two, the bells fall permanently silent, while the human voice escapes.

And still: pull the focus back to a simple, practical explanation for the constant separation of bells and voice, and one sees that the bells were powerless all along. Mozart's "instrument of steel"—the protocelesta in the wings—despite its manly name produced sound too weak to prevail over full baritone force. For the bell sounds to be heard at all, the singer needs to be quiet, and the play of voice and bells began with this acoustic fact of life. Yet, the fact of life evolved into the symbol, a phenomenon that left its imprint on the prop forms of the bells over time. In a set of 1793 engravings thought to represent the original Viennese staging, the prop is a box on a strap, hiding whatever is within.[41] Thereafter, the more familiar form turns up, the rotisserie or tennis racket of bells, the "Schellenbaum" that Papageno holds close to his head, as it were his head in another form. As early as 1795, whatever had been in the box jumped out, assumed the guise of little bells, and started creeping up toward Papageno's face, as if propelled by its symbolic power to shut his mouth.

Example 2.2. "Klinget Glöckchen, klinget"

Example 2.2. (*continued*)

II

VI

The sunny major mode of the Glockenspiel aria obscures the nocturnal role of the magic bells. The conversion of human voice into instrumental sound or metallic piping is played out more audibly in the arias sung by the Queen of the Night. Her coloratura has been read as a representation of baroque affect, signaling her alignment with an outmoded absolutist order.[42] More globally, however, it can be read as representing an absence of rationality, an excess of passion, and thus as essentially female speech. This particular truism has come to constitute a psychoanalytic, literary, and musicological monolith, tugged along by a critical armada.

To appreciate its dimensions, one need only cite accounts of the Queen's voice as summarized by Michel Poizat.[43] For him, her voice is something that "makes present the imaginary 'maternal,'" constituting "a musical version of sheer high-pitched cries" that bear evidence to a "will to destroy the word."[44] As a figure of "maternal bliss" initially accorded positive value, the Queen bans the "law of the Word and the Father" from her realm.[45] Her voice quickly becomes the focus of a profound ambivalence, once its suasions must be renounced in favor of "culture, architecture, and the Temple, which in act I must be substituted for the realm of savage nature."[46] Or, in Clément's famous phrase: "this is a losing song; it is femininity's song."[47]

Within the dramatic fiction, of course, the Queen is demonized in terms that reflect deep cultural anxieties about female rule; the historical bases for these anxieties are patent and were reflected in many contemporary allegorical readings of the plot. Her habit of metamorphosis can be understood in this economy of anxiety as a transsexual symptom, the sign of her masculine aspirations.

Perhaps her darkest literary association is with the figure of Cybele, as noted earlier. Schinkel recognized the connection: in his famous neoclassical designs for the 1812 Berlin production, he dressed the Queen in a peplum and, significantly, in a *Mauerkrone*, the characteristic headdress in Cybele's iconography. Cybele herself has musical overtones. In legend she was accompanied by eunuchs who carried boxes containing their missing body parts; this entourage sang and made music on flutes and drums, surrounding her with shrill sounds. That instrumental pairing in turn suggests two further mythological sources. These are the instruments played by the Maenads who murdered Orpheus, flutes and drums that were capable of drowning out Orpheus's music and neutralizing its magical protections. And they are the instrumental pair that is conjoined in the legend of Apollo and Marsyas: the faun, daring to challenge the god in a musical competition, played the flute against Apollo's lyre. For his boldness he was flayed alive, his skin hung on a tree, thus becoming, as skin next to wood, a kind of protodrum. Much of the humming mythic backdrop that is channeled through the Queen, as a reference to Cybele, cries out for the pairing of flute and drum in a reminder that, in certain backwaters of Greek legend at least, flutes are not nice.[48]

The female king who covets power, the irrational and unstable terror: is she there as sound? Of course, there is that immense critical drive, which makes all the music associated with the Queen of the Night "bad," or at least, into the "losing" sound in an allegorical battle between assumed stylistic extremes. This is not how her singing is perceived within a performance (in any competent performance), where her voice becomes an object of intense desire, and her arias an occasion for celebration: the winning song. Perhaps, however, this merely demonstrates that opera-as-sung is recruiting the listener to several wrong alliances, one more time.

The point is nonetheless more complicated: Ulybyshev, for instance, wrote "the contrast of light and dark, musically speaking, is simply not present. Those characters that are supposed to personify darkness—the Queen of the Night, the Three Ladies, Monostatos—have nothing black about them, with the exception of their costumes and their skin. Their singing does not evoke the shadow at all, and is not capable of doing so."[49] If Ulybyshev's aesthetics of musical "darkness" was historically conditioned—possibly, he imagines *Der Freischütz* act 2—his claim nonetheless suggests that there is a musically embodied Queen of the Night whose relation to her onstage personification is tangential.

This particular Queen—the one in the depths of the music—is curiously resistant to banishment or misogynist caricature or defeat. In his penultimate engraving for *The Magic Flute*, Slevogt captured this musical object as a visual symbol, as women who are about to escape into transfigured flight. Slevogt's engravings, which dismembered a score for optical material and seem to illustrate a plot, thus create their most striking effect when translating music into visible form.

VII

The Queen appears during an orchestral passage that accompanies her arrival in act 1 and serves as a prelude to her opening recitative. In this *creatio ex nihilo* opening, a quiet B♭ pedal point in the basses and cellos builds into a third on B♭ and D, then a triad, then some louder arpeggios, finally ending in an annunciation, the fanfare of descending B♭ major triads (see music ex. 2.3). Her first vocal line is not just a new beginning after this prelude, but also its completion, the closing flourish to a great instrumental crescendo that the vocal entrance repeats in miniature. An instrumental pyramid finds its end in a human voice, and a human voice seems to come into being as an arpeggio born of instrumental sound.

But the orchestral prelude also sounds familiar, as if it were a memory of something already heard. Moments before, in the middle section of the portrait aria, Tamino sang "Oh! Could I but find her!" to a similar syncopated B♭ pedal point (see music ex. 2.4). Tamino's "her" is Pamina; he is gazing at her portrait and wishing that "she" could appear in his presence. The woman who appears moments later is the other one, but the music is repeated nonetheless, and the musical correspondence thus elides Pamina and the Queen, constructing their acoustic genealogy. This genealogy assumes another form in two vocal motifs, the descending D-C-B♭-A-G that opens the Queen's act 1 aria (in G minor, 6/8), repeated and varied as Pamina's opening line in her aria (G minor, 6/8) in act 2. Horace Vernet's drawing of the Queen and Tamino, in which a very young Queen hands Tamino the magic flute, seems to reflect these musical alliances (see fig. 2.5). Vernet transposed a moment from the act 2 finale, where Pamina is reunited with Tamino and restores the flute to him, into act 1 as the meeting of Tamino and the Queen. Yet the vignette's confusion of mother and daughter is not simply imaginary: it is there in the opera, just not visibly.

Example 2.3. The Queen's entrance music, act 1

In the portrait aria, Tamino's desire to see the absent woman is phrased in the subjunctive. His "she" is not there, as provisional as the B♭ pedal point against which he sings, a bass fixed on a pitch, which, despite its position in the lowest register, at the bottom, cannot be secure against the A♭s in Tamino's vocal line. Those dissonant sevenths between voice

Example 2.4. From Tamino's aria, act 1

Figure 2.5. Vernet, "La flûte enchantée."

and bass create a pervasive instability, whispering about the bass's imminent move to E♭. With the Queen's appearance, however, the same B♭ bass pulse is no longer "in the subjunctive," no longer the lowest point in a sonority that "must be resolved." Desire is erased, but not in the way the aria imagines, not by resolution but by reinterpretation of the B♭ bass: as the last word. As music, the dream image in the portrait aria walks directly into reality, sooner than Tamino had imagined.

This link between premonition and unexpected materialization represents the Queen and her voice as a miraculous precipitation from that which was immaterial, only imaginable or implied, the perfect B♭ pulse hidden within the unstable one. She is positioned as the transcendent, and this will reflect upon all her other manifestations, upon her habit of metamorphosis, and her reversion to coloratura, the aspect of her musical embodiment most subject to being demonized.

Dolar's characterization of the voice without words, cited earlier, can stand for the loud critical consensus that has read the Queen's coloratura as a manifestation of hysteria, as proving her sensuality, as irrationality, as sinister feminine attraction (vocal variety), as ancien régime, as a cry from the presymbolic order. Ulybyshev's perception that her singing cannot be evidence of "darkness" seems odd, given the counterweight of twentieth-century interpretation. What would it mean, however, to imagine a music that is incapable of darkness? For some, this simply involves a journey away from the fiction of the stage world, and from the opera as a transcendent work, to the immediate phenomenon of the performance. The Queen's second aria, the "revenge" aria, represents a triumph of musical execution.[50] Ulybyshev remarks upon the common contemporary practice of trans-posing the aria, which he supports, since otherwise "the only instance of powerful and sustained passion" in the opera might have to be cut.[51]

Still, one need not necessarily depart from the fiction to avoid the darkness. The Queen's second aria, that dwarf star that emits so much musical evil, is several different aria fragments as one. Radically different kinds of singing appear within it, a brief declamatory opening verse void of ornament, a final section in recitative, and a big coloratura center. In the whole aria no single vocal style is sustained for more than a minute before being superceded; and the aria, though incredibly short, accom-modates shifts of musical shape second by second.

Even more extreme: the coloratura singing is set apart from that in the first aria, as from Mozart's other bravura soprano arias, in one signifi-cant technical way. In her act 2 melismas, the Queen sings only arpeggios, no scales at all (see music ex. 2.5). There are no conjunct melodic runs up or down some diatonic ladder or other, no conventional operatic *passaggi* of the kind familiar from eighteenth-century *seria* arias. And with this technical departure, an unprecedented voice comes into being, one with no capacity for melodic conjunction. In this—and not in any simple loss of words—voice metamorphoses into an impossible device, a wind in-strument unknown in 1791, unknown ever since. When this instrument-voice is echoed by the high violins and doubled by the flute in measures 73–79, the equivalence of voice and instrument is expressed as a set of mir-rors exactly parallel to one another, in which one cannot say what is reflected, and what is really there.

This is not, however, simply a moment of passion, hysteria, rage, irra-tionality, babbling, essentially feminine noise, not a shriek, not a degrada-

Example 2.5. From the Queen's aria, act 2

tion, not the philosophical nightmare of *logos* dissolved into *melos,* nor any natural sound, not a losing song, not at all. Voice is suspended in a sonic overworld, as if it wanted to linger there for a few seconds, in itself serene but at the same time, to the listener, strange in a way that disarms the very fear that threatens one's astonishment: it is cold. This cannot possibly be sustained. Conventional operatic vocalism returns along with perceptible human speech, right before the end.

One could therefore say that the Queen's habit of metamorphosis, her symptom, manifests itself in her second aria in two forms. There are juxtapositions, the many vocal idioms that succeed one another without the luxury of gradual transition. And there is the moment in which voice becomes instrument in a mutation that outlines the affinity between unlike characters, Papageno and the Queen. This mutation, in the Queen's case, remains both an instance of transcendence and of peril and cannot be fixed as one or the other. Her voice emerges from the instrumental as a marvel, and, transmuted from organic to metallic, reverts to the instrumental as an uncanny sound.

VIII

Music in which human voice balances between instrumental and vocal represents metamorphosis, which in the historical context of the Enlightenment reflects at once anxiety about sexual fluidity, and the lost barrier between human and mechanical. In *The Magic Flute,* instances of metamorphosis have a glow predicated on a sense that, as signs, they cannot be fully deciphered. Those who reject mimesis as an aesthetic precept have been content to view music itself this way: as a hieroglyph, as meaning concealed by the very form of its manifestation.

In one scene in *Magic Flute,* however, hieroglyphs (real ones) play an important part: the Trial scene in the act 2 finale, where the stage directions call for a pyramid on which hieroglyphs are inscribed as "transparent writing." In 1791, Egyptian hieroglyphs had not yet been deciphered; breaking their code had become a scientific obsession for eighteenth-century Egyptologists. So the fact that the two armored men can translate the hieroglyphs and read them out loud is a scholarly insider joke, staging pure impossibility for those who knew enough to appreciate the jest.

What happens is magical not for *what* the writing says (which is standard stuff) but because it can be read at all:

> Der welcher wandert diese Strasse voll Beschwerden
> Wird rein durch Feuer, Wasser, Luft, und Erden.
> Wenn er des Todes Schrecken überwinden kann,
> Schwingt er sich aus der Erde himmelan!
> Erleuchtet wird er dann imstande sein
> Sich den Mysterien der Isis ganz zu weihn.—

> [He who wanders on this way full of peril / Will be purified by fire,
> water, air, and earth. / If he can overcome the horrors of death, / He will
> raise himself from Earth to heaven! / Illuminated, he will then be capable
> / of consecrating himself fully to Isis's mysteries.]

One last lexographic frisson: because the armored men also *sing* what they read, the scene suggests that music itself—pitches and rhythm—is encoded in the Egyptian ideograms on the pyramid. And this marvel rightly draws our attention to the readers. The figures are never required to lift their visors—to be deciphered—and reveal their true faces.

There is much at stake in a scene where reading an inscription out loud is brought so prominently into play, thus staging a musical perform-ance with all necessary elements in place, the written script, the perform-ers in full costume, their voices, and the acoustic materiality of the realization. When the white-gloved hand lays things out with such care, the dead object problem inherent in performance occupies the spotlight.

For instance, the armored men have been made into media. They "read out loud," something not every different from repeating something one has heard. That, of course, is the sin committed by chattering women and by sound-reproduction machines. Both "vorlesen" and "nachsagen" involve a text and its repetition as live sound, though the two activities are not equivalent in status, since repeating what one reads suggests higher intellectual powers than repeating what one hears, the culture of writing as opposed to that of analphabets and oral transmission. And nonetheless, if the chattering women are easily reconstrued as "deadly machines," mechanically transmitting something a priori, what can save the armored men? In this, there is no distinction between women and men, and the metal plating covering the men is symbolic.[52] Turning the tables, one could say that text that is visibly present as an inscription speaks through the two armored men. The men do not sing the text—rather, the text switches them on, directs their vocal cords and lungs. Like two phonograph needles they sense what is graven into a recording medium and vibrate with its sound, which they transmit at high volume, and once the inscription has run out, they fall silent.

A famous comic parataxis follows the transmission. When Pamina's voice calls from offstage, the musical mood shifts instantly to opera buffa and, released from the inscription, the armored men sing in cheery tones: "Yes, yes! That is Pamina's voice!" Their new voices are completely unlike their old voices, a quick vocal costume change, disorienting and funny, but also perplexing. Are the figures merely conduits for sounds that are not theirs? Gothic or sunny, chorale prelude or opera, it does not matter what they sing, since they sing without volition. Having thus been exposed as devices, the armored men remain under suspicion of repeating scripts by rote, shifting instantly and perfectly from one sound to another. That is why their visors are closed: they have no faces of their own.

IX

The Trial scene is a double-exposure: a scene about Tamino's and Pamina's final meeting and how the hero and heroine undergo their trials, and a scene involving the performance network, highlighting the human and inhuman values performance can represent. Mozart has even inserted himself into this network and its mechanisms. Just as the armored men perform their a priori text, so Mozart (famously) repeated preexisting music in setting their reading, placing a Lutheran chorale tune in the armored men's mouths. Observing two male conduits, he put himself in their position: as a stylus that transcribes music from somewhere else, as a hand whose motions are prescribed by a musical text, as the third armored man in the scene. His quotation of the chorale and the chorale prelude and fugue in this scene have often been interpreted as a musico-historical invocation of J. S. Bach, appropriate to the serious quasi-religious ritual onstage.

But the extraordinary effect of this music derives not just from humane implications of artistic homage, but from a nocturnal quality without which it would cease to be so transfixing or to feed the antitriumphalist interpretations and their doubts. Once more Ulybyshev comes up with a morbid idea:

> The mysterious pair sings to themselves, while at the same time the fugal entrances, each in turn oblivious to every other, grip each other like the gears in a clock that ticks and ticks, but whose face is blank, bearing neither numbers nor hands. The terror creeps gradually into the strings, extends and reproduces itself, shared by every voice, flowing from one instrument to another. It frees itself from the orchestra like a mourning song, which echoes in contrapuntal imitations, dull whimpering or suppressed sighing, into infinity. This alien music, thus struggling with death, engenders theater in the eyes of the soul, a theater that gradually elides into that present on the stage, until the music produces a kind of intellectual phantasmagoria.[53]

The armored men—singing "to themselves" though seeming to address Tamino—lack the natural exhibitionism of human performers and the will to communicate. The famous fugue is produced by cogwheels, from inside an unreadable clock with a featureless face. What is perverse about this description is the nature imputed to the performance network that has been pressed into the work. If fugue is something that replicates itself, stamps out copies from voice to voice, then the echo effects of counterpoint symbolize the passage of musical works into performed reality as an industrial process, as the work of machines. If this music reflects on performance as repetition, it also tells what is lost in a blinding, pure, and exact transmission of the work from inscription to realization. That purity is both the magical promise, and the terror, implicit in devices that reproduce music.

This sets terms for subsequent sections of the Trial scene, though they often suggest a completely different mood, merry or ecstatic, far from severe. But throughout these shifting moods, across the formal bricolage that is common in operatic finales, repetitions, mirrors, and echoes proliferate and refer back to the prologue.

Some hold out intimations of escape. Right before Tamino and Pamina enter upon the Trials, they and the two armored men give voice to an epigram about musical power, twice singing the words "we will wander, through the power of sound / joyfully through Death's shadowy night." This rhapsody is beautiful beyond reproach, the musical heart of the opera—what is deepest in, and seems strongest against despair, against closed visors. The music conjures up blind reproduction in order to defeat it in extraordinarily subtle ways.

There are two parallel musical statements corresponding to the repeated text (see music ex. 2.6). The harmonic design is the same both times; though some flutes and bassoons are added the second time around. Four characters sing the same words, and the same four vocal melodies are repeated: aspects of blind reproduction. The melodies are exchanged between the voices, so that Tamino's melody with its leaps to A is assumed by Pamina in the reprise, while he sings her initial intoned Cs. Similarly, the two armored men take over each other's parts transposed by an octave. This contrapuntal device speaks strongly of the mirror, of course; voice exchanges are an inversion technique. Even on the page, one sees the double helix of notes in each pair of vocal lines, turning round its center.

Yet the exchanges themselves are far from exact—even as the voices suggest the mirror, they break it. Tamino, at first repeating music given to him as a script by Pamina's voice, devises a different ending, as does she with his music, as do the armored men with each other's lines. No repetition is exact: everyone is improvising. Once more, the hand lays out the inscription and the performance, the text and the repetition. Inscription and text, however, now only serve as a point of departure for something they have not ordained. Just as Papageno's voice will separate from the magic bells, so the four voices in their improvised flight play out a similar escape, with human autonomy set against capture and duplication. Singing the word "night," they fly their highest.

Ulybyshev and Stravinsky nonetheless note that a deadly mechanism appears instantly, as soon as this rhapsody fades away. The March for the Fire and Water Trials has a distinct status within the opera, appearing at one of the few places where the 1791 libretto calls for music from the stage that is not played exclusively by the magic flute, the bells, or the panpipes: "Tamino plays his flute; muffled drums accompany him at intervals underneath." This is implicitly realistic music, music within the stage world.[54] The accompaniment "underneath" is as if played by imaginary unseen instruments.

The March seems automatic by virtue of its captured and repeated improvisation. This quality, however, is suggested most clearly not in the

Example 2.6. From the act 2 finale

Example 2.6. (*continued*)

II

Example 2.6. (*continued*)

III

notes, in the melodies and rhythms, or the *da capo,* but in the orchestral sound, in the essence of a material object that has been made present by a unique timbre, as Bloch describes such phenomena in "Magic Rattle." An odd instrumental group accompanies the magic flute melody: tympani, along with trombones, trumpets, and horns, all playing softly. Muffled drums have funerary implications, and for the first and only time in the score there is a prominent flute-drum pair, a charged combination whose acoustic symbolism (Cybele, and so forth) is far from benign.

The instrumental snapshot, besides being mythic-poetic, also captures a specific contemporary reference. A solo flute is accompanied by a quiet drum, by brass instruments that hoot and puff as if they were an organ whose pipes were heard from behind closed doors. This sound leaves a distinct thumbprint: that of a "Flötenuhr," a cylinder-driven clock-organ that typically allied a flute stop with other wind stops (sometimes adding drums) and hid all the mallets, skins, and bellows within an ornamental case. Such instrumentation suggests the March's kinship with K.608, the fantasy and fugue Mozart wrote in 1791 for a Flötenuhr that played in a mausoleum.[55] The Flötenuhr itself, however, was a predecessor to bigger machines. By the decade of the 1790s, automaton builders had their sights set on reproducing human instrumental performance in its most elaborate collective form. The panharmonicon and orchestrion, developed in the last decade of the eighteenth century, were fruits of this ambition. The March in *The Magic Flute* makes a human orchestra labor to produce an automaton timbre at the very moment that late eighteenth-century science headed in the opposite direction. As far as it is devoid of the human, of sounds that suggest live bodies and laboring musicians, the March is perfect, and in being perfect, is dead.

And this is black comedy. Solemn rituals take place onstage, while a grinning compositional jester—the Mozart one never wants to see— makes human forms and their musical sounds into toys. There is even a visual reference to such toys. If the dancing slaves in the act 1 finale are ornamental moreschi, Tamino and Pamina, going in and out the gates, suggest another eighteenth-century objet de vertu, the clock with porcelain figurines that march into one door, circle around, march out, and march into another to repeat their ritual motions. By 1791, this object is no longer merely quaint: it has become nocturnal.

One may acknowledge that the music for the Trial scene has intermittently strange undertones but suggest that these straightforwardly reflect the perilous activities being pursued in the stage world, the fact that Tamino and Pamina are at a serious juncture. Such a claim—this would be the highest and most pointed irony—dismisses operatic music as mere repetition, fallout from the plot, an argument that accounts for operatic music in the saddest possible way: as a form of mechanical reproduction. The Trial scene represents mechanical reproduction in disquieting forms, defeated, resurrected, and contemplated once more. Musical inscriptions produce repetitions, in a series that allows one escape. In this back-and-forth, however, musical representation pays no attention to "good" and "evil" in the plot. This is true elsewhere as well. The Queen of the Night has a voice that transmutes into the instrumental, and then back into human singing; why such insistence that her "steel laughter" represent only messy emotional babble, or feminine rage? There is a story about happy magic bells, whose actual sounds nonetheless have a capacity to suggest, as Ernst Bloch knew, the occasion for despair. To see musical gesture as lying athwart the moral premises of fictions onstage of course postulates music's own escape from blind contingency, from a script. The *Magic Flute* music escapes because it imagines what the stage drama does not: the possibility of a nocturnal sun.

Yet in opera, music's metaphysical flight often—paradoxically—occurs simultaneously with a gesture of intense physical grounding, of the fall back to the earth. Papageno and the magic bells are a paradigmatic instance. If the bell sounds and their symbolism elude or subvert the libretto, those sounds are, nonetheless, represented as something anchored to the singer's body and throat, as if they and he were one. Music transcends narrative, or image, or philosophy, yet remains wholly tied to the material means of its production. And the latter, perhaps, is what we are least likely to honor.

X

Jankélévitch's "nocturnal sun" is not an inversion, the cinematic trick of "day for night," but rather seeks affinities between unlike terms, playing them off against one another. Inversion as a simpler gesture has nonetheless shaped postwar concepts of the European eighteenth century. As Terry Castle points out, intellectual fashions have created a "sense that the myriad transformations of the epoch [signified] something other than the unproblematic, unassailable triumph of Reason's 'sufficient light'." Ever since Horkheimer and Adorno's *Dialectic of Enlightenment*—and après Foucault—"it has been difficult to maintain, without a devastating infusion of Swiftian irony, the once-conventional view of the eighteenth century as an era of unexampled social, political, and philosophical progress."[56]

Reading accounts of *Magic Flute* written since the mid–twentieth century, one is struck how completely the idea of counter-Enlightenment, the "dialectic of Enlightenment," critiques of rationalism that are commonplace in history of science and philosophy, have been successfully kept at bay, and for so many reasons. Contemporary listeners experience *Magic Flute* after indoctrination in Romantic aesthetics, which still shapes habits of music appreciation, and which associates sunshine and simplicity with all major-key numbers. There is the pseudo-Wagnerian habit of seeing operatic music as contingent, as a factotum or massive leitmotif that routinely endorses the most obvious moral precepts within librettos, as well as the distinctly non-Wagnerian habit that ignores orchestration and physical gesture. Mozart's music occupies a privileged position as a pure aesthetic object that is, in its purity, unable to embody critical refusals. When Sarastro sings the music Max Slevogt pasted into his penultimate engraving, nothing seems tarred with ambivalence, though in Slevogt's case, doubts about rationality and Sarastro's triumph are sketched in a form that is openly perverse. Listeners are easily overcome by acoustic beauty, especially when it appears as the last word. Overcome, the listener defends operatic music as something protected from the instance of doubt, and as something that in turn erases doubts about the narratives with which it coexists. Mozart's music most of all: alone among the Orientalist texts assailed by Edward Said, *Magic Flute* and *Abduction from the Seraglio* are largely praised and excused.[57]

Perhaps, finally, there are critics inclined by misogyny to endorse eighteenth-century fantasies about women and to claim that music proves the truth of their hatreds or, conversely, inclined by outrage to repeat those fantasies and the point about their musical endorsement with offended relish, which quickly becomes counterproductive. The result is similar thinking on both sides of the fence. Thus there has been a broad triumphalist consensus about *Magic Flute,* oddly repetitive and closed. One nonetheless needs neither the *Dialectic of Enlightenment* nor late-twentieth-century historical revisionism to seek a nocturnal *Magic Flute.* Implications that familiarity with postwar intellectual fashions alone inspires nuance vis-à-vis Enlightenment artworks will stumble awkwardly over the counter-narrative that accompanies the opera and has done so for two hundred years.

"Le roi magicien" was written in 1698, *Magic Flute* in 1791; Max Slevogt's engravings date from 1912–18. Their collision suggests that metamorphosis, which in the fairy tale stands for unstable sexual iden-tity, also stands for the mutation of human into machine. Staging this collision serves to identify a historical moment at which anxieties about the performance network and perfected reproduction of music begin to inflect opera. From a perspective at the beginning of the twenty-first century, musical mechanism is patently disquieting; it was patently so by the time E.T.A. Hoffmann wrote his famous stories about musical automata, after 1810. *Magic Flute* lay at the point of the turn, when the magical instrument was first revealing its obverse. There is a skull in its musical garden.

A skull? But there is also an escape, and both are there as well in Slevogt's engraving, and Mailly's fairy tale. And still: two images—the unknown bird flying out of the story and the transfigured women flying out of the engraving—turn out to be quite different. Perhaps Mailly's screaming bird circled the skies of Enlightenment Europe for a hundred years, before falling back to the earth as the bad Queen in Schikaneder's plot. Slevogt's bird-women on the other hand, seeming unorthodox as illustrations of the *Magic Flute* libretto, reflect subterranean notes in the opera's music. They stage an escape from a scene of deadly order, whose prison bars have been broken by chattering women in flight—the most unlikely heroes of all.

CHAPTER

3

METEMPSYCHOTIC
WAGNER

Theodor Adorno and Preston Sturges, philosopher and Hollywood director: they are not matched bookends, so one does not expect to find them paired. Yet in their separate ways they saw that Wagner's operas are marked by an obsession with eternal returns expressed most vividly in *Tannhäuser* and *Parsifal*, and that the obsession is far from benign. Both operas toy with the idea of metempsychosis, the phenomenon in which an individual soul's eternal essence is imagined to travel unchanged through its residence in this body or that, human or animal. For Adorno, metempsychosis is the narrative counterpoise to phantasmagoria, a sign of Wagnerian cunning typically involving

> characters [that] cast off their empirical being in time, as soon as the ethereal kingdom of essences is entered. If, in his last years, Wagner flirted with the idea of metempsychosis, there is scant need to attribute this to the stimulus provided by Schopenhauer's Buddhist sympathies. Phantasmagoria had already enabled the pagan goddess Venus to migrate into the Christian era; she is reborn there just like Kundry.[1]

Wagnerian phantasmagoria entails musical or acoustic illusions of eternity and collapsed space—effects involving harmonic stasis, or "near for far" orchestration. Other musical tricks reflect the textual device even more directly, in the form of motifs that travel from one work to another. Some of these motifs, however, have changed significantly by the time they arrive at their terminus:

> All these motifs, like the musical idiom of *Parsifal* as a whole, have something broken and self-alienated about them: music wearing a closed black helmet. Out of the exhausted remains of a primal inventive force, Wagner creates the virtues of a late style, which (according to Goethe's maxim) retreats from the appearance of things. A comparison of the fanfare motif for Parsifal—simultaneously muted and wreathed in shadow—with the fanfare for Siegfried reveals the former's character: a motif that is as if already only a citation of the past.[2]

Motivic repetition across operas betrays passing time, age, and change. Wagnerian metempsychosis in general, however, entails an erasure of time and history in favor of repetition, representation of "the moment as that which endures."[3] Adorno points to several instances in Wagner's librettos. Kundry (as Klingsor says) has gone through multiple reincarnations in her journey from biblical to medieval times, as "Herodias" and as "Gundryggia." Brünnhilde evinces a "detachment from time" and expresses love for an "eternal" Siegfried who, she declares, existed well before the empirical Siegfried's birth. The Dutchman is a myth frozen into oil and canvas, and one day he simply steps out of his frame, as he has, invariably, every seven years. Along with phantasmagoria, metempsychosis marks the decadence of Wagnerian music drama, as spiriting away "its own origins in human labor" and with them, history and social meaning.[4] Alerted to the Wagnerian intent, one is thus enjoined to vigilance against the socially debilitating Wagnerian effect.

Kundry could hardly escape being the most important exhibit in Adorno's cabinet of Wagnerian shape-shifters. Not only does she endure through a thousand years, she also appears in *Parsifal* in three different forms, one for each act: wild woman, fatal woman, penitent. Such litanies do begin to sound like the peroration in *Faust zweiter Teil* with its laundry list of female archetypes, "Jungfrau, Mutter, Königin, Göttin," all of us solemnly enjoined to "remain merciful" in the face of masculine offense. Kundry's manifold forms, of course, reflect her genesis as a composite character based on separate figures in Wolfram's *Parzifal* epic.[5]

But wait: is she merely a page from the book of Wagnerian decadence, expressing a fantasy of eternal essences? Maybe she is instead a
specific product of *Parsifal's* historical time, a commodity, fractured by
capitalism's imperatives.[6] Or a female hysteric straight out of Charcot's
theater, who acts out a series of identities to which she is indifferent. In
this view, Kundry's various forms symbolize critical resistance, a sort of
crazed yet heroic skepticism, manifesting itself as role playing and
directed against the suffocation of patriarchal society. Her physical con-
vulsions, all the writhing and flailing, are a form of writing that is legible,
but inscrutable to the Grail knights.[7] Yet as "the split, hysterical woman"
she may also be a symptom of male sexual (shall we say) problems. Resist
her blandishments and you cure the problem; the symptom disappears.
The plot of *Parsifal* would appear to support this analysis rather straightforwardly, since once Parsifal turns Kundry away in act 2, the magic garden withers, Klingsor's power is destroyed, Parsifal gets the spear back,
Amfortas is cured, and Kundry is reduced to mutism.[8] And then again, it
may be that Kundry redeems Parsifal by "feminizing" him with her kiss,
at which point he becomes an instance of "the human genus" by dropping
a masquerade of maleness like "a snake getting rid of its skin."[9]

To cite so breathlessly so many different interpretations of Kundry's
meaning, gathered from a collection of philosophical and psychoanalyti-
cal writings, is not merely to make the unremarkable point that when one
looks at critical readings of Wagner, the choices just keep coming. Several
writers analyzing Kundry—each imputing a certain meaning to *Parsifal*—
make no mention of music. What is going on here? The dramatis personae of *Parsifal* are collectively so gaudy that staring at them with
complete attention may seem completely reasonable. Thomas Mann
exclaimed over the castrated villain, the sickly knight, the idiot-savant
hero, kidnapped Christian rituals, a wound that will not heal, and Kundry.[10] There are anti-Semitic undertones and misogynistic overtones in
the plot, competing to attract the gaze. Perhaps *Parsifal's* musical sound is
just the elephant in the room: a thing so overwhelming that no one need
bring it up. Or is this an extreme instance, an exaggerated form of a habit
familiar in readings of opera as text: music is not subject to questions, not
onstage. Though musical sounds may have shaped a whole series of

beliefs, and while this fact may well be openly acknowledged, they nonetheless make no appearance in the critical regimen. The writers just cited are at times so convincing; one cannot imagine that music has not been assimilated: *Parsifal's* libretto (a little voice is saying) cannot have inspired this on its own.

Parsifal's music, however, has also been praised for circumventing and ignoring the very aspect that is central to such readings, the drama onstage and the people that inhabit it. This is the essence of Claude Debussy's famous comment on Wagner, that *Parsifal* "is one of the most beautiful edifices in sound ever raised to the eternal glory of music."[11] It is important to remember what precedes this line: a scathing précis of *Parsifal's* plot and cruel witticisms about its characters. Debussy gives no credit to Wagner for his musical results, and mockery of the plot reveals a belief about intent. The beautiful monument came into existence despite Wagner, despite his naive affection for a bizarre onstage drama, despite his lack of irony, despite his oft-expressed aesthetic convictions that music, poetry, and visual image should merge into a symbiotic whole.

Debussy's comment is not merely another way to articulate familiar bad-faith clichés of Wagnerism: that his music excuses or transfigures all dubious politics, bad poetic style, and harsh caricature in the librettos, or more broadly that the works and their author must be balkanized, as separate republics subject to separate standards. Adorno declares that Wagner's music engenders a mesmerizing illusion of "unreal reality" (which implies transcendence), yet such music colludes fully in schemes articulated within the stage world, as within Wagner's aesthetic theories. What Debussy identifies, however, is a far more radical phenomenon: that there is a fundamental gap, a misalignment between sound and what it accompanies, as if music has collided almost accidentally or casually with everything else. With Wagner's other works, including the one that is hardly in second place for "beautiful monument in sound," this sense that component parts are disjointed never arises. *Parsifal* is different, and this difference is one aspect of its flavor, its special strangeness. Hence the silence that meets music in several accounts of *Parsifal* as drama may be evidence not that tongues have been tied by disciplinary modesty, nor even that music has been broken down and absorbed into a belief about characters and their actions, supplying invisible calories for an intellectual mise-en-scène. Rather, the silence is evidence of the truth in Debussy's claim.

There is a standard rejoinder to Debussy. Michael Tanner for instance reassembles *Parsifal* into a whole, defending it as a *Gesamtkunstwerk* in which fusion equals perfection: "I shall eschew polemics and instead produce an account of *Parsifal* which shows it at once to be a supreme dramatic masterpiece."[12] Thus all those who account for the opera in skeptical ways merely produce "nonsense" and "insanities" and evince a surprising "grossness of misunderstanding." Nietzsche and Thomas Mann (one might as well add Adorno) are worst of all in this regard; in harping upon decadence in *Parsifal,* they merely expose themselves as mentally and physically sick.[13] The means by which Nietzsche's and Mann's biographies are mustered to defeat their arguments are instructive:

> There can be no doubt that Wagner's urgent desire in *Parsifal* is to find a treatment [for sickness] of the most efficacious kind; there is even less ground for attributing to him than to Nietzsche a fascination with sickness, decadence or depravity for their own sakes, and very much less than in the case of Mann, who would have suffocated in clear air.[14]

Again, the same mortal blow, the same attack on the unenlightened, dismissed as illogical or secretly deformed, "gross." At what price is society cured of morbid aliens who are sick and sicken the environment by their presence? Such classic Wagnerism, with such a familiar ring, probably no longer amazes anyone, so putting more of it on exhibit would be superfluous. But it is still worth wondering whether Wagner's operas are not ill served by absolutism.

Debussy might instead be taken at his word. He implies that the misalignment in *Parsifal* is an aesthetic enigma, one that splits an experience of the opera into many registers, perhaps too many to count. This phenomenon is captured in Hans-Jürgen Syberberg's famous film version of the opera (1982). The film's soundtrack is gleefully uncoupled from the image track, most notoriously in using both a man and a woman to lip-synch Parsifal, and its visual landscapes are overcrowded with distracting objects, what David Levin calls "heaps of ambivalent *ur*-German bric-a-brac."[15]

Syberberg's technique is the means to two ends. The rift between visual and sonic domains is a polemical device, a co-conspirator in his representation of *Parsifal* as sum of its "cultural, historical, and political saturation."[16] Yet it also reflects the enigma—the misalignment—which is part of an experience of the opera as it was from the first, with Debussy, when much of the moss gathering and saturation had only begun. The French Symbolists loved *Parsifal* for precisely this reason: because it was a fractured *Gesamtkunstwerk,* and material was spilling out in more directions than one could be expected to analyze soberly, encouraging fantastic and irreverent synapses. That one could be sardonic about Amfortas as a "whining shop girl" and still give oneself completely to the work is an experience that many reject as alien a hundred years later, as demonstrated by outraged responses to Syberberg's film. For the Symbolists, it was no particular trick. One might even say that Debussy has put his finger on a *Parsifal* that seems at odds with the *Parsifal* decried by Nietzsche, in his now familiar critique of the opera's stasis and glorified quiescence. Debussy's *Parsifal,* with its bad lip-synching between music and stage drama, is anything but finished off and over with.

I

One should not however give too much credence to Debussy's overarching appraisal of the music. While the opera's misalignments can be appreciated as a mystery, there is also music conveying the sense of having been written at one remove, as if something from somewhere else had been quilted into place: the dying swan in act 1 (replay *Lohengrin*), the flower maidens, and Kundry's singing in act 2 (replay Venus from *Tannhäuser*). Eduard Hanslick, whose attitude toward Wagner is more subtle than rumor would have it, compared Kundry's act 2 music with Venus's, to the later Wagner's discredit (Hanslick had been one of *Tannhäuser*'s earliest supporters). He wrote that the big seduction scene in *Parsifal* is "profoundly unreal" in relation to its predecessor in *Tannhäuser* act 1.[17]

The first scene in act 2, above all, seems inflated by artificial resuscitation. Those chromatic minor-key rumblings associated with Klingsor the great magician replay—slightly—music from the opening of *Siegfried* act 3, as a late Wagnerian take on *basso nero* and Mephistopheles, which has little of the force conveyed by Hagen's music in *Götterdämmerung* acts

1 and 2. Klingsor thus seems an excessively impotent adversary, easily defeated: an operatic antique. This could be the evidence of artistic exhaustion, with Wagner, an old man, stealing vaguely from an earlier self to cover a temporary stammer. For this reason, something sung by the knights in the act 3 funeral procession may seem sad: "What has defeated him [Titurel], whom God once favored? Old age has felled him, as it fells us all."

Yet the listener's stance toward such passages is inflected by the assumption of a flaw, that artifice—seeming "unreal" or alienating—is aesthetically meaningless and unintended. A late style creates virtues out of necessity: the opening of act 2 is conceived differently if one assumes that the music is, instead, a calculated representation of creative failure. As the pale imitation of operatic genre music whose vigor and reality were once unmistakable, it reflects cruelly on Klingsor as the acoustic parallel to all the outmoded magical devices that festoon his lair, the obligatory bric-a-brac of necromantic decor. The arrow hits its mark when Kundry laughs at his mutilated body, and he howls in rage. While Wagner's flirtation with the idea of writing Klingsor's part for a castrato appears simpleminded, the decision to employ a low male voice instead was more than a bow to practical necessity. Klingsor, being a small part, is sometimes cast with an older singer, those who graduate from Hagen or Alberich. In addition, the role's tessitura is a little high for a true bass: some straining will be involved. Thus even the singer's sound quality can become unreal, a remnant that refers to what was once a fully diabolical timbre.

Such assumptions of intent impute to Wagner a critical stance that might well seem biographically improbable, above all because to expose a magician as a poseur, and magic as a "commodity," might strike too close to home. Such musical commodity fetishism or weariness may suggest Wagner's artistic evils, or his exhaustion.[18] But it may also suggest qualities in the fictional scene he has chosen to portray, since in *Parsifal,* unwitting aesthetic missteps have become indistinguishable from a necessary embrace of an illusory failure, of aesthetic dishonesty, to some larger end. This is a fracture in another form, one that makes it possible for the listener to stumble over symbolic gestures without thinking to question intent. The music's place in interpretation is thus particularly fraught. One may leave music silent or allow it to remain looming yet unmentioned.

Or one may accept with Debussy the belief that *Parsifal*'s music simply has not much to do with what is happening on stage. But the complications along that way are of course impossible to lay to rest. This music would not have come into being without this plot and these words and these stage actions. Wagner still composed measure to measure, according to precepts of correspondence he had articulated decades earlier. There are all the famous gestural moments, like the wild descending string figure that is the audible form of Kundry's stumbling entrance in act 1, and that turns out to be the violin double of her crazy laughter as well. There are many elaborate linguistic-musical parallels. In one passage from act 3, Parsifal sings his epigraph to the "Good Friday Music" and refers to the human flowers of act 2: "I saw them wither, they who once laughed at me. / Do they long for redemption?" The turn of the rhetorical question—the grammatical caesura, the strange idea that flowers, metamorphosing from human beings to mere flora, might desire or mourn—is traced musically in several registers (see music ex. 3.1). There is a switch of motifs (from echoes of Flower Maiden Music), and a corresponding harmonic shift. Certain techniques have not changed much since the 1850s.

Over the years that separate *Parsifal*'s composition from a present witness, even more has stuck to the music that cannot be stripped away. Thus the sounds, the characters, plot, and text, the work's reception history, Wagner's intentions and his writings are locked up with one another "for all time," like Kundry and her curse.[19] The occult anti-Semitism of the plot trails along, for some, screaming loud enough to drown out any musical sounds.[20] Yet the opera was banned in Germany from 1939 to the end of the war, a historical puzzle. As Saul Friedlander points out, this puzzle demands that we ask who is hearing which allegory, at which precise cultural moment. If Kundry is Jewish, and the opera is about the triumph of an Aryan elite, there would be no reason that *Parsifal* should not have been displayed during the war as a choice morsel of aesthetic propaganda. But that reading evidently never occurred to Hitler. Obsessed by

Example 3.1. *Parsifal,* act 3, "Ich sah sie welken"

the opera, he may nonetheless have been anxious about motifs such as pity, about a future ruler who began as a "pure fool," or a current head of state who is handicapped and frantic.[21]

In fact, Wagner's last work is either defended against or condemned for what has stuck or might be leaking out, starting with Bayreuth's first preemptive strikes against external performances, against secularization or the possibility of illicit interpretations. The regime that controlled *Parsifal* was unusually strict. And discomforts about *Parsifal,* despite a wartime ban that seemed to affirm its social innocuousness, grew stronger in the postwar years.[22] Music and all the rest are together even as the music intermittently repels itself from the rest, as if aligned with magnetic south, warding off by its very nature everything aligned with magnetic north. But with such magnets there is always a trick: turn them another way, and they will attract each other. What is there to hold in one's hands is a sense of *Parsifal's* grave condition of contingency and separation, a condition that affects the relationship of music to all that Debussy wanted to forget. If psychoanalytic readings of the drama are subject to pressure for their silence about music, should Debussy's ardor not be subject to question for its dismissal of everything not "in sound"? The paradox of contingency and separation might mean, in other words, that music goes off and yet is frequently looking toward traveling companions, across distances that attenuate relationships to greater and lesser degrees.

II

Looking toward something may imply longing, but it may simply be investigative, implying a search. This motif is shared between *Parsifal* and *Tannhäuser* in ways that Adorno was quick to understand. He points out, for instance, that Tannhäuser seeks a *fata morgana,* an ideal whose remaining embodiment within the opera is the Shepherd's song in act I scene 3: "The only surviving trace of what had originally led him to rebel is the beautiful song of the shepherd who celebrates the productivity of nature herself, beyond dream and captivity, as the work of the same power that had seemed mere slavery to the enchanted Tannhäuser."[23] His other objects—Venus and Elisabeth—are imperfect avatars and, as such, secretly aligned with one another. Adorno's impulse to save the Shepherd's song, to recreate it as something "not by Richard Wagner," is worth investigating, but so is the puzzle of two women seen as essentially the same.

Their alignment has not gone unnoticed. In his 1972 staging for Bayreuth, Götz Friedrich cast Gwyneth Jones in both roles, which is possible (though extraordinary) because the two characters are never onstage at the same time. Clues about Elisabeth and Venus are scattered throughout the opera in the form of a series of apparent flaws in logic, theatrical miscalculations, and musical jests. Several times in the opera, Tannhäuser or Wolfram cries out a woman's name, and the cry has instant consequences.[24] At the end of act 1 scene 2, Tannhäuser obtains his release from Venus by invoking the Virgin; his "Maria" is sung to a high fifth D-A-D, and he is transported to the upper world. In act 1 scene 4, Wolfram is able to convince Tannhäuser to remain with the knights by cutting through their babble and getting to the point: "bleib bei Elisabeth" [stay for Elisabeth]. Her name is sung on the descending fourth D-A, and a harp scatters fairy dust. So far, at least, the musical gesture seems to have some ethical sense; the Virgin Mary and Elisabeth belong together in the plot. But in the Song Contest (act 2 scene 4), Tannhäuser goes out of his mind and sings a hymn to sensual love, throwing a bomb at the words "zieht in den Berg der Venus ein" [go to Venus's mountain]. Again a name, and again the same tenor high fifth, D-A-D. But what is Venus's name doing in acoustic company with Mary's and Elisabeth's? Finally in the last moments of act 3, Wolfram once more uses Elisabeth's name to distract Tannhäuser from disaster, singing almost exactly as in the act 1 septet, now a half step higher on E♭-B♭.

That Venus's name is smuggled into the coterie of virgins might seem irrelevant if the repeated musical gesture is taken to be pure acoustic structure, or, less austerely, to be an amorphous and recurrent signal that precedes any big scene change or plot twist. Yet women are conflated and collapsed into Woman in more than one way. When the little Shepherd sings in act 1 scene 3, he begins with "Dame Holda came out of her mountain," referring to yet another Venus. Even in the 1840s, *Tannhäuser*'s first critics had noted the paradox of the Shepherd's song to "Frau Holda," who is bringing spring and rebirth. Isn't this "Frau Holda" the same demonic Venus who had just disappeared?[25] And what about Wolfram's "Song to the Evening Star" in act 3, in which the celestial body is enjoined to watch over Elisabeth? Her otherwise blameless troubadour is now directing his efforts toward the planet Venus.

These things are inconsistencies, or even absurdities. Worst of all was Joseph Tichatschek's behavior as Tannhäuser in the original Dresden production of the opera in fall 1845. During the Song Contest, he actually turned to Johanna Wagner (Elisabeth) and addressed the Song to Venus directly to her—"to you, goddess of love!"[26] Yet perhaps Tichatschek's excess, which frustrated Wagner, got straight to the point that the male characters mysteriously sense an essence that is one Woman. This essence is only poorly concealed by differences in outer form, behavior, degree of sexual experience, status of hymen, name, voice range, vocal style, moral convictions, or amounts of chromaticism in one's orchestral accompaniment. Men have been granted the blinding insight that Venus is identical to the spring, the star, and the virgin, and after that the move to Kundry was easy. All this is worth some concern.

III

The "same woman" problem was what Preston Sturges found in *Tannhäuser* when he transmuted the opera into a movie, *The Lady Eve* (1941) and in doing so took on metempsychosis in order to expose its potential for disaster. In the movie, fatal Venus and virgin Elisabeth, one metaphysically essential Woman, become one woman who secretly pretends to be another. The film is a critique of Wagner's eternal returns, a satyr play to Adorno's tragedy (the *Versuch über Wagner,* written in 1937–38). Both works came into being at a historical moment when Wagner's operas had begun their slow mutation into theme music for fascism, and both raise a similar, specific alarm about the social dangers associated with stasis and eternal return.

The satyr play: Jean Harrington (Barbara Stanwyck) is a professional card shark (fatal Venus) who targets millionaire Charles Pike (Henry Fonda) on an ocean voyage; instead she falls in love with him and he with her. Transformed by her affection, she mends her ways. But when Charles is informed of her true "criminal" background, he jilts her before they dock in New York (leaves the Venusberg). Thirsting for revenge, Jean reinsinuates herself into his life by penetrating the courtly world of upper-class Connecticut and posing as an English aristocrat, "Lady Eve Sidwich" (virgin Elisabeth). Charles falls in love with her again. This time they are married, but on their wedding night, Lady Eve (now Venus) inventively confesses to a series of prior sexual antics calculated to mortify her priggish husband. They are divorced, and Charles takes another ocean voyage, only to meet Jean (now Elisabeth) again and embrace her as his true love. He does not figure out that the two were one, but Charles's skeptical valet, who suspected it all along, is given the movie's final line: "Positively the same dame."

The Wagnerian plot lurks within the movie plot, and that presence is made explicit in the wedding night scene, when the *Tannhäuser* overture is heard on the sound track at a critical moment in the conversation. Here the "secret" text, the opera, erupts into the movie as a voice without language, whose capacity to convey "secrets" is thus not subject to challenge. The opera makes one other appearance, however, disguised as a speech about metempsychosis. On the boat to New York, Charles makes a romantic declaration to Jean, identifying their love as an eternal return: "You see—every time I've looked at you here on the boat, it wasn't only here I saw you. You seem to go way back. I know that isn't clear but I—I saw you here and at the same time further away and then still further away and then very small—like converging perspective lines." This seems sincere. It ceases to do so, however, once Charles repeats the speech, word for word, while courting Lady Eve. As Stanley Cavell has pointed out, it would be easy after this mechanical repetition to understand the speech as proving Charles's fickle nature, his susceptibility to all women, even his hollowness as a subject. As a poststructuralist might put it, he is not producing the speech; rather, the speech is producing him. But the speech, delivered both times in a kind of trance, may reveal his unconscious sensitivity to the hidden truth that both women are—really—the "same dame." Their sameness engenders a mysterious, involuntarily identical response.[27] Pairing speech and repetition is fundamentally Wagnerian as well, in that it suggests a repeated leitmotif. Less abstractly, this pairing is a specific allusion to Wagner's opera, since Sturges is restaging Tannhäuser's disastrous error, his repetition of the Song to Venus from act 1 in front of Elisabeth in act 2. Charles (Tannhäuser) imagines he is addressing his performance to Lady Eve (Venus?) when he is really addressing it to Jean (Elisabeth?). And in Jean's (Elisabeth's!) ears, the repeated speech (song) demonstrates a new, more awful aspect of Charles's (Tannhäuser's) character.[28]

When *Tannhäuser* turns up in the wedding night scene, the comic inversions are multiplied. Alone with her new husband, Lady Eve tots up her previous sexual partners, beginning with "Angus the stable boy." Charles is shocked but strives for magnanimity. There is another speech: "Eve, if there's one thing that distinguishes a man from a beast, it's the ability to understand. And in understanding, to forgive: sweet forgiveness." Suddenly the opera makes its appearance, with the opening sixteen measures of the overture on the sound track. In the opera, this music is eventually sung by the Rome Pilgrims in act 3 (fortissimo): "The balm of forgiveness has been granted the sinner; he now goes to the realm of joyful peace." The words are there, below the instruments in the overture, pinned to their music; one hears them even though they are not being sung.[29]

Once the *Tannhäuser* overture comes into play, the metempsychotic substitutions go wild, and even gender distinctions disappear. Shocked yet forgiving, Charles becomes Elisabeth. Lady Eve, who began as Elisabeth and came to seem like Venus, has become Tannhäuser, the sinner who dallied with "Angus"—a name whose assonance with "Venus" now leaps to the ear. Eve responds to Charles's words: "I knew you'd be that way. I knew it the first moment I saw you standing beside me—I knew you'd be both husband and father to me, I knew I could trust and confide in you. I suppose that's why I fell in love with you." Now which woman is talking? Not Lady Eve—the British accent has been laid aside. Another acoustic mark is added in its place. Just as Charles's sweet forgiveness speech is delivered to the overture's first theme (mm. 1–16), so hers is to the second theme, chromatic minor-key music that wanders around harmonically (mm. 17–32). There are unsung words here as well, anguished words given to the Pilgrims in act 1 scene 3: "Ah, the burden of sin presses heavily upon me, I cannot bear it any longer!"

But the "sin" is not the fictitious sexual misadventure; it is the vengeful heart, and the consequent masquerade that multiplied Jean into Lady Eve. The minor-key theme from the overture causes a short circuit, erasing Eve and her voice, and converting Jean's anger into remorse. After exacting her revenge—confessing as Lady Eve to many more Venusbergs—Jean cannot bear Charles's dismay. Lady Eve agrees to a divorce and refuses a monetary settlement. This leads magically and quickly to the happy end. As a precondition for that happy end, all the shape shifting must be put to rest. This is demonstrated by the movie's plot, but in a strange way it is also true of the movie's relationship to the opera. If *The Lady Eve* merely reembodies an essence that once inhabited *Tannhäuser*, then the film would end as the opera does, in tragedy. But it doesn't: it isn't "the same dame."

Differences matter. A critical stab at Wagner thus is aimed precisely at the mystical "same woman problem," now multiplied irreverently into a shell game of essences and vessels, "Jungfrau, Mutter, Königin, Göttin," father, husband, Elisabeth, Jean, Eve, Tannhäuser, Charles, Venus, Angus—we can hardly keep track of who is embodying whom. Sturges's mockery is a reflection on "sameness" that parallels Adorno's critique, and others since. Wagner's taste for endogamy, his affection for racial marks that are passed from generation to generation, are expressed symbolically as mythic repetition in characters who are "universal symbols," who express the "standing-still of time and the complete occultation of nature."[30] The end is disaster.

IV

Playing the shell game one last time, one could say that if Kundry is a single Woman who embodies both Venus and Elisabeth, then—as a reprobate, as someone despised by a society that excludes her—she must have a bit of Tannhäuser in her as well. Her masculinity, like her double nature, is obvious. Perhaps there is no aspect of earlier Wagner that does not find its way into *Parsifal*'s plot or dramatis personae, with the parallels to *Tannhäuser* merely the "most obvious" among many.[31] One could even see these textual parallels as a meta-leitmotivic system, a "mythological system" that transcends any single work and reaches its summa in the last one.[32] The eternal returns were catalogued long ago, like the leitmotifs, and like the leitmotifs came to be seen almost neutrally, as structure or schema. Which Wagnerians thought to question their broader implications? Those in Los Angeles circa 1941, it would seem, were first in line after Nietzsche.

The parallels between the operatic plots need not be reviewed, but the first instance of recapitulation, Charles's repeated speech in *The Lady*

Eve, is worth revisiting. Such repetition suggests hollowness, because when words are repeated exactly in different circumstances, they suddenly seem impotent as an expression of true feeling. Their sonorous aspect, however, their duplications of earlier phonemes and sonorities, leaps to the ear. Mechanically repeated speech slides easily into musical sound. At the same time, Charles's speech—the embarrassment of the duplicated apostrophe—refers explicitly to Tannhäuser's Song to Venus.

The two speeches, however, also suggest a particular kind of musical hollowness, an absurdly exact formal recurrence. After a certain point (about 1850), this particular absurdity would be practiced only by the worst of Wagner's people. Mime in *Siegfried,* for instance, chides Siegfried's lack of gratitude by singing a song in act 1, "als züllendes Kind zog ich dich auf." He sings it even though it has been sung countless times over the years (Siegfried's irritation makes this clear) and though his audience has had more than enough: he is harping. It is no secret that such empty formalism, though the librettos present it more harmlessly as the outmoded or antique, was what Wagner had in mind in 1851 when he decried Jewish music, its "false mimesis" and artistic incapacity.[33] Before 1851, Senta can sing three more-or-less identical verses in her ballad, and that is just an operatic convention, at most a sign for erotic obsession. After 1851, only Wagner's most demonized characters harp, and, as David Levin points out, their harping "stand[s] in embodiment of language gone astray as language (that is, language that has lost touch with nature)."[34] The biographical implications are enticing, since *On Jewishness in Music* was written simultaneously with *Opera and Drama* and the first parts of the *Ring,* at a time when Wagner was shedding the skin of an earlier, conventionally operatic self.

Perhaps mechanical repetition is the musical form of a sinister "figure" against which the ground of Wagnerian rhetoric must be played out.[35] Philippe Lacoue-Labarthe makes the argument that Wagner needed such a "figure" to organize his political and historical theorizing, and Levin has extended that argument to the realm of narrative. In Wagner's works in general, "a good character is marked . . . by aesthetic qualities that the work endorses, while a bad character is marked by aesthetic qualities the work loathes."[36] Wagner's demonization of Jews, in Slavoj Žižek's alternative view, reflects his ambivalent stance toward modernity as a "reign of exchanges, of the dissolution of organic links." He "needs a Jew" so that he can reject the figure embodying "all that is disintegrated in modernity" and, by rejecting him, keep the "fruits" of modernity while discarding the rest.[37]

Accordingly, one could argue that the principle of pure repetition (the figure) would need to be contested wherever it might crop up, in order that its delightful "fruits," which would include narrative metempsychosis and transformation of leitmotifs (as forms of repetition), might best be savored.

One contests it with what is furthest away—noise, sound that conveys the illusion of being tapped directly from some untainted source; such music, what Goehr calls a "negating aesthetic experience," springs the prison bars of modern social artifice and alienation.[38] Wagner was master of blurring the lines between natural sound and music. The artless songs, forest murmurs, sunrises, storms, Rhine journeys, and the "world breath" are of this order. Of course, they are in fact elaborate contrivances, which Kittler was first to describe as a Wagnerian "technology" of nature sound.[39] As Thomas Grey puts it, "Wagner's ideal of art tends always to regress toward the imagined roots or origins of things, toward a utopia of absolute, unmediated expressivity, even while it remains, in practice, thoroughly committed in so many ways to the techniques and technologies of modern culture."[40]

In the arguments just cited, such nature scenes are evidence of general Wagnerian tendencies: sentimental reverence for unspoiled first-growth forests, racial coherence, and a time before industrialization, before the corruption of language by the imperative of representation. Through them, Wagner is attempting to recruit the listener to regression, and hence to an alliance against all that is demonized within his works, whether it is social alienation, modernity, exogamy, or Jews as signs of these phenomena.

And still, scenes involving natural or primal sounds are not just that, or rather, within them there is a reproach directed at all that Wagner appears to endorse most fully. There is an alternative natural music, which belongs to the same domain as the pastorales and the sounds of nature, and nonetheless represents primal sound and any regression toward it as a horror. This second genus of natural music—a kind of negative primal music having nothing to do with forests or birds—is a radical phenomenon in Wagner's works. Such music flows from musical techniques analogous to those present in the positive forms and involves a similar reversion to acoustic constructions that suggest unmediated sonority and transcendence. There is, in other words, a shared aesthetic apparatus or technology, something similar in figure and ground, and this twinship undermines the positive term. Certain great Wagnerian precepts are thus subject to a claw that tears from within. In *Parsifal,* the coexistence of two natural genera subverts values assigned to the positive form, and with this, any ambition that unmediated sound expresses the refusion of language and nature, an ideal so prominent in Wagner's theoretical program.

V

What may seem unsurprising in Adorno's critique of Wagner—given his own nostalgia—is that he is ready to approve two scenes in Wagner's operas, the voice of the Forest Bird in *Siegfried* act 2, and the Shepherd's song in *Tannhäuser.* They are scenes that involve natural sound, but that otherwise are similar only in being songs. The Forest Bird, by singing coloratura, is a properly artificial operatic bird-voice, and in this consciousness of inhabiting operatic theater, the least dubious musical presence in the entire *Ring.*[41]

The Shepherd's song, however, is part of an operatic soundscape that was unprecedented in 1845 and would remain avant-garde well into the twentieth century. In act 1 scene 3, Tannhäuser is transported from the Venusberg to the upper world, and when he arrives, the pit orchestra drops out. Almost everything audible during the next ten minutes comes directly from the stage: the Shepherd's song, his piping, the voices of the Pilgrims that approach and then fade away realistically, cowbells that imply unseen flocks, and finally tolling bells from the Wartburg tower and the Landgraf's hunting horns. Aside from a tremolo wake-up call when Tannhäuser comes to, and some discreet background accompaniment to the reprise of the Pilgrim's chorus, the orchestra remains silent.

In its place, the landscape itself shimmers with musical sounds.[42] The approach and retreat of the Pilgrims' voices laboriously trace the physical reality of spatial distance, as if it were the deliberate antithesis to all that made Adorno most wary, the Wagnerian conflation of near and far, the "occultation" of geographical and historical difference. To complete the illusion, Wagner's song for the Shepherd is no ordinary onstage song. It is filled with unpredictable pauses and calculated to sound as if a singer were going off-key and correcting himself, not strophic, not formal, but entirely improvised: "I'll sing this—a little higher—now maybe something else, maybe not" (see music ex. 3.2).

The stage music in short suggests that nobody produced what one hears other than the figures that sing it and play it or the objects that clang and blow, and this is a critical point. Human beings and instruments are equated, in a prelapsarian scene that makes what people sing as inevitable—as rooted in their being—as the tone of a bell whose weight and shape determines the unique note it sounds. This music is unperformed: no one has learned it or repeats it, no *paradis artificiel,* no proclamation of ironic distance with every melodic turn. Wagner has thus labored very hard to produce something that short-circuits consciousness of his presence, that therefore lies beyond reproach, seeming to erase the truth that what is present as sound, after all, is a representation: something someone had to have made. How ironic that Adorno should have been lulled by a scene that reflects, among other things, a German nationalist fantasy that musical expression is indeed grounded in the *corps sonore,* in a physical being that is unalterable: in blood.

Such sounds proliferate in *Parsifal,* with means and ends, too, like those in *Tannhäuser.* There is a lot of sheer noise from the stage— Kundry's groans and cries and stammers, and the backstage bells used in acts 1 and 3. There is vocal sound that only borders on composed melody, music sung by Titurel. And at the pinnacle of this pyramid, there is the noise that got to Debussy and under all his defenses, the Good Friday Music in act 3 that is represented as a meadow that laughs, the celebratory resonance of all living things. This is a sort of Shepherd's song with cowbells to the twentieth power or so, and of course it is not stage music at all—but within the poetic and acoustic fictions of the opera, it has

Example 3.2. *Tannhäuser* act 1, the Shepherd's song

Example 3.3. *Tannhäuser* act 3, the "Dresden Amen"

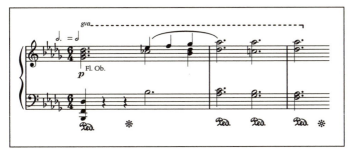

become music as if from a mystical onstage presence, and not from the orchestra pit.

Time, then, to confront the elephant without flinching. There is a particular compositional device that turns up in the Good Friday Music and transforms an instance of musical representation into an illusion of natural and primal sound. This device involves the famous Dresden Amen motif, which migrated from *Tannhäuser* into *Parsifal*, another instance of melodic metempsychosis. In *Tannhäuser*, the motif is heard in the act 3 prelude, in Tannhäuser's Rome Narrative, and in the chorus of young Pilgrims at the end of the opera (see music ex. 3.3). In *Parsifal*, the same rising melodic fifth becomes the tail end of the Grail motif (see music ex. 3.4).

This similarity is obvious and direct and has been duly recorded in many musical analyses, which also point out that the motif was real music, a melody used for singing the "Amen" at the Dresden cathedral in the nineteenth century, quoted by composers besides Wagner (Mendels-

Example 3.4. *Parsifal* act 1, the "Dresden Amen"

sohn used it in his "Reformation" symphony). All this means that the motif has become semiotically supersaturated: it functions not only as an intriguing echo of *Tannhäuser* within *Parsifal,* but also as an invocation of the ecclesiastic and Catholicism, with implications appropriate to both plots. Finally, the motif suggests history by invoking Wagner's past, his Dresden period (1843–49), when *Tannhäuser* was written and *Parsifal* first conceived, and when he was listening to his local cathedral choir. Semiosis is doubled up, and then tripled up. The motif is thus close to becoming something like a word, surrounded by a large brood of tangible associations. Such heavy baggage, by converting music into a sign, constitutes quite a lapse, at least for Wagner after Schopenhauer. Musical ineffability has disappeared into the lesser mode: philosophy.[43]

The Good Friday Music, appropriately, will sweep all that away, pushing the motif back past its extramusical implications to prelapsarian musical purity, and further. First of all, the motif is given an alternative local provenance, as if it had gotten into a witness protection program. It is reinvented out of a chromatic rising figure (E)-A♯-B-B♯-C♯-D, which morphs into the diatonic rising major fifth from (B)-E to B (see music ex. 3.5, mm. 1–2 and 10–11). This diatonic figure is the "Dresden Amen," the end of the Grail motif, and the harmonic setting reinforces the mnemonic synapse. But at the very moment this motif is conjured up, it is denied. The diatonic figure E-B, newborn with an innocent past, is not isolated as a unique object but rather repeated over and over, in waves without rhythmic profile, an oscillating prelude to the bass's big vocal moment. From word, to motif, to motivic fragment, to sound waves— and what would happen in the next step, the one not taken? The sound waves would freeze into stasis, become a great humming fifth E-B, then perhaps a single note E, receding back into a realm before music, the place where *Das Rheingold* began.

This symbolic regression away from language into music, toward a primal vibration, writes the Good Friday Music's fundamental illusion into a detail. The fundamental illusion is simple. Natural sound, the singing of flowers and grass, is brought to the ear as an astonishingly beautiful orchestral interlude, in which Gurnemanz's voice blends with the instruments and finally holds a high D for seven long beats, as if poetic

Example 3.5. From the Good Friday Music, act 3

Example 3.5. (*continued*)

II

descriptions of magic were simply dissolving into pure breath and sonority, once more correcting a lapse into philosophy. The music no longer originates literally in the onstage landscape (as such music did in *Tannhäuser*) because it no longer needs to. The hand has fooled the eye in another way, and the game with a motif remains, as a clue to the practice.

Astonishingly beautiful: this is the passage where the tigers and the lions simply cannot meet. Either it is the most beautiful music ever written (speaking with Debussy), or it is what Adorno loathed, "faded light," accompanying a distasteful stage tableau in which Wagner's stock recipe for "inauthentic . . . theatrical illusion" has merely given one last gasp.[44]

Even Syberberg's film wants magic. For this stretch in act 3, Syberberg invents a stunning optical sequence that opens with Kundry's baptism—and the famous "sound of annihilation"—in which Kundry (Edith Clever), recognizing that her baptism is her end, walks grimly from the stream past an open grave.[45] But at the same moment, as the Good Friday Music begins, a phantasmic image looms in the black sky behind her, looking at first like an unfurling demon from the "Night on Bald Mountain" sequence in *Fantasia*. One realizes quickly, however, that it is a projected film in which a conductor, suffused with light, conducts an unseen orchestra that is playing the music we are hearing. This sudden reminder about the Good Friday Music's means of production is a sly reference to its separate existence as a concert piece, ripped from its operatic context.

But then there is another twist: the conductor (Armin Jordan) turns his face to the light and is thus revealed as the man who portrays Amfortas and lip-synchs his voice in the film's image track. This is a face and body that have been witnessed in great suffering, wounded, incapable, sick and pale and drained. To see this face and body existing in another place, bathed in golden light, physically vigorous, is to see a single human being rescued from the fate that elsewhere overtakes him. It is deeply moving, like a dream of children saved from annihilation. Yet it is also a cinematic projection within a projection and presents the apparatus at a slight angle that makes Armin Jordan look anamorphic, "not there" to a degree that removes him once from Kundry and the sadder space she inhabits. While the Good Friday Music is performed, annihilation sits silently downstage and stage left in the form of the open grave.

VI

Music that was never composed but simply resonates, the Good Friday Music is a hyperpastorale in which a prelapsarian moment is both manifest, ready to be captured, and already lost. This reversion to the fundamental involves in this case very diverse means: orchestral textures, poetic allusions, and an elaborate game with a motif. Elsewhere in the opera, things are done more straightforwardly.

As sheer voice, Titurel's singing seems more real and less constructed than any other in the score, even though the body that produces it is hidden, and the voice "comes from a vaulted chamber behind Amfortas's couch, as if from the grave." This vaulted chamber (like Jochanaan's subterranean cistern) acts as a megaphone, increasing volume and bringing the voice forward physically in a peculiar way. Like the Shepherd in *Tannhäuser,* Titurel at first sings against total orchestral silence, and once again the absence of the pit orchestra, as well as the vocal line's free, unforced declamation, suggests a voice that emerges from a place prior to operatic composition, unframed (see music ex. 3.6). Now, however, there is anything but a pastorale. Titurel is a grim object, Wagner's big birthday present to psychoanalysis, "undoubtedly the most obscene figure in *Parsifal,* a kind of undead father parasitic on his own son," representing the "morbid, cruel side of the Grail's temple."[46] Žižek associates Titurel's disembodied commands with Amfortas's superego, as a paternal voice that enjoins the son to duty. In this, Titurel's position is self-evident: he is part of the symbolic order, a necessary aspect of subjectivity.

As a voice that sings, however, as musical sound, and most importantly as one among several related regressive moments, Titurel's noise is something else. This is a voice before music, before symbolization, from a lost sonic realm never revisited but conventionally assumed to be the acoustic domain of the feminine. His singing thus embodies the "other" primal voice: the "law itself, in pure form, before commanding anything specific," rattled into being as a sound that "commands total compliance, although senseless in itself."[47] In an alternative psychoanalytic reading, Titurel's voice is not the superego—which expresses itself in symbols or words and belongs to their "order"—but something older and a priori. This voice is a purely sonorous "remnant of the dead Father, that part of him which is not quite dead, what remained after his death and testifies to his presence—his voice—but also to his absence, a *stand-in for an impossible presence,* enveloping a central void."[48] Dolar's description refers neither to Wagner nor to opera, but to another music entirely, the sound of the shofar, the "primitive horn" of Jewish religious ritual. In a coincidence whose irony must be savored, his analysis of this unusual sound hits one Wagnerian narrative mark with complete accuracy. Well might Titurel represent unaccountable terror within the Grail knights' domain: his funereal aspect is bizarre. More than this, however, his effect in the opera is predicated on travesty. Anyone who eavesdrops at this particular closed door is conditioned to expect the distant sigh of Nature and Mother. Instead, he or she gets this half-dead basso.

Example 3.6. Titurel's voice, act 1

Titurel's singing voice might well be a good stab at representing the Real: the terrible remnant, what is left over, ungraspable, when the subject acquires language and "enters the symbolic order." In Lacanian terms, the Real stands for what is lost under that pressure—a prelapsarian state—and it can be only imperfectly conceptualized, usually as certain uncanny, intensely material, and occasionally revolting objects.[49] In this respect Titurel's only rival before *Parsifal,* in a scene whose general musi-

cal effect is very different, is Hagen's big noise, his loud singing to dissonant backstage steer horns, which opens *Götterdämmerung* act 2 scene 3.
Here, too, a once encumbered and musically elaborate motif has
regressed to a more basic form (the half step in Hagen's voice), as sheer
sound.

Wagner's ambition to open gates, to recover sounds barred from
representational grasp, thus took a sharp left turn with Titurel, after
decades of right turns featuring paradise lost and Schopenhauer, and
before a big right turn in the Good Friday Music. The two things face
each other, perhaps, as Syberberg understood. The Good Friday Music's
miracle is visible above, while Kundry walks past the grave. Within the
opera, the two are literally next to one another in act 3, since the Good
Friday Music is followed directly by the funeral procession for Titurel.
They are paired not only by proximity. Both share a metaphysical ambition that propels resonance anchored in bodies onstage toward an illusion of noumenal sound, and that seals the gesture with elaborate
musical games.

The funeral procession is the most radical passage in all of Wagner's
operas, seeming to expose what should never have been seen, heard,
imagined, or represented musically. The only possible way to contain this
music is to cram it into the historical juggernaut proposed by Viennese
modernism, see its noise as an intimation of atonality, Schoenberg avant
Schoenberg. But this is not music that points ahead: it points down.

VII

At the final performance of *Parsifal* in Bayreuth during the
1882 season, on 29 August, Wagner suddenly decided to lead the orchestra—the last time he would ever conduct. Hermann Levi described what
happened: "During the [act 3] Transformation Music, the Meister came
into the orchestra, and he crawled up until he reached my podium, took
the baton out of my hand, and conducted the performance to the end."[50]
Just as the funeral procession is about to begin, an old man appears at the
bottom of the steep orchestra pit as if summoned, creeping upward
through the instruments on hands and knees. What had animated
whom?

VIII

The regressive devices in the funeral procession have strong affinities with those in the Shepherd's song, in Titurel's voice, and in the Good Friday Music, especially the last. One way in which it might be seen to disclose what "should never have been seen" involves a particular Wagnerian technique, one frequently dissected in music-theoretical writings on his music, a trick involving exclusion.[51] The act 3 prelude opens with interlocking melodic fifths and tritones, and within the first melodic phrase, a consonant B♭-F-B♭ is followed by the dissonant note E♮, a grain of sand in its eye (see music ex. 3.7). This grain, right from the start, signals an odd technical feature of the prelude: though the key signature, and the opening melody, point toward B♭ minor, there is no unequivocal cadence to B♭ minor and no instance, anywhere within the prelude, of a root-position B♭-minor triad. Other grains of sand keep getting in the way.

There is in fact only one root-position triad in the entire prelude: the E-minor chord (spelled E-G-C♭ and played by violins and viola) that is heard for the space of an eighth note in the strange eighteenth measure, marked "softer still," "slower still," and "exhausted." This sound is extraordinary, standing out from all the chromatic agitation around it like a sudden apparition from some alien place. One could say that the note E, the "wrong note" in the opening melody, represents an instantly excluded presence that nonetheless is irrepressible, and that will return in a more disquieting form. The B♭-minor key, as implied terra firma, is excluded in a fundamentally different way than the "figure" E.

Example 3.7. The act 3 prelude

In the act 3 transformation music and the funeral procession, these two absent objects are summoned, magnified, and made very loud. E minor, fortissimo, is the key of the transformation music, acclaimed by the entire orchestra (except the harp), playing together this one time—all the winds, trumpets, horns, trombones, tubas, bass tubas, and the onstage bells, with the lowest of the four sounding the pitch E. When the knights march on, they sing their funeral hymn in B♭ minor, following upon the transformation music across an only minimally mediated schism between the two keys. Once the knights clamor for the Grail, however, things disintegrate. Ground and figure, right note and wrong, are brought together simultaneously in a passage where some knights sing in B♭ minor while others drag the collective painfully upward into E minor, and the entire orchestra (but no harp) bellows again, and the bells, tolling much faster, drape everything in reverberation that seems to contain every note ever imagined, all at once and almost louder than one can bear.

The harmonic game that brings once unrealized objects into our presence resembles other Wagnerian techniques for invoking impossible sounds or impossible instruments (remember Elsa's telephone call in *Lohengrin* act 1). Like the Good Friday Music, Elsa's impossible sigh leaves a sweeter taste behind. Yet even though the mood is quite different, the funeral procession is like the Good Friday Music, the negative within the same domain. Thus the knights' atonality is not an ascent into modernist idioms. One cannot contain the passage by restyling it as music conscious of a place in history, music that self-consciously points to its own compositional artfulness. Rather, the funeral procession music is an arabesque, tracing a downward trajectory that dead-ends in pure and terrible sound.

This sense depends on intersecting phenomena. It is not just the elaborate promise that this massive amalgam brings forward something unheard that was once kept behind closed gates, excluded B♭s and Es. When the bells toll so fast, the collision between their fundamentals and overtones creates a panharmonic instrumental clangor that is in fact produced directly from the stage, and that merges with the knights' voices with their many and conflicting pitches, as their double. Once more, the physical world onstage shimmers with sound. Whatever the orchestra plays is inhaled, pulled into the stage world by superior volume. And the bells' authorless sound, as double to the knights' bell-voices, intimates that those voices—like the little Shepherd's—emerge from some more primal musical domain, unframed. This regression is complete when the knights cry out after Titurel's corpse is revealed, an unscripted, barely musical cry in the bass registers where screaming, so we have imagined, is never heard.[52]

　　And then: what "nature" makes this kind of music? Not paradise lost, the one cited by the little Shepherd. In a psychoanalytic analogy with Titurel—who is finally present, carried in a box—this music is a last echo from the absent Father, Titurel's voice to the twentieth power. Somehow "absent Father" seems too harmless, too conventionally mythic or tame, too safe, in the face of such musical terror. Like Titurel's voice, then, the funeral procession is not simply about Titurel or the knights, not a sign for the cruel underside of the Grail kingdom. Music has taken account of all that and at the same time is farther away, looking at something else.

Wagner's last nature scene takes shape as resonance that eludes reason, as music—and now, as a horror. In all the gestures that pair Good Friday Music with this music, there is thus a hidden caveat: the Grail celebrations, the consecrated male societies, apotheosis and redemption, and the laughing meadows are predicated upon the wretched existence of something whose name is undisclosed. It is what makes the laughing meadows so astonishingly beautiful.

This juxtaposition of two natural genera thus clears a ground where tiger and lion might meet, for a brief moment. Beautiful sound exists, not despite, but because of an instance of terror. Understanding what they share, the common aesthetic-technical palette, gives the beautiful sound another meaning, yet does so (paradoxically) without perturbing that beauty. The juxtaposition also reflects on opera's final scene, the famous apotheosis, and its effect. Are endings always convincing, and always the last truth, just because they are last? Though the opera's final choruses and the orchestral postlude are collectively so splendid, their capacity to erase the memory of the funeral procession is uncertain. In an odd way, the choral textures, the presence of the very same knights' voices, help to keep that memory alive as an afterimage left on one's aural retina. Few writers have sensed that *Parsifal's* musical end is the "undialectical 'resolution' of all conflict in general and sacred harmony," as described in Nike Wagner's critique, a critique that nonetheless postulates an overpowering force that has made an end.[53] This is, to the contrary, an end that perhaps cannot be made, except schematically. Or, as Arnold Whittall put it, "Closing a work integratively does not mean that the disruptive forces are 'cured,' retrospectively reduced to insignificance."[54] Even though the music of the final scene follows the music of the funeral procession, even with the last word's terrific advantage, it has to overcome what came before, that which is not easily or quickly healed.

If works engender images of their creators, then many "Wagners" have been implied by Wagner's oeuvre, the choices that just keep coming: the devious exhausted one, the anti-Semitic one, the homosocial one, the misogynist, the Hegelian triumphalist, the German nationalist, a musician-genius, a decadent sensualist. What "Wagner" is created by a radical phenomenon, by negative primal music? Perhaps one that has not yet been identified.

IX

And now, for Kundry. She has been seen as the Woman and all Women, as bisexual (qua Dutchman or Tannhäuser), as Mary Magdalen, as the Wandering Jew (Wagner himself started that one), and, in recapitulating so many different essences, she is one of Wagner's great originals. She is hysterical; she plays too many roles. She embodies a critique of the Grail society, a spirit of resistance, but because men have the last word, she is also mortified, humbled, and doomed. In act 3, she dies three times, first by falling silent, then by being baptized, then finally by dropping dead. Once Cosima Wagner's anecdote about Wagner's "sound of annihilation" at Kundry's baptism became common knowledge, the race was on to determine just what was being annihilated: desire, sin, a woman, or a Jew? As the only starring female character in the opera, it would seem significant that Kundry is subjected to such treatment, and much can be made of her muteness in act 3 and her death as silencing the feminine voice or signifying the pleasures of all-male society.[55]

This, of course, overlooks the fact that women's voices are alive and well everywhere in the opera, even in the Grail kingdom. There are the two young esquires in act 1 (sung by women). And there are the invisible "Boys" who roost in the temple dome and sing the Grail choruses at the end of acts 1 and 3. Some of them—in the top rung—are real boys. But an equal number are Dome Girls, female altos and sopranos in the "middle heights." At the original performances in 1882, some of these celestial sopranos doubled in more unsanctified roles, as Flower Maidens in act 2. A Dome Girl gets a final solo in act 1, and they almost outlast the boy sopranos in act 3, but not quite: the children "from the furthest height" sing the last sustained vocal note in the opera. Replacing Wagner's esquires and Dome Girls with boy sopranos in a dull stab at homosocial perfection (No women allowed! Anywhere!) would eliminate delicious ironies in Wagner's casting.

Such a laundry list of Kundrys emphasizes an obvious point: interpretations of *Parsifal* have sought an essence, a single, palpable Kundry, but come up only with imperfect avatars. Yet without attempting to trap yet another Kundry, it is still worth considering the moment of her death. As Nike Wagner describes it:

> This marvelously scintillating work, a work in which paradox has enabled the philosophical articulation of truth, in the end enforces an unequivocal Christian salvation, which shuts out everything else. The single death, the sacrifice of Kundry, only discreetly and schematically recalls the terror that had to be survived, the evil that had to be exorcised. We reach the end of the world. The reign of Good—without the collaboration of the feminine—has arrived. The Grail, the quintessence of a search for salvation, is found, rescued, illuminated forever. We find ourselves outside history, in a pure state: the terminal state. This is a kind of euphoric deadness.[56]

That the end of *Parsifal* might display euphoric deadness is an idea worth savoring—and worth turning back on the claim that Kundry's death is somehow discreet. Though it is certainly quick, it is marked. In this, Kundry stands alone among Wagner's women: the rest of them die indeterminately and inaudibly.[57]

This is how Kundry dies. The last hundred-odd measures of the opera are a spiral, a sequence starting in A major and falling through subdominant harmonies to reach A♭ major at the end. Wagner does this with a daisy chain: A major through F♯ minor to E major, through C♯ minor to B major, through G♯ minor to F♯ major, through E♭ minor to D♭ major, where things pause for a moment as the dove appears above the Grail. If the pattern were unbroken, the next keys would be B♭ minor and A♭ major, the terminus. What happens instead is this: "Kundry, eyes raised to look upon Parsifal, sinks, lifeless, to the ground." And the entire harmonic pattern breaks. Instantly something not in the plan, an A-minor triad, sweeps down and up through the orchestra as if played by a giant harp. D♭ is recovered a moment later, and the sequence glides on, as prescribed, through B♭ minor, to A♭.

One way to read the strange measure in A minor is to see it as movie music, as an orchestral shudder (or, for Nike Wagner, shrug) that points a finger at Kundry's final collapse in case the audience had not noticed. Her body's descent becomes music, and the two things are knotted absolutely to one another, as if the orchestra were a humming electronic field and the falling body a hand that had drifted into that field, altering its sound as surely and as naturally as wind shaping a wave.

As a shrug, the A-minor measure is a momentary interruption in a serene harmonic juggernaut that simply continues on its way once the woman is dead. The chain overrides the interruption. Yet perhaps the interruption also calls into question the force of the chain, which has been broken this way before, for instance, at the end of act 1. That one is quieter—no monstrous harp is brought into play—but harmonically it involves the same unanticipated descent, the same correction. In act 1, the interruption also coincides with a visual effect, as the Grail's light fades and the esquires cover the reliquary.

The point, however, is not that music works the same way two times, to reflect a visible phenomenon on stage, but that the musical chain has a wonderful flaw, a place where one of the links is baroque. If one associates this baroque flaw with Kundry's presence in Grail society, then the daisy chain and its interruption become something more indirect, symbolic representations of Kundry's critical resistance.[58] Saying that music is a symbol for Kundry's resistance detaches music from her falling body. This is nonetheless another way of understanding that music as contingent upon the stage world, conventionally so, as a sound-comment on aspects of the plot. Debussy's insight that plot and music are far apart would suggest another experience entirely.

If the musical effect is not registering the drama onstage, then maybe it is registering something else entirely, the listener's position within another world: the one constructed by music. The A-minor "shudder" measures how deeply that listener has been drawn into a web of sound, how deeply, therefore, he or she assimilates the narrowest and most disquieting fantasies of the stage action that unfolds in step with it and remains unprovoked by anything else that spills out. The musical effect is indeed somatic, reflecting the inner secrets of a body, but the body is one's own and not that of any character on stage.

Thus the end comes, and the listener is floating along euphoric, lulled by subdominants, drowning, sinking. Then, for an instant, he or she returns to awareness, to realize that such music is dissolving all consciousness and reason, irreversibly. A great Wagnerian ambition has been reproached, from within. The A-minor measure is so strange, and so indelible, so unlike the narcotic daisy chain: an alarm, the briefest act of mourning, a shudder that wakes a sleeper from dreams of falling, right before he or she falls asleep for good. Debussy's impulse serves the opera well, after all.

X

One way of understanding Parsifal's or Tannhäuser's quests would be to see them straightforwardly as the search for a receding ideal, a Grail, forgiveness, something that keeps them both wandering for a long time. In both operas, the act 3 prelude represents passing time, the *Wanderjahre* from which one hero returns empty-handed and dies, and one returns to find what he had sought and becomes king. In an odd way, the medieval Grail legend meets post-Lacanian psychoanalytic theory in the Grailish notion of the Real, which eludes symbolization because symbolization was its cause, and because it is symbolization's leftovers. Or, maybe it is Amfortas's wound that is Real, as it surely is in Syberberg's film, in which the wound is carried around on a white pillow like an especially fine cocktail tidbit.[59]

Kundry is looking too. In act 2, she tells the story of her encounter with Christ in stammers, beginning in medias res with the traumatic moment: "I saw him, and laughed." In being so coy about the crucifixion and the "him," Wagner seems to operate under an Old Testament prohibition against representation, anticipating all those Hollywood Bible epics, those *Ben Hurs* that show only the back of Christ's head, and the crucifixion—if at all—at a distance, fuzzed up.[60] At least Kundry's narrative is fuller once she comes to her curse, which, like all curses, is metempsychotic: the "same laughter" afflicts her all the time. Before she mentions laughter however, she alludes to the aftermath of her trauma in one of the libretto's oddest lines: "Now I am looking for him, from world to world."

That "world to world" is arresting as a poetic line, because while we have been informed that Kundry reappears in Judeo-Christian history (Gundryggia, Herodias, et cetera), the line suggests that her quest has dragged her to places not even Klingsor knows about, places outside the opera she otherwise inhabits. Thus when she sings her line, we are treated to another bit of musical metempsychosis. What she sings resembles a passage from *Tannhäuser,* specifically, the Pilgrims' music from the *Tannhäuser* overture, which turns up during Jean's wedding-night speech in *The Lady Eve.* To give the words for this music from act 1 scene 3: "Ah, the burden of sin presses heavily upon me, I cannot bear it any longer!" And the Pilgrims go on to say (to the same music, again), "Therefore I want neither peace nor rest, and gladly choose to toil and to be tormented."

When it appears on Kundry's lips, the Pilgrims' music has its visor down, and the new incarnation is "as if already" a motif from the past. This effect is most pronounced in one transoperatic echo without any narrative import. What is measure eighteen in *Parsifal's* act 3 prelude, the sudden apparitional E-minor chord, when its face is visible? The E-minor triad for Brünnhilde's awakening in *Siegfried* act 3, so alarming that the sound itself is the shock of opening one's eyes after all those years. The same sound in *Götterdämmerung* act 3, when Siegfried opens his eyes before he dies. Muffle them, transpose them from the winds to the strings, and they are the distant hortatory instant, an E-minor chord that remembers how loud and bright it was, before it was felled by age.

Kundry's line about searching from "world to world" strikes the ear, finally, because it expresses the grave condition of *Parsifal's* music. As Debussy understood, the music is somehow unanchored, as if the beautiful sonic monument were restless, seeking its proper narrative ground and the characters it properly expresses, because the ones it has are somehow wrong.

This is a symptom, of course, the defining ingredient in *Parsifal's* special strange flavor. This symptom is what makes Nietzsche's critique—his accusations of euphoric stasis—seem unduly shut-in, as if he were hostage to transcendent works and their eternal essences, and no longer the imp of the perverse. Yet such restlessness also constitutes a general condition of all opera, even of music itself as a phenomenon. An operatic work is silent without material realization in interpretation and staging. No single interpretation, however, is the terminus, and still the unique mise-en-scène, the unique live performance, is what is there, to experience, to be held briefly in one's hand.

Indulging in the fantasy of a "Leibowitzian reversal," seeing the work as a "being," one could then say that all operas are anxiously seeking physical forms, reanimating singers and instrumentalists, mustering conductors and stage directors, attempting to manifest themselves in the world: to become audible. In the process, an opera passes through one staging to another staging, from one interpretation to another, at different speeds, with different voices. With *Parsifal,* this restless condition was written into a last, late operatic work.

This is by no means a rearticulation of Adorno's insight that Klingsor the magician stands in for the magician of Bayreuth, that Wagner, when he surrounds Klingsor with "magical tools and necromantic apparatuses," has at last admitted that to cheat theater of artifice cheats it of enchantment. Adorno turned *Parsifal* into *Zauberoper* years after Hanslick had come to the same conclusion, which is now regularly recycled.[61] And at that point, the wound that does not heal, the castrated villain, the whining shop girl, and especially Kundry rise up in protest, since in radical ways *Parsifal* defeats efforts to hold it to an essence. As does music: scripts will be restaged and replayed. Operas manifest themselves in shifting forms, positively never the same, even from one night to the next.

This restlessness is nothing to fear or regret. Opera may well be metempsychotic, but metempsychosis is not merely the regressive fantasy of a permanent essence that prevails over time. The alchemy of change is there as well, in the differences between occupied bodies, the differences that matter. In "Le bienfaisant, ou Quiribirini," another fairy tale by Louis de Mailly, a kind Prince can transpose his consciousness from one forest animal to another. An evil rival usurps the Prince's human body as it lies unoccupied, condemning the Prince to a series of animal forms while he seeks a remedy. In the finale, the various original bodies become irrelevant, and the Prince, as sheer consciousness, begins to metamorphose. Reorient assumptions about metempsychosis along such lines, and a parable about music's state of being can emerge, with an equally ambiguous and far from tragic end. A script may be permanent, but the shapes the work assumes in being performed are variable, as are the meanings that will be imputed to it at different times. One's sight line to any "eternal essence" (itself of course a moving target) is through the bodies that have been occupied, the physical forms that have been taken over. Or, which have taken over the work, and bring it back to life.

4

∞

DEBUSSY'S
PHANTOM SOUNDS

In the middle of a life spent thinking about music, Vladimir
Jankélévitch wrote that "music is the silence of words, just as
poetry is the silence of prose."[1] With this lapidary remark, he bottled up
essences of French Symbolist doctrines, their elevation of music above
language, an impulse to urge poetry toward the condition of musical
sound, and the sense that music is ineffable. "And the ineffable," for
Jankélévitch "cannot be expressed because there are infinite and inter-
minable things to be said of it." Denying that music was inarticulate—
denying that it conveys something *indicible,* unable to be said—he saw
instead a hall of sonorous mirrors, saturated with implications and suggestions that draw the mind on to a vanishing point that can never be
reached.[2] Music has the perfect apparitional quality that others regarded
as characteristic of symbols per se, as that which materializes in the distance and cannot be caught in a journey toward its meaning: it will always
recede, leaving a glowing trail of assumed connotations.[3]

Symbolist literature, with its rhapsodies to musical mystery, dealt
profitably in poetic images of suggestive but unimaginable sound. Such
sounds have their most famous incarnation in the melody of Mallarmé's

faun's flute, repository for all that cannot be thought, said, or remembered. Mallarmé created a poetic symbol that as symbol per se borrows the ineffability of music. It is a mirage whose connotations are lost even as they are approached. By choosing a *musical* object (a flute melody), Mallarmé drew doubly upon music's apparitional quality—as if to say, even if the impossible could occur, and we were to grasp the symbol and its single luminous meaning, hearing what the flute plays, that sound like all music would merely send us wandering onward again.

These literary conceits demanded hard labor of composers who took inspiration from them. Poetry or theatrical scripts may describe ineffable sounds, but inventing such sounds is a programmed failure of sorts. When the poet insists so heavily upon fugitive music, realization of such music in setting the text risks being anticlimactic at best. Thus Debussy wrote not *L'après-midi d'un faune* but a *Prélude,* declaring his flute melody separate from the mystery described by Mallarmé and possessed of a wholly independent capacity to stir mental flights. Composers faced with the faun's flute or, like Rimsky-Korsakov, the bells of the city of Kitezh, or any such spectrally freighted images usually devised similar evasions. For Jankélévitch, such sounds can *only* exist somewhere else, and he observed an interesting pattern: fictions describing them always insist upon their paradoxical quality of being "absent and omnipresent," upon their geographically indeterminate origin.[4]

But of course live theater demands a practical attempt at realizing sonic mysteries. One of the most famous mysterious sounds in the European theatrical repertory occurs in act 2 of Chekhov's *The Cherry Orchard,* as Lopakhin and his companions sit at sunset in doomed pastoral fields. They hear something (these are Chekhov's stage directions): "Everyone sits sunk in thought. Silence. All that is heard is Firs muttering quietly. Suddenly a distant sound rings out, as if from the sky, the sound of a broken string, dying away, sad." Startled, the characters begin to discuss this noise: "What was that?" "I don't know. Perhaps somewhere in the mines, a cable broke." "Perhaps it was a bird—a hawk or something. Or an owl . . . or the hissing of a samovar." Chekhov's sound symbol, since first twanging in 1902, has resonated in the minds of those who witness the play performed or who read the text. Exegeses of the broken-string sound and its greater meaning have been varied: as a warning of impending downfall for the Russian upper class; as a premonition of saws being bent for the ferocious tree felling that will end the play. Indeed, the sound recurs right before the final curtain. But what the sound is, no one can know. No one can see the place where the sound originated, the body that gave it life, and so it engenders a cascade of associations, a motion that cannot be frozen into place. As Jankélévitch understood, in fictions about music ineffability goes hand in hand with invisible origin.

Anyone who has seen *The Cherry Orchard* realizes that directors cannot make this sound come to life, because such sounds must indeed exist only somewhere else, not here and now where they can be heard. In three different productions, I have heard an amplified broken mandolin string, a computer-generated vibration, and an offstage harp, but they fail, as they perhaps must, because they are acoustic realities, and Chekhov's invisible string sound is silenced in any realization. Two different texts—Chekhov's "sad, dying" sound as well as Jankélévitch's writings on music and language—propose the ineffability of disembodied sound, the difficulties inherent in its recreation as sound effect, and finally, how music that lingers in this territory may express such conceits without falsification.

I

The Cherry Orchard was hardly alone in demanding spectral sound: European Symbolist theater returned frequently to the motif of noises "not from here," which, because of their disembodiment, command mystery and resist interpretation.[5] Symbolist theater can, however, be seen as articulating a pretechnological fantasy that preceded by decades the penchant for disembodiment common to both electro-acoustic music and sound cinema. Perhaps in consequence of their technological complications, later genres have given rise to a serious theoretical literature that attempts to account for the epistemology of decorporealized sound. Taking this theory as counterpoint to philosophical writings on Symbolist art underlines how close and suggestive (and yet distant) a historical connection between Symbolist theater and sound film may be. In film theory, however, discussions about invisible sound quickly move from the Symbolist and philosophical focus on invisible music and infinite reveries, to a generally psychological focus on how invisible sound sets up a situation of mastery and submissiveness. In other words, what becomes interesting is the situation in which the listener's capacity for speculation is repressed even as it is being ignited.

The very issue of disembodiment and omnipresent yet invisible sound was a foundational issue for electronic music and *musique concrète*, as well as talking movies. Pierre Schaeffer's *Traité des objets musicaux* first popularized the notion of sound from behind an "acousmatic curtain," referring to *musique concrète* whose invisibility forced the listener to concentrate on the morphology of sounds rather than their origin. At issue here is not just sound that engenders a series of interpretations, but sound that becomes a master voice because of its invisible origin. Schaeffer invoked the figure of Pythagorus, recalling how one of the cults of disciples surrounding the great mathematician listened to him teach from behind an arras, so better to focus their thoughts upon his words and not be distracted by his body or his gestures, or by him. Power then accrues to the utterance and not to the person. The words are freer, something more than the sound of a human being, thus pointing not merely to Pythagorus and his earthly form, but detaching themselves entirely from an agent of utterance to take on other meanings.

Pythagorus's curtain is also a visual motif that expresses a hoary truism, one with a long history: invisible speech is equivalent to divine speech, and God's authority is predicated on the presence of his voice in the absence of his body.[6] Once the curtain is torn, mystery is deflated and authority inevitably lost. The ancient Pythagorean insight would come to be recycled many times in the twentieth century, in the movies—think of God's voice in The Ten Commandments (that "I am!" swooping around Charlton Heston's head) or the wizard in The Wizard of Oz. In the scene where Dorothy and her companions have their final confrontation with the spectral wizard (all floating head and green smoke), they begin to question his wisdom and resist his injunction to "go away." As if echoing their boldness in motion, Toto trots to the corner and draws back the curtain hiding the real wizard, the Kansas con man, exposing a humble source for all that acoustic thunder. "Pay no attention to that man in the booth!" shouts the wizard voice at the moment of its own physical grounding and consequent demystification.

What force, however, is associated with voices whose source is obscured, seeming without ground in physical reality? Omniscience, veracity, the power to convince. If so, the effect would seem antithetical to sound as symbol: bodiless sound is an answer or explanation and not a mysterious sonic invitation. Is this the difference between disembodied *voice* speaking in words, and invisible *music* (whether vocal or not) and its beckoning resonance? Opera confuses those categories, assigning a truthful or proleptic thrust to disembodied voices, the ones that trill from above, like Wagner's Forest Bird, Strauss's Falcon, or the *voce dal ciel* in *Don Carlos;* the ones that boom from below or from one side, like Titurel or that strange Shepherd in act 4 of *Pelléas.*

This association is evident in one operatic scene where the character is alternately on- and offstage. In act 2 scene 1 of Chausson's *Le roi Arthus,* Lancelot hears a peasant sing a song about the giant Rion and his defeat by King Arthur. At first, the peasant is invisible, but then he crosses the stage, disappears, and reappears once more.

This is a neat test case. The peasant's singing seems automatically "different" as he walks out of sight, at which point whatever he says assumes greater mystery. In one instance, however, the assumption that invisible voices possess superior knowledge has shaped the libretto itself, and what the peasant says the moment he disappears is literally different from what he was saying when he was visible. Near the end of the song, the vanished peasant suddenly *quotes* another voice, referring to the distant future: "'Merlin, awake, and awake the king as well.'" The great magician's encounter with Morgan le Fay, Merlin's magic sleep, and Arthur's mythic final disappearance from the world have unexpectedly gotten into the game. This double ascent into invisibility and omniscience is unsettling, as if someone else, some prescient being just out of sight, had instantly assumed control of what is being sung, though the music has not changed in the least (see music ex. 4.1).

Not surprisingly, Symbolist opera in France and Russia, with shared Wagnerian roots, has a special fondness for offstage voices of this sort. Being offstage is one way to guarantee a disconnection between body and

Example 4.1. Chausson, *Le roi Arthus*, act 2 scene 1

I

Example 4.1. (*continued*)

voice, but the association between disembodiment and mastery does not depend simply on sending the singer into the wings. Compelling operatic voices also speak through vessels and mediums or emanate from ghostly bodies and inanimate objects. Though in *reality* produced onstage by a human body, they preserve their authority because the operatic *fiction* declares that a human body is not actually there: the apparatus, the physically present singer, thus paradoxically produces an effect that traditionally demands the body's absence.[7] So the Commendatore, or Nino in Rossini's *Semiramide,* or Antonia's mother in *Tales of Hoffmann* are not *Wizard of Oz* voices that have been embodied and deflated, but rather voices fantastically amplified by their fabulous corporeal media, as if marble, canvas, or ectoplasm had strong megaphonic properties.

Reembodying the voice within inanimate matter will produce not just the usual epistemological effect—omniscience—not just the psychological effect of increased persuasiveness, but an imaginary increase in sheer volume as well. The sound engineering for such apparitions in operatic recordings is symptomatic. Recordings made in classic LP stereo sound (such as Colin Davis's performance of *Don Giovanni* on Phillips) tend to distort such voices with acoustic devices that amplify sound without literally increasing volume, such as echo effects. This habit of enhancing disembodied speech with synthesized resonance characterizes Hollywood cinema as well. The pervasiveness of the gesture is one reason why the disembodied voice of the omniscient Hal in Stanley Kubrick's *2001: A Space Odyssey* is so peculiar. Hal's voice is muffled and acoustically dead, as if his lips were planted close to one's skull, within a tiny space.

Yet the phenomenon begs pause. A medium's speech is at once convincing and suspect: there is always the danger that it has been produced by trickery, by the magician's black machine, and that the ultimate speaker behind the vessel is merely human after all. Even when there is a clear warning within a plot, the operatic phenomenon, as heard in the performance, countermands common sense. In *Tales of Hoffmann,* where the listener knows to distrust Dr. Miracle, the mother's disembodied voice—heard within a trio lacking any musical irony whatsoever—erases all reservations, making everyone within earshot into an Antonia.[8] The difference is that while she dies before she can reconsider her gullibility, the listener survives the consuming moment, perhaps to wonder how he or she could ever have been so deceived.

If film theory assumes the association between disembodiment and authority, operatic practice seems to confirm the happiness of this traditional marriage. Yet neither theory nor opera is monophonic, and the overarching patterns of agreement are only one part of the story. Though the disembodied voice can be read as supernatural, it is worth recalling that taking away the body in order to lend power to the voice is a tricky move, because meanings do proliferate more freely under such circumstances. You want to convey authority or otherworldliness, but without a body your means backfire and may defeat your ends.

This is the alternative significance of the free-floating voice, the instance of doubt. What disembodied voices stand for in a disenchanted world is illusion, the trick of the performance: they suggest not God, but the apparatus and the set. This interpretation shapes Syberberg's *Parsifal* film, where we actually see Titurel: he is King Ludwig II, fat and sick, sitting under the stage that he has paid for. Thus modernist reversions to speaking at moments when God is saying something—in operas like *Moses und Aron*—are reversions to the rational modality of the voice. They may ironically express this disenchantment by converting what fiction presents as otherworldly voices into ordinary speech.

There are disembodied voices, moreover, that create uneasiness by making a noise that is nothing more than the sound of their own indecipherability, just as the sound from *The Cherry Orchard* leads listeners into interpretive riddles that have no answers. Disembodiment may secure trust in some instances, but in others it construes voice and music as a perfect symbol, propelling those who are listening off down a hall of mirrors.

II

Consider the Sailor whose song begins act 1 of *Tristan*. This brief minute or so from an opera notorious for so many other reasons is one of the crucial turning points in operatic history. It represents a rare example of a totally unaccompanied song, for while unaccompanied cadenzas or virtuoso vocalizations are common, self-conscious songs were, up to this point, sung to instruments. In this sense, Wagner's song is hyperrealistic, since sailors singing from high up in the masts would be using their hands to hold on, not to play the lute. One never sees the sailor who sings, though he is presumably an ordinary man and no magic bird, so his invisibility is pointed. And his singing, unlike the singing of magic birds or divine fathers, is full of ambiguities, disturbing for lacking the sureness, that sense of reliable information, habitually associated with invisible voices from above, off, or below. The song places a sign at the opening of *Tristan,* one that hints at a confusion of sonic origins and meaning that ricochets through the entire opera.

This Sailor was anticipated in other Wagnerian works, of course. The Steersman in *Flying Dutchman,* who has a song in the first scene, sings the first phrase of his opening melody without the orchestra, which chimes in only for phrase two. Senta, warming up for her ballad, has some a capella "johohoes." In *Tannhäuser,* the young Shepherd sings alone. All three differ from the Sailor: they are visible, and they have instrumental backup here and there. The Shepherd goes off only at the end of the scene, and he accompanies himself between lines by playing his shepherd's pipe. There is nonetheless a similar effect of hyperrealism joined with harmonic oddities and verbal non sequiturs. Wagner had a nascent intuition about the strange partnership between unaccompanied song, a disappearing body, and a node of uncertainty that is literary as well as musical. The Shepherd's song in *Tannhäuser* whispers that Venus and what she represents cannot be surgically cut from the overworld of *Tannhäuser* and restricted to a demonized space for a demonized Other, though this fluidity is nowhere openly articulated by any character who inhabits the narrative, not even by Venus herself. Post-Wagnerian opera began to reconsider the custom that defined simple divinity or authority—master voice—as moods of invisible speech, thus catching up with an insight present much earlier in Romantic literature: that disembodied voice and mediumistic speech could be suspicious.

Even in film, the disembodied voices are not uniformly informative or imbued with power to compel belief in their utterances. While classic voice-overs hector the spectator with useful information, other disembodied voices are not merely disorienting but terrifying and have achieved notoriety for this reason. In *La voix au cinéma* (1982), Michel Chion explored examples of voices that have no bodies, all of them with negative connotations. Chion borrowed his term for invisible sounds—*acousmatique*—from Pierre Schaeffer, but he modified Schaeffer's cool insistence that concealing sound simply meant enabling a concentration on acoustic morphology.[9] He discussed instead the psychology of disembodied voice, its connection to mastery, God, and religious ritual, in turn defining a particular acousmatic *voice* in film, one not yet hooked to its visible source, or one detached from it: "When the acousmatic presence is that of a voice, above all a voice that has not yet been given visual embodiment—when one cannot yet assign a face to it—one then has a being of a peculiar sort, a sort of talking and acting shadow, to which we shall give the name *acousmêtre*."[10] The word "acousmêtre" is untranslatable (and has entered Anglo-American film theory as such) but invokes the idea of voice as creature, as a being with existence independent from any visual embodiment.

Chion divided acousmatic voices into types, an *acousmêtre intégral,* the one not yet seen; the *acousmêtre déjà-vu,* a voice belonging to someone who has momentarily disappeared from the visual field; and the *acousmêtre commentateur,* the narrative voice-over. Finally, he compared this cinematic phenomenon to disembodied voice in radio, and to the *voix des coulisses* in theater and opera. He argued that in the latter there are significant differences, most importantly, that offstage voices in theater and opera are clearly localizable as emerging from a space *other* than the visible scene. Generally in film the voice offscreen, in terms of the listener's perception, is emitted from the same real space as the visible voice.[11] Later, the fundamental and conventional association of disembodied voice with authority was reaffirmed: "fiction films tend to grant three powers to the acousmêtre, to the voice that speaks over the image but is forever on the verge of appearing in it. First, the acousmêtre has the power of *seeing all;* second the power of *omniscience;* and third, the *omnipotence* to act on the situation. Let us add that in many cases there is also a gift of *ubiquity*—the acousmêtre seems to be anywhere he or she wishes." *Deacousmatization,* Chion notes, strips the voice of these gifts.[12]

Yet acousmatic sound can also be a ghost, drawing attention to unanswered questions about body and origin. *Acousmêtre,* referring to the voice-being not grounded in an object, becomes in many cases a sonic cousin to the phantom, condemned to eternal wandering like the unburied dead, to float in the sound track. In Chion's most disturbing cases, such voices never find their final resting place. His discussion of one famous example, the voice of Norman Bates's mother in *Psycho,* has become a flash point for interrogations of the uncanny in cinema. Žižek, for instance, cites the example of *Psycho* in limiting the acousmêtre to a floating voice that is neither omniscient nor opinioned, as a voice

> which cannot be attributed to any subject and thus hovers in some indefinite interspace. This voice is implacable precisely because it cannot be properly placed, being part neither of the diegetic "reality" nor of the sound accompaniment (commentary, musical score), but belonging, rather, to that mysterious domain designated by Lacan as "between two deaths."
> . . . [A]s was demonstrated by Chion in his brilliant analysis, the central problem of *Psycho* is to be located on a formal level; it concerns the relation of a certain voice (the "mother's voice") to the body for which it searches.[13]

Norman's mother's voice, Chion pointed out, cannot originate in Mrs. Bates's body (she is dead) and is made technologically spectral by the sound apparatus of the film; for though the plot reveals that the rampaging Mrs. Bates is really Norman (Anthony Perkins), Mrs. Bates's voice was not actually the voice of Anthony Perkins in disguise. Chion wrote, of the great frisson in *Psycho,* that this particular acousmatic voice greedily seeks out a resting place but, with nowhere else to go, embeds itself in the wrong body, in Norman Bates himself, who at the film's end is possessed by his mother's voice. But since there is no proper grounding, the voice remains a symbol, and its sound continues in an acoustic afterburn, as an audible apparition that continues to beckon, even after the movie is over.

One could luxuriate for long hours in similar acousmatic conceits and their morbid implications, all those sinister telephone voices. Telephone terrorism shapes the plots of *Sorry, Wrong Number* and, best of all, *Midnight Lace,* where a bizarre eunuch voice menaces Doris Day.[14] Like the voice of Mrs. Bates (and unlike *When a Stranger Calls* or *Sorry, Wrong Number*), this voice is never suitably interred. Though the police finally identify the stalker and bring him to justice, the voice on the telephone is not glued to the culprit's body, never exposed and demystified as the disguised voice of the actor who plays him. In the end the eunuch, heard only tele-phonically, hovers as an unresolved cipher over the movie's apparent safe conclusion. Telephone answering machines, with their double threat of disembodiment and mechanical capture, began to proliferate in films where evil is associated with disembodied voices at a very early stage. In *Kiss Me Deadly* (1955)—from an era in which such machines, hardly yet household fixtures, still have a dangerous feel to them—the machine becomes an in-home repository for the villain's voice.[15]

The sexually ambivalent timbre of evil telephone voices is an excep-tion that only affirms the general preponderance of disembodied male voices in classic Hollywood films, where narrative voice-overs almost invariably belong to men.[16]Given the prevalence of bass-baritone timbre for disembodied speech in film, the conceit of floating maternal speech in *Psycho* and later in James Cameron's *The Terminator* (1984) is set in stark relief to custom. *Terminator* is a movie in which telephones and answer-ing machines—benign domestic appliances—are sly reminders of the movie's nightmare villain machine (played by Arnold Schwarzenegger), the one who cunningly looks and talks (almost) like a human being. For instance, in an early scene, Sarah Connor (Linda Hamilton) listens at her apartment to her answering machine tape; hearing a message from her mother; she pointedly ignores the voice and talks to her pet lizard instead. For the moment, the business with the disembodied maternal voice seems there merely to establish character, to tell us that Sarah has more calls from her mother than from potential mates.

But later that sound will be recast as another acousmatic voice, not simply waiting to be associated with its body (Chion's *acousmêtre intégral*), but rather, a voice with no chance of being properly anchored, one con-demned. Toward the end of the movie, Sarah is on the run from the Ter-minator and reaches the apparent safety of a run-down motel. Warned not to let anyone know where she is, yet alone and weak-willed, she tele-phones her mother, longing for a voice with the associations attributed in myth (and psychoanalytic theory) to maternal sound. She wants the plen-itude, the safety and bliss.[17] The tinny maternal speech familiar from the answering machine pours from the receiver: "I've been worried sick, honey." Then, as Sarah listens and replies, there is an acoustic and visual exchange. The camera cuts from her hotel to her mother's house; correspondingly, Sarah's voice becomes thin, and the mother's voice becomes rich and full, present very nearby as the spectator's ear moves closer to the yet unseen body who speaks.

Panning over the scene, the camera glides toward a place where the movie's starring acousmatic phantom is now due to be caught, glued to the safest vessel of all, the mother's body. There is such hopefulness in this motion, as if the spectator's eyes were the eyes of a distressed child who knows he is about to see his mother and sigh in relief. Then, something goes wrong: the house is dark and disarrayed, and sinister music, a tympani figure in a low bass register, washes into the soundtrack. What happens next is a profound shock that comes at the precise moment the camera makes its final move and pins the voice to a face and a form. The acousmatic voice takes residence in the worst place imaginable, the nightmare body, the Terminator whose thin lips form the words the mother-voice speaks: "I love you too, honey."

III

Theories of cinematic sound acknowledge that acousmatic sound can be omniscient, assumed to originate with a narrative or organizational principle, and conversely disturbing, taking form as a terrible beckoning symbol. The possibilities of mood or meaning are as varied as the wealth of film examples, their narratives, and their acoustic techniques. Yet cinema, and the theory attached to it, reproduces without any consciousness of historical belatedness an earlier Symbolist-theatrical insight that complete absence of material origin can release an untamable proliferation of significance, and that until a voice is buried, its enigmas remain subject to pursuit. And while music theorists like Schaeffer, with his emphasis on morphology of sound, aimed to neutralize the spectral quality of disembodiment in electro-acoustic or computer music, film theorists like Chion at least acknowledge that disembodiment creates a psychological effect. What is left unsaid is whether that effect is always the same, historically uninflected, inevitable.

Chion is also one of a small number of film theorists who consider even fleetingly the nature of disembodied voice in live theater. Such voices emerge physically from somewhere else, somewhere other than the visible stage, from the wings or the catwalks—or, one might add, from the orchestra pit, locus for a voice of another kind entirely. For what is the orchestra in opera, if not a source of invisible sound? Musicologists have one professional deformation in their habit of treating the orchestral continuum of opera as if it were one acousmêtre and not the other, not disorienting or misleading or sinister. Operatic orchestras, so it would seem, deliver a commentary, a statement by some coherent persona who articulates truths about image, plot, or character.[18] In this, the operatic orchestra is the equivalent of a male voice-over in film and often is explicitly gendered as masculine.[19]

Nondiegetic film music, at least in classic sound-film practice, is assumed to be similar: given exegetical capacities as a continuous stratum that renders absolute or accurate judgments in sound, set powerfully against all that is fractured or heterogeneous in film.[20] Film music is, in this reading, another close relative of the male voice-over, belonging to the category of disembodied sound with a consoling or explanatory function. Like the voice-over, it is technically separate from any visible resonant body but secure as a source of information: it tells the spectator-listener what to believe or feel. In traditional film music, this effect is so familiar as to seem inaudible or imperceptible.[21] Examples are legion. In *Terminator*, there is that sinister music in the deacousmaticization scene that is heard seconds before the camera actually reveals what is "wrong," and that proleptically conveys "wrongness" in a form (music) that compels belief in its message as "right."[22] If, however, orchestral *music* in opera possesses the same epistemological capacity as disembodied singing *voices* in opera—if it knows the answer—that same orchestral music is, like the voices, also subject to the same doubts. Like the disembodied Sailor's song, the disembodied operatic orchestra may be more than it first appears to be.

Finally, any distinction between disembodied sound (voice or music) in film and disembodied sound (singing voices and orchestral music) in opera or theater depends on possibilities for realization historically available to a posttechnological art, as opposed to a pretechnological one. Acousmatic sounds or voices in film are the responsibility of sound designers with mechanical means at their disposal, and of course spoken theater or opera today can also demand technological crutches like amplification or computer-generated sound for the performance of antique, pretechnological works.

To address this question of realization, I want to back up to the era of Symbolist theater and ask what was involved in creating disembodied sounds or voices in opera. There is the technical question: as Chion noted, invisible sounds in live theater are acoustically oriented in ways fundamentally unlike acousmatic sound in film, whose physical point of origin is identical to that of visible sound. Both originate in the same sound track and, at least before the era of elaborate Dolby and surround-sound effects, both are projected from loudspeakers near the screen. For Chion, the peculiar force behind disquieting acousmatic gestures is predicated upon the very fact that the acousmêtre originates from the same space or point of origin as the embodied voices. This is what can be exploited to undermine the impression of omniscience. Live theater and opera, it follows, are technically incapable of duplicating this kind of psychological disorientation. When their voices are "off," they are really "off," in another space entirely.

Does opera, however, fail in the creation of phantoms precisely because it is not an imaginary signifier, fail by virtue of its live physical presence and the surfeit of acoustic possibilities that entails? This is a fundamental question: while it may be true that opera and theater confine disembodied voices to spaces offstage, physical placement is not the only means for defining an apparitional sound that inspires hermeneutic wanderings. Opera and theater have a kind of hyperacousmatic potential. To say how this could be so, one need not necessarily pursue the suggestive resonance between theories of film sound and operatic sound. Two works by Debussy, a song and the opera *Pelléas et Mélisande,* confront the older Symbolist paradox of inaudible and unrealizable music. And in their own ways, they create phantom sounds.

IV

This is the foundational paradox of opera, the paradox of Orpheus's singing. Yet it became a favored trope of Romantic and Symbolist literature as the Song, where a transcendent moment of singing works magic that cannot be recalled or repeated. Sometimes the Song was heard only in the past, its melody now imperfectly recalled or lost. This conceit had been explored by German Romantic writers, whose musical metaphysics were (via Wagner) one wellspring of French Symbolism. In *Heinrich von Ofterdingen*, Novalis described such a song as "the gentle tones of an unbelievably beautiful voice that seemed to issue from a primeval oak tree," sung by an "uncanny stranger," a song "the like of which had never before been heard."[23]

Debussy of course set hundreds of Symbolist texts, from the early songs of the 1880s to his last opera, *La chute de la maison Usher,* and more than any other composer of the fin de siècle returned obsessively to this literature for its impossible musical proposals. *La chute de la maison Usher,* Poe's short story, was the most difficult of these texts, full of trouble when transposed into a libretto. Debussy encountered the story sometime before 1890; work on a libretto and music extended from 1908 until 1917. Famously, the operatic setting was never finished.[24] Numerous biographical arguments have been advanced to account for this failure, but no argument has noted that Poe's story, like *The Cherry Orchard,* demands sound effects whose realization seems to defy all creative effort. *The Fall of the House of Usher,* for example, ends with a scene in which Roderick Usher's friend reads to him from a "story of Sir Ethelred," a medieval tale with elaborate descriptions of brass shields and swords falling to the ground, of gates grinding open, and creaking hinges. While reading the tale out loud, Roderick and his friend hear certain sounds that match these descriptions and they interpret them in different ways, while the sounds' unseen source allows their significance to remain indefinite. For the friend, they are random house noises, and he concentrates on their morphology without much wonder about their source. Roderick Usher, with more acuity, hears them in all their acousmatic terror; they are wandering noises whose origin he cannot yet identify, to which his morbid imagination assigns increasingly sinister significance. And he is on the right track, for they are revealed later as sounds made by his sister Madeleine as she breaks out of the family vault, where she had been hastily deposited, before her time.

Poe's house noises are Chekhov's broken string a hundred times over. Debussy actually multiplied ambient noise further in his libretto, in which Roderick brings a second book to the reading scene, one with accounts of "ancient African satyrs and Aegipans" that cause him to imagine a "passionate and funereal dance" accompanying their ceremonies. His stage direction: "As they are reading [silently] one hears, vaguely, the music Roderick Usher imagines."[25] This direction demands the impossible, a phantom sound from time past, one not even described by a fictive text that is, itself, invisible to our eyes and inaudible to our ears, a book we cannot read. Such a sound is so buried within the imaginary that any attempt to make it directly present and concrete would inevitably commit violence upon its essential distance and silence. Debussy left its realization in music to a compositional alter ego unable to complete the task.[26]

For the story of Sire Ulrich (so rebaptized by Debussy), musical sketches reveal how he conceived the "house noises" as melodrama, as musical utterances by the orchestra underneath the friend's spoken narration.[27] What Debussy managed to write is exhausted and silly, for while what he provides is not directly onomatopoeic, the music has the gestural redundancy reminiscent of bad film music. This final failure—suggesting the difficulty of rendering a script for disembodied sound into music—is nonetheless atypical given his many elaborate successes in the same domain, which include *Pelléas et Mélisande* and his song settings from as early as 1884. Preceded by years of song composition in which Debussy realized heard and unheard sound, *Pelléas* was an operatic flower from this proving ground of *ariettes, chansons,* and *mélodies.*

One of his earliest songs, "Mandoline" (1884) is famous (and occasionally denigrated) as a bagatelle, a favorite recital encore. The song sets a poem by Verlaine from *Fêtes galantes* that refers to sounds equally as lost, past, or interred in fictional layers as those funereal African dances. In making music for these impossible sounds, Debussy in 1884 succeeded where the Debussy of 1916, staring at one last libretto, would fall silent and fail.

Verlaine's *Fêtes galantes* are ekphrases of landscapes by Watteau. Both paintings and poems deal with the same series of images: courtiers in a garden, talking, singing, and playing, or listening to music. In "Mandoline" Verlaine adopted an ironic voice that reflects the belated mood of Watteau's iconography: these are not real shepherds and shepherdesses, but "givers of serenades" and "pretty listeners" playacting at pastoral identities, who talk in an eighteenth-century aristocratic garden far removed from prelapsarian Arcadia. Their fascinations are not in their speech, "insipid remarks" that have replaced music, but in their colored silks, which twist into a visual explosion, "whirl[ing] in the ecstasy of a rose-gray moon":

> Les donneurs des sérénades
> Et les belles écouteuses
> Echangent des propos fades
> Sous les ramures chanteuses.
> C'est Tircis et c'est Aminte,
> Et c'est l'éternel Clitandre,
> Et c'est Damis qui pour mainte
> Cruelle fait maint vers tendre.
> Leurs courtes vestes de soie,
> Leurs longues robes à queues,
> Leur élégance, leur joie,
> Et leurs molles ombres bleues
> Tourbillonnent dans l'extase
> D'une lune rose et grise,
> Et la mandoline jase
> Parmi les frissons de brise.

[Givers of serenades / And pretty listeners / Exchange insipid remarks / Under the branches who sing. / There is Tircis, and there Aminte, / There the tedious Clitandre, / And there is Damis, who for many / Cruel ladies makes many a gentle poem. / Their short silken vests, / Their long dresses with trains, / Their elegance, their joy, / Their soft blue shadows / Whirl in the ecstasy / Of a rose-gray moon, / And the mandolin chats melodiously / Amid the shudders of the breeze.]

At the word "tourbillonnent," the wind tosses the human figures, the same wind that blows on the mandolin in the final lines. While human music making has fallen silent in the poem—the singers have abandoned the mandolin, hung it up in the tree—objects in nature are performing, reclaiming music at high volume. The branches in the tree are not "ramures chantantes," singing branches, but "ramures chanteuses," literally, singer-branches. In the final line the mandolin, without benefit of human intervention, "chats melodiously" as the wind sweeps its strings ("jase," a French cognate of "jazz," can mean half-melodious, improvisatory speech). Of course, this is a reference to an aeolian harp, the string instrument played by nature. And still, there is something not quite right about this picture: the wind gives a "shudder." At what? The inanimate objects, the branches and the strings, which have perhaps become a bit too lively, with the spectral human figures by comparison a bit too dead? As an ekphrasis, the poem also stares at the blurs that are memento mori in Watteau's paintings.

Setting "Mandoline" entails one instant dilemma, similar to that of *Usher*'s African satyr dances. Since the poem alludes to human serenades past and silenced, and since any and all songs produce real human music making in their performance, making a song out of this poem must resurrect the very singing it has dismissed as lost, giving it present life as if time had been run backward. In one sense this dilemma has been ignored in Debussy's song setting, since the insipid serenade appears explicitly as the cheerful voice, as a piano that has become a mandolin with broken chords that create a simulacrum of strummed strings. Innocence is everywhere: the major mode, the hypertraditional pattern of statement, contrast, and recapitulation for Verlaine's four verses, nothing the least avant-garde in formal terms. Even ecstasy is firmly straitjacketed, since the poetic explosion at "tourbillonnent" coincides with a return of the opening theme and key.

This is all pointed, however, since the serenade is unreal: such sounds are from time past, the typical product of "serenade givers," done with even as one hears them, in a serenade framed by its own silent future. At the beginning and end of the song, there is a strange noise, almost wild, completely unlike anything that follows or anything pianos usually play: the grace note and single loud G♮ held ad libitum, fading into a long, long silence (see music ex. 4.2).

What is this? One reply is that it is the sound of a broken string, sad, dying away, the last string of a mandolin long ago abandoned, in a garden that has withered. There is an odd brush of hands between Chekhov's sound and Debussy's, broken-string sounds associated with doomed pas-

Example 4.2. Debussy, "Mandoline"

toral worlds. Yet if Chekhov's play ends with the destruction of the trees, Debussy allows the natural music makers, the singer-branches and the talking mandolin, a momentary afterlife in the piano postlude of the song.

After Verlaine's text ends, the song continues with verbal nonsense, "la-la-la," as the voice sinks through three keys, from G, to E♭ to C at the end (music ex. 4.3). This postlude stays within insipid serenade territory; the strumming continues; the singer has not yet fallen silent, though his voice gradually dissolves into pure resonance, and at that point the insipid serenade begins to metamorphose. The alternative music, the music of the inhuman objects, is present within human singing, displaced not so much onto music per se, but onto that sound, *la-la-la,* phonemes lying exactly midway between word and music. The "La"—a nonsense syllable, paradigmatic glossolalia—also has a specific sensible meaning in French as the pitch A♮. This pitch is marked in the song: the first sung note, touched upon momentarily in the last vocal roulades, hovering in the treble in those final polytonal chords, the key cited immediately before the formal return of the opening.

And A♮ is more still, the musical note suggested in Verlaine's poem as the tonic pitch of the aeolian mode, the traditional pastoral mode, and the ancient lyre sounds that abandoned mandolins would make could one ever really hear their speech.[28] This is the pastoral A♮ cited in "L'après-midi d'un faune," where Mallarmé's faun tunes his pipes in a search for the symbolic note. He searches for a prelapsarian past when breath had not

Example 4.3. Debussy, "Mandoline" (end)

I

yet gone out of the world, "Inerte, tout brûle dans l'heure fauve / Sans marquer par quel art ensemble détala / Trop d'hymen souhaité qui cherche le *la*." [Inert, everything burns in this tawny hour / without noting the art by which, together, they escaped / him, who, dreaming of union, is searching for the A.]

Example 4.3. *(continued)*

II

In the postlude and its "La," a symbolic A-aeolian hides as a transverbal-transmusical sound, and survives any transposition, for in whatever key you sing the song, this particular A♭ is ineradicable. Thus the postlude becomes a node where, as Jankélévitch's would put it, impossible music that is "always elsewhere" can be both absent—for giving it real form is

Example 4.3. *(continued)*

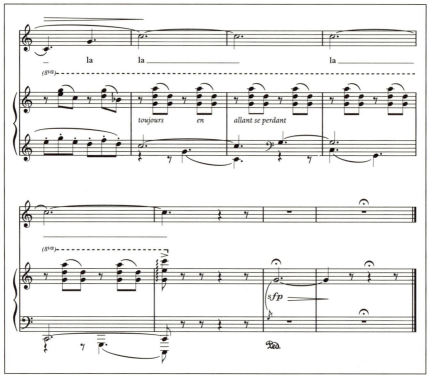

III

impossible—and omnipresent.[29] What the phonemes conceal—the music of the animated instrument and branches that have morphed into chanteuses—is marvelous, but also troubling. One hides it for two reasons: to save it, and to avoid shuddering at its presence.

Yet the song also turns a final screw and brackets all of this la-la nonsense with the snapping noise of the piano's Gs, as if something had been broken after its purpose had been exhausted.[30] "Mandoline" captures in real time at least two imaginary times: the absent past, when simple serenades were heard all the time, and the present of dead and silent gardens. In cinematic terms, however, the song represents sound that is "not there" symbolically, layer after layer. While one such symbolic representation, "la," invokes the aeolian harp as conduit for a divine or natural voice, the other, the broken string, wanders without getting pinned down and is unsettling beyond the end of the song.

These representations of disembodied noise nonetheless appear to the ear as music that cannot possibly be disembodied, the real music emanating from a piano and a singer performing the song. And still: the material apparatus, the song concert, the piano, the tenor in white tie, or the gowned diva, are these things not also banal even as they are a reminder of mortality, just like the serenade?

V

After "Mandoline" in its brief conceits, Maeterlinck's *Pelléas* play might well have seemed overwhelming. The play gives directions not for one or two but for numerous incalculable noises, and tallying them up would give rise to a very long catalogue. As in *The Cherry Orchard*, there are required sound effects and verbal stabs at explanation (as in act 4 scene 4 of the operatic libretto, "What is that noise? They're closing the castle doors"). Mallarmé, reviewing the 1893 premiere of the *Pelléas* play in London, not only wrote of the play's purely musical essence—gesture, word, and image have become ineffable—but suggested that actual musical additions would be in the truest sense superfluous, implying that acoustic phenomena in reality are no match for the silent music engendered by poetry, and also that realizing the sound effects noted by the characters would destroy their essence as well.[31] Yet among the sound effects demanded by the *Pelléas* play are several explicitly musical sounds connected with the human voice, as in act 3 scene 2 (scene 1 in the opera) where there are two Mélisandes singing in the dark, and a preverbal chant from Pelléas:[32]

Mélisande:

Mes longs cheveux descendent	My long hair falls
jusqu'au seuil de la tour,	To the tower's threshold,
Mes cheveux vous attendent	My hair awaits you
tout le longue de la tour,	All along the tower,
Et tout le longue du jour.	And all the day.
St. Daniel, et St. Michel,	St. Daniel, and St. Michael,
St. Michel, et St. Raphaël,	St. Michael, and St. Rafael,
Je suis née un dimanche,	I was born on a Sunday,
un dimanche, à midi.	A Sunday, at noon.

Pelléas:
Ho-la, Ho-la Ho!   Ho-la, Ho-la, Ho!

Mélisande:
Qui est là?   Who's there?

Pelléas:
Moi, moi, et moi. Que fais-tu là   Me, me, and me. What are you
                                              doing there
à la fenêtre, en chantant comme un   At the window, singing like a
    oiseau qui n'est pas d'ici?   bird who is not from here?

Mélisande:
J'arrange mes cheveux pour la nuit.   I'm arranging my hair for the
                                              night.

Chekhov's sound *is* a broken string. Mélisande's singing on the other hand is described as *"like* a bird who is not from here." Reversion to simile acknowledges explicitly that this sound-object cannot be represented: what it *is,* as opposed to what it is *like,* remains immune to decipherment.

Pelléas's opinions about his own voice, however, are another matter. "Who is there?" Mélisande asks of the chanting, and Pelléas answers by knotting his voice tight to his body; three times, he assures her, it comes from "me, me, and me." This same semiotic hard-liner has judged the origin of her singing quite differently. His poetic figure detaches sound from the woman in the tower and assigns it to a being whose nearest approximation is a "bird" who is literally elsewhere, not from here, not here. Thus both characters produce music; both voices issue from the dark, but though Mélisande sings recognizable words and Pelléas emits pure phonemes, he characterizes her voice as a sound that cannot be represented, and his own voice as the sound of reason. To him, her words are *lingua ignota,* unknown language issuing from an unknown place.

This same claim—with its charged reference to birdsong—was reproduced in ironic guise in Jean Cocteau's 1943 film *L'éternel retour,* a modern retelling of both *Tristan und Isolde* and *Pelléas.*[33] In the operatic scene, questions of optical and acoustic spectatorship have already arisen—who is being observed (the conventionally female role), who is observing (conventionally male), and where the audience's ear or eye is located within the fiction. The operatic scene intimates that conventional borders between masculinity and femininity are disintegrating, a consequence that Pelléas's own analysis would deflect or rearrange. In the film, the names Pelléas/Tristan are conflated as "Patrice" and the androgyny of the character (played by Jean Marais) is overt. Patrice has a distinct acoustic marker: he whistles and imitates birds—this is his favorite party trick. Later, he uses the same whistling as a secret signal to Nathalie (the Mélisande/Isolde character), to call her to their assignations. The mutation of human voice into birdsong and *lingua ignota* has been grafted on to a male character, who is in fact "being observed" in more ways than one. The Melot character (renamed "Achille" and played by a dwarf whose face resembles Debussy's) spies on Patrice. But Patrice is also an object for the camera and the sound-recording device, a status only made clearer by Jean Marais's immense beauty, by a plot that puts him at the center of attention, and by a sound track that records his whistling in acoustic close-up, as if it were as glorious as a Wagner opera.[34]

For modern ears, of course, that bird simile and all it implies seems an irresistible invitation to dwell at length upon gender trouble. That women babble, shriek, trill, or emit music while men co-opt the word was a notion venerable in 1902, even in 1802 or 1702: one need only remember the Queen of the Night. Yet in 1791, avian men were no surprise, and *Pelléas* as modernist opera may thus recapture an earlier, pre-Romantic attitude toward male plumage.

If so, the opera also expresses a distinct modern, and even radical, attitude toward male and female speech. The representation of Mélisande's voice within the opera does not match the one made by Pelléas: this alternative image is unconventional and remains ironically separate from the hero's means of listening and understanding. Alien birdsong, an operatic cliché par excellence, is a game generally played according to certain rules, especially in French opera of the nineteenth century. An exotic woman trills wordlessly in supersonic registers (Esclarmonde, Lakmé) or vamps down low (Carmen, Dalila). Mesmerized male characters listen transfixed and, just to make things more obvious, may even comment on the cause of their enchantment: "ta voix, ta voix." This game has also possessed, or acquired, implications about the female body. Creating the alien operatic bird means grounding female voices more securely in crude physicality, in the labor of the actress or singer. Put another way: the usual forum for hearing exotic alien birds in theater is when they are down at the footlights, sweating and vocalizing on open vowel sounds.

In this particular operatic scene, however, Pelléas is the one whose voice cannot float free: it is the product of his body, "me, me, and me." Mélisande is elevated above the stage and invisible to Pelléas (and barely visible to the audience). By now it is commonplace in gender theory to allege that female voice is "embodied" by nature, either as a fact of life, or as a sad consequence of representation, something foisted upon listeners and readers by fictions.[35] Yet this may be no more than dogma based on selected texts. Unlike that of her cousins in classic film, Mélisande's voice, at least in this scene, is like any male voice-over, sensible and disembodied at once. Unlike Pelléas, she sings words, not just siren-song la-la: sly words. She names three saints, Daniel, Michael, and Raphael, a king and two archangels, great and muscular male heroes from the Old Testament, famous for casting out demons and resisting temptation—predicting the next turn of the plot. Even her illogical poetic jumps work toward her figurative masculinization; in their suggestion of improvisation, they suggest her authorship of what she sings. They also align her verbal style with that of Maeterlinck himself, master of the suggestive non sequitur.[36]

Two versions of Mélisande's voice are present: the phenomenal reality of that voice in the theater; and Pelléas's experience of the same voice, as expressed through his poetic figure. One can reconcile the two with the trite explanation that Pelléas hears exactly what the theater audience hears, but describes it in a peculiar way conditioned by his romantic intoxication, or by his clichéd views about feminine speech. But there is a more provocative assumption: a dissimilarity between the two representations means that Pelléas hears something concealed from the theater audience, something "not there" in reality. His characterizations posit that sound or present it to the imagination, but it is not subject to capture: sounds made by an alien bird.

Debussy's musical realization mediates the two, finding a musically indirect approach to a sound that verbal representation also approaches indirectly, by saying what it is like, and not what it is. His musical setting of Mélisande's singing is hyperrealistic beyond any operatic norm, since

Example 4.4. Debussy, *Pelléas* act 3, scene 1

Example 4.4. (*continued*)

II

Example 4.4. (*continued*)

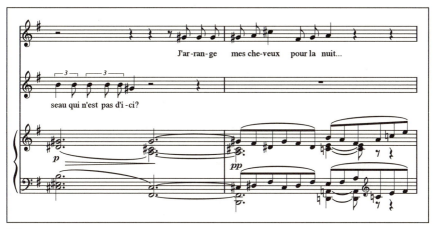

J'ar-ran-ge   mes che-veux   pour la nuit...

seau qui n'est pas d'i -ci?

III

he has the orchestra drop out entirely—real Mélisande in a real tower would have to sing unaccompanied, unless she had her own mandolin and stopped combing her hair to play it. The correspondence between this unaccompanied song and its Wagnerian predecessors is concealed, even tongue-in-cheek, for there is no concrete musical resemblance between Méli-sande and Wagner's various hyperrealistic singers. But this hyperrealism—the long orchestral silence—creates a shock effect that changes any perception of the orchestral music preceding and punctuating Mélisande's vocal lines, reanimating a deadened sense for a fantastic absence of verisimilitude endemic to operatic music. Called into question is the very plausibility of the orchestral voice in opera. How did that orchestra sud-denly get to a forest in the middle of the night? Mélisande's unaccompa-nied singing radically defamiliarizes opera's orchestral continuum, so much so that there is a sense of deflated mystery when the song ends and the voices join the orchestra, a sense of operatic business as usual (see music ex. 4.4).

The real singing, the song about combing long hair, is not the alien birdsong Pelléas hears and cites. Mélisande's hyperrealistic song, resound-ing in the theater, conveys no sense of apparitional magic in an unknown tongue. But Debussy could displace the poetic notion of impossible music "as if" from an alien voice metonymically onto an orchestra whose impossible singing becomes the phantom form of the concealed song.

VI

Pelléas discovers different ways to hear Mélisande's voice and expresses them in acoustic similes that become increasingly fanciful, divorced more and more from a reality heard during the opera's performance. The schism between two registers of sound, one concealed and one audible, widens as the opera unwinds toward the catastrophe of Pelléas's murder. In act 4 scene 4, he says that Mélisande's voice is "cooler and more candid than water." What could he be hearing? Her lies, her bleak admissions of infidelity, seem so obvious.

Repeatedly characterized as sound of uncertain origin and as an acoustic cipher not requiring or admitting the possibility of being deciphered, her voice becomes the focus of a problem in language philosophy that is aimed specifically at music. Both voices however, hers and his, serve as a reproach to gender essentialism.

Pelléas, not noticing what Mélisande says, instead hears music: a grain that for him drowns out the literal meaning of her words. It is not the Tale, but how she tells it. In act 4 scene 4, when he rhapsodizes about the sheer beauty of her voice, he breaks off to ask her whether she is being truthful. Her reply goes ethically and logically awry: "I never lie; I lie only to your brother." But he does not perceive her words, only the texture of the sound she emits, and thus responds, "Oh, how you say that! Your voice, your voice!" This "how" declares radically that when truth is at issue, text is irrelevant, and execution paramount. Pelléas's line does not bring the classic "performative" aspect of language into play: that aspect, adhering to words in the form of something spoken, is also present "on the page," in written statements. Pelléas is not concerned with any words, nor whether grammatical form implies a certain force or truth, nor with any part of the statement that can be captured by being written down. He seeks, and analyzes, the wordless music of live speech, the element that exists only when words are said out loud, especially when they are sung: something in excess of grammatical signs.

What Pelléas hears in Mélisande's voice is analogous to what Symbolist poets wished to hear in poetic language: sonority, not philosophy. Thus his poetic figures in act 4 scene 4 complete what began with his ornithological remark in act 3, decorporealizing and dispersing her voice until it becomes a rustling sound that "travels over the sea in spring." In a play whose echoes of Wagner's *Tristan* libretto are so transparent, Mélisande's voice ends as sonic cousin to more famous sighs rhapsodized in the Sailor's unaccompanied song, sighs that fill ships' sails with wind.

Once more, however, the operatic scene as performed produces an effect that reverses the genders that seem so essential within poetic representation. Though it is Mélisande's voice that Pelléas's intoxicated exclamations would convert into pure grain, it is the rich high baritone of the singer playing Pelléas—and not anything the soprano sings—that beckons the listener as an object of desire. A formal trick multiplies the effect: the rhapsody to Mélisande's voice ("on dirait que ta voix a passé sur la mer au printemps") sounds like a sudden aria, an unexpected mélodie that drops in on a post-Wagnerian sound web. The rhapsody follows a full stop, in a gesture that recalls recitative and aria from opera past, a degree of separation that evolved from a compositional fact of life: the rhapsody was the first fragment of the play set to music by Debussy, in a sketch dating from late summer 1893. The precomposed passage was integrated into the whole scene at a later point, retaining its character as a foreign body. One still senses this, as the slide into formal lyricism, the aria effect when Pelléas begins to sing. Words make the woman into the singing bird, but their sung performance demonstrates that male vocality can rival any woman's for embodiment and intoxication, as a voice whose own words can easily go unheard.[37]

After this final scene in act 4, however, something mysterious happens to Pelléas—more precisely, to one part of him. He dies. But his auditory peculiarity—a capacity to hear sounds that are inaudible to everyone else—survives his death. It is transferred, through music, to the audience. A representation of Mélisande's voice that had been present only as a description becomes a representation of that voice in sound, as Mélisande's voice changes to the ear, assuming for everyone within earshot the force of undecipherable sound. Thus act 5 is harrowing not just because

Golaud is so tormented, or because Mélisande is dying, or because her infant daughter is left to survive without consolation. Once Mélisande's voice as audible reality is newly stylized as distant and incommensurable, the audience's ears have been positioned in a peculiar way: the new point of hearing is the one once occupied by Pelléas. One hears the phantom voice, at last, but at a price: one sits in the place of the dead.

Mélisande's voice, in being converted from one initial extreme form to its opposite, implies that any ear perceptive to her sound has been repositioned in this way. The first time she sang in act 1, she answered Golaud with her famous exclamation, "Don't touch me! Don't touch me!" This happens without any orchestra in the background, in free speech bordering on something unmusical, even unsung. Her first vocal presence is thus nothing at all, no inspiration for a rhapsody, and as far from some traditionally apparitional or enchanting voice-object as one could imagine. In fact this vocal entrance anticipates the unaccompanied song that opens act 3, and its practical artlessness. Golaud on the other hand sings along with a series of ardent orchestral exhalations that mimic his voice, as if they were his breathing to a higher power, magnifying the sounds he produces. Thus Golaud quite sensibly reacts to Mélisande's image and not to her voice, exclaiming (with an exclaiming orchestra), "Oh, how beautiful you are!" upon first catching sight of her face and body.

By act 5, Golaud attacks Mélisande on her deathbed, trying to elicit meaningful speech from her and instead getting showered with verbal signs that have become opaque to understanding, incomprehensible to everyone, even to Mélisande herself. "I no longer understand everything I say, you see. I no longer know what I know. I no longer say what I wish to." Her dialogue with Golaud in act 5 is a clash of irreconcilable voices, in which the balance of act 1 has been precisely reversed. He sings humbly and freely, without the instruments. She sings quite differently. In three peculiar instances, Golaud's free recitative, starkly unaccompanied, is set against highly formal, even hieratic, triple-meter replies by Mélisande (see music ex. 4.5).

In their strange precision and formality, the three replies simultaneously construct and take up residence within musical reliquaries, as an untouchable vocal object in a rare and precious ornamental housing for remnants and parts. In act 3 scene 1, the orchestra worked as a displace-

Example 4.5. *Pelléas* act 5. First reliquary

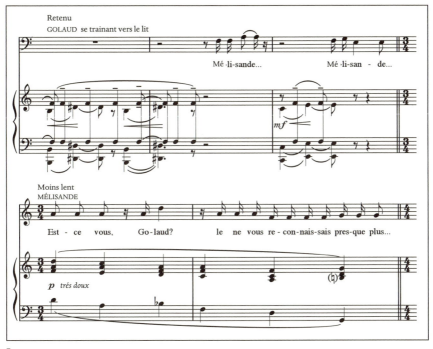

I

ment for alien singing attributed to Mélisande, a phantom form of what
could not be realized. Mélisande sang without the orchestra, as she had in
her first vocal entrance. In these instances from act 5, her voice has moved
into alignment with its phantom orchestral form. The two merge as the
parallel string chords assume the timbre and register of the soprano, and
the soprano intones synchronously with the hieratic six-stroke pulse of
the strings. As this happens, her voice becomes quite audibly an object
that recedes to far distances, away from human discourse, at one with the
instruments. Debussy recreates Mélisande's voice as a perfect symbol,
seeming (in Blanchot's words) "prodigiously far away, like a strange
apparition," unattainable and unknowable.[38] That voice thus approaches,
as much as any voice that exists as sung reality could approach, the unrealizable sound of a song that can never exist, sung by a creature no one
can identify or see with human eyes.

Example 4.5. Second reliquary

II

Example 4.5. Third reliquary

III

VII

And this is frustrating: the flight was so fast and high, the material remnant is so small. Such frustrations are endemic to Symbolist art, which can succeed only when the remnants, like the reliquaries that contain Mélisande's voice, are themselves instantly transfixing because they seem to express to perfection what has escaped. Interpreting Symbolist opera nonetheless runs the risk of seeming to net a butterfly in an iron mesh: speaking about an imaginary music that cannot be realized, fixing the eye on this music, looking above the head of music that actually exists. This can seem like a parody of hermeneutic interpretation, as one seeks not just for an obscure meaning, but for something more fugitive still, something that is not anywhere represented within the text.

Symbolist literature, however, proposed a fiction—an inaudible musical object—that descended through many paths from the Kantian idea of the perfect noumenon. In reality, this object can only be echoed in displaced musical forms. Debussy was manifestly attracted to this conceit and finally defeated by it, though more than any other composer he located the staging grounds, in collisions between text and music, for paradoxes like Jankélévitch's absent omnipresent. Such oxymorons, along with the association of ineffability with physical phenomena such as disembodiment, resonate fruitfully if obliquely with later cinematic ideas of acousmatic voices, which are invisible yet as present as visibly embodied sound. Invisible voices that emanate from the visible stage would constitute a paradoxical physical condition that would parallel the paradoxical metaphysical condition of ineffability, of saying everything yet remaining silent. If Debussy's operas and songs, along with fin de siècle theater, cannot literally create the physical condition, they seem nonetheless to aspire in alternative ways to both paradoxes. Chekhov's famous sound, for instance, is described oddly as both "distant," that is, from a single point at the edge of audibility, and "as if from the sky," as if from everywhere—corresponding to Jankélévitch's "from everywhere and nowhere."[39]

What should one call such musico-poetic fantasies? Should film-theoretical notions be grafted upon them, making them analogous to acousmatic sound? Perhaps Symbolism dreamt proleptically of something that only technology and sound cinema could accomplish.[40] That claim, however, shrinks opera and theater into technically incompetent predecessors of cinema, while the impulse to create impossible song and sound "everywhere and nowhere" led to elaborate artistic stratagems, which are only distant cousins to cinema's technical tricks. Opera's talking statues and singing paintings were one such stratagem, as were spoken theater's scenes of ventriloquism (think of *The Cherry Orchard,* act 3). The mechanisms of "Mandoline" or of *Pelléas et Mélisande* go further still.

Symbolist opera needs no genuine technology, or, rather, it makes a fascinating pseudotechnology out of a temporal alliance, the simultaneity of poetic implications and musical gestures, a collision of fiction with present musical sound. Such present sound, of course, is the one thing film, as an "imaginary signifier," cannot possess. As Christian Metz wrote in a classic essay:

> In the cinema as in the theatre, the represented is by definition imaginary; that is what characterises fiction as such, independently of the signifiers in charge of it. But the representation is fully real in the theatre, whereas in the cinema it too is imaginary, the material being already a reflection. Thus the theatrical fiction is experienced more—it is only a matter of a different "dosage," of a difference of economy, rather, but that is precisely why it is

important—as a set of real pieces of behaviour actively directed at the evo-
cation of something unreal, whereas cinematic fiction is experienced rather
as the quasi-real presence of that unreal itself.[41]

The lack of live bodies and present noise in cinema means that the
medium itself is "swallowed up" by that which is represented, the imaginary: little distance remains.[42] Cinema is a bit flat in this respect.

Metz remarks in an aside that music, as a signifier, has little "affinity"
for the unreal or the fictional and "finds it particularly uncongenial."[43]
This is interesting because in effect, he is putting music on the side of performance and presence—the real—and setting aside the possibility that
music can constitute a representation of the imaginary. Extending his
remark to opera would mean splitting operatic works apart, with dialogue and staged action taking on sole responsibility for conjuring up the
fictional world. Music on the other hand would bring the audience back
into full consciousness of opera's theatricality. As a phenomenon, then,
operatic works engender a constant pull between the performance and
the object of representation and thus lay claim to depth contours that are
not there in film, or even in spoken theater.

But of course music is a representation as well as a performance, and
classic idealist arguments about operatic verisimilitude come to conclusions that are exactly opposite to those implied by Metz's aside. Operatic
music smoothes the listener's way into the stage world and creates an
unreal, more potent world that dialogue or action can represent only
rather poorly. This is what is demythologized in Metz's bland reminder
that the musical signifier is a performance, and what it signifies are the
musician's bodies and gestures, the presence of theater.

Pelléas et Mélisande abounds in musical "fictions": absent omnipresent
sound, disembodiment to a higher power, alien birds and their singing.
Yet some of these fictions come about through a "double work," the performance / representation, in which intoxicating baritones rhapsodize
about the voices of uninteresting sopranos, an irony that does not eliminate mystery. The unusual marriage of irony and mystery was what
Jankélévitch found both artistically brilliant and fundamentally moral in
Debussy's works.[44] Yet Debussy combined the two in one other way, in

reacting to technical challenges without any technology other than the acoustics of stages, voices, and orchestras. Composing an opera at the close of the nineteenth century might well have involved following a script, translating what Symbolist literature proposed as ineffable sound into inadequate reality. Yet it also entailed, as in Debussy's case, an act of courage, shrugging off the threat of futility implicit in attempting a great coup: to represent the sound of Chekhov's broken string.

OUTSIDE
THE TOMB

Having begun with a decapitation and a singing head, it seems appropriate to end with an amputated hand, an icon representing the nocturnal elements in musical performance: the threat of mechanism, that performers are lifeless animated objects. The literary and philosophical texts cited in chapter 1 dealt with the possibility as an abstraction or fantasy, but it also existed in reality, in the form of musical automata, music boxes and other mechanisms, player pianos and reproducing pianos, and finally gramophonic devices. Such machines are the most completely material forms of the performance network, in which musical execution has become entirely inhuman. And yet, by the early twentieth century, their implications were not just grim: the music that reflects them, if it constitutes a modernist interpretation of subjectivity in music and humanity in performance, and their loss in mechanical reproduction, also suggests the futility of seeking lost objects by breaking open tombs. Such music intimates that what is kept hidden should not be exposed, that music itself is always behind a closed door, invisible to the eye, of course, but also in flight from reason.

But first, the amputated hand, the one on Jean-Jacques Rousseau's last tomb. Immediately after his death, Rousseau was laid to rest at Ermenonville, on a small private island surrounded by poplars, in a neoclassical marble sarcophagus. This first site was Arcadian in keeping with Rousseau's pastoral interests as well as his aspirations to "tear away the hideous mask" of death.[1] But in September 1794 the corpse was transferred to the Panthéon, to join those of other great men. Many were uneasy about consigning Rousseau to the eternal indoors, and for two days his coffin rested in the Tuileries garden before reaching its final destination.[2] For the site in the Panthéon a new wooden sarcophagus was devised, still in place today: a miniature Greek temple, whose columns are carved to look like living trees. On two sides, temple doors stand ajar, and out of each stretches a bare fist holding a lighted torch (see fig. 5.1). Some thought this sarcophagus merely ugly.[3] Perhaps the symbolism of the torch was too obvious: enlightenment, Rousseau's influence after his death. Yet Friedrich Meyer, a German visiting Paris in 1797, experienced a frisson of horror on seeing the sarcophagus and the hand that pushes so importunately against the door:

> The two sarcophagi, in which *Rousseau's and Voltaire's* remains rest, stand in the middle of the dome across from one another. They are wooden, adorned with poor bas-reliefs; in the near future they are to be replaced with black marble. On *Rousseau's* tomb there is the beautiful epitaph that appeared on the tomb at Ermenonville, on the Island of Poplars: *Ici repose l'homme de la nature et de la vérité.* Emerging from both narrow sides of the sarcophagus is a dead hand, holding a torch, as if out of the grave. This is a somewhat ponderous symbol of the idea of enlightenment engendered by the philosopher after his death—an idea that a poet might well find use for, but that is no model for the visual arts. This hand, coming from the grave, inspires more horror than benign feelings.[4]

A German writer from a culture whose fondness for grotesquerie peaked a few years later with E.T.A. Hoffmann could well appreciate the monument's bizarre aspects. He saw obligatory motifs from German Romanticism: animation of the inanimate, the fragment that suggests limitless enigma and the noumenal. What unknowable arm supports the hand, what unknowable eye looks to the outer world, from inside? The most mysterious place on Rousseau's sarcophagus is the narrow bar of

Figure 5.1. Rousseau's Tomb.

shadow in the doorway, an opening to the interior, or perhaps merely a
dark inset creating that illusion, mounted with a hand that ends abruptly
at the wrist. Those who conceived of Rousseau's first tomb at Ermenonville self-consciously had rejected the "lugubrious apparatus" of death,
with its implications of decay and the ossuary, and instead had consecrated the illusion that Rousseau rested in the midst of a natural garden.[5]
How ironic that he should end not in white marble but in a sarcophagus
whose *Todtenhände* suggest how the body, prey to death, might irra-
tionally be understood to rise from the grave. There is something nightmarish about the tomb; it remains in the imagination, as it surely did for
Jean Cocteau. That famous *défilé* of amputated arms in *La belle et la bête*,
pinned to a wall and waving their candelabra, refers to Rousseau's sarcophagus by multiplying its most surreal feature.

Rousseau's tombs and their settings entered into contemporary
debates about forms of funerary architecture and cemeteries. A horror of
mid-eighteenth-century urban cemeteries as packed infernos of putrefac-
tion had helped to spur a reform that envisaged the cemetery as a garden
and place of contemplation, in which the ashes of the departed slept,
peaceful and unchanging. Several aspects of Arcadia were reproduced in
this vision. For one, much is eternal in the cemetery garden. Mortal
remains do not decay, but stay, as they are, in sustained sleep, or as cinders
safe from mutation. And like Arcadia, the immutable dead recede from us
as we age and change and experience passing time; their immutability, like
that of the pastoral Edens we visit in imagination, is comforting.

In its primal iconic form, however—as a box and the hand that inhabits it—the sarcophagus might be read as a symbol for musical mechanism,
as a provocation to ask what traces were left within music by the music
machines. In baroque music, they appear as tombeaux, instrumental
pieces celebrating a dead master; in the eighteenth century, in *The Magic
Flute;* in Romantic music, in other forms. In the twentieth century, however, in Maurice Ravel's music especially, they are everywhere. His opera
L'Enfant et les sortilèges (1925) tells of a child who in a fit of anger destroys
furniture, books, and other objects in his room, and how these things
then come to life, reproaching him for his violence. *Le Tombeau de
Couperin,* the piano suite from 1917, similarly involves dead objects and the

act of bringing them to life. In these two works, music mirrors all the unquiet tombs, automata, performer-puppets, and devices for reproducing sound. I would go even further, though, and argue that such objects, and the performance network they represent, constitute a hidden trauma in the history of music, of opera in particular. They are fellow travelers, accompanying and inflecting music from the eighteenth century to the early twentieth, when modernist works (most spectacularly, *Petrushka*) seem suddenly to stop and stare them in the face. Thus any consideration of musical mechanism, as the most brutally material form of the performance network, reflects on concepts of voice and of subjectivity, and their representation in opera as in instrumental music over two centuries.

I

"Tomb" can have many meanings, and in the eighteenth century different senses were assigned to the words "monument" and "tombeau."[6] In the *Encyclopédie,* the article "Tombeau" first defines the word symbolically, as "speaking . . . of those things which cause us to lose our memory of some other object, things that cause its destruction, which, so to speak, swallow it up." When funerary architecture is discussed, the common meaning is given: a vessel containing a body. An ancient Roman distinction between kinds of tombs is invoked, "sepulchre" being an ordinary tomb "constructed to preserve the memory of some person, without any particular funerary solemnities," and monument being "more magnificent," perhaps not housing an actual body.[7] This distinction, along with the Roman custom of the cenotaph, is explored at length.

But the *Encyclopédie* nowhere mentions tombeau in a sense familiar to musicians, as a work written in memory of someone who has died. Such tombeaux are familiar in French baroque art; they could take form in verse or as instrumental works. Literary tombeaux first appeared in France in the sixteenth century and were usually collections of poems. By the mid–seventeenth century, French composers adopted the conceit. Musical tombeaux, almost always a single movement, were written for various instruments, most commonly lute, harpsichord, or viol. Dedicatees included patrons or relatives, but more often the tombeau was consecrated to a dead teacher or master, whose style would be invoked in an act of "commemorative mimesis."[8] Such tombeaux had all but disappeared by the mid–eighteenth century and perhaps for this reason were not mentioned in the *Encyclopédie* article.[9] The word could, then, have two meanings that precisely exclude one another. The tombeau destroys or consumes memory; conversely, it remembers someone who has died, reflecting on his artistic utterances by reproducing them in altered form.

Saying that musical tombeaux are in effect a form of reproduction is undoubtedly eccentric, since this definition makes the tombeau sound like a phonograph, though not a particularly faithful one. Similarities between baroque artwork and industrial invention exist nonetheless. Thomas Edison wrote about the usefulness of his new machine for preserving the voices of aged and dying relatives, and bringing back sounds of dead people speaking or singing.[10] Musical tombeaux, through repetition, also bring back something that is gone; they are in principle "strongly inspired by the spirit and style of their dedicatees."[11] The analogy between phonograph and dance piece is suggested by the notion of "commemorative mimesis," which defines tombeau as a genre. Besides the phonograph, however, there are other boxy images suggested by the tombeau: not only the literal tomb, but also a kind of miniature theater, a rectangular prism, containing something that has been brought to life. Thus the tombeau involves two ideas that are inversions of one another. Tombeaux play back a lifeless work. But they are also inspired by that work: they are lifeless objects set in motion by the hand that moves from within. The living composer plays his imperfect recording of a dead master's sounds; at the same time a past master brings a present composer back from stasis or death. There is a double exposure, a sound that is gone—concealed or lost—and yet is audible through a present sound. Tombeaux repeat sounds from the past without repeating them phonographically as a facsimile.

But can a phonograph experience grief? Metaphorical descriptions of tombeaux as "laments" have a long pedigree, though the description may simply reflect the fact that tombeaux are written in honor of the dead.[12] Yet as allemandes or pavanes, lacking vocalisms, showing emotional restraint, often seeming objective—not mourning at all—they are far from being instrumentalized song. Those that avoid dance tropes or imitate vocal gestures are oft-cited exceptions to the rule. Marin Marais's *Tombeau de M. Ste Colombe* (1701) has a free melody and form in imitation of song; Froberger's 1652 *Tombeau fait à Paris sur la mort de Monsieur de Blancrocher* is to be played "sans observer aucune mesure," aiming at the improvisational rhythms of speech.[13]

Furthermore, tombeaux are disquieting where ordinary vocal laments are not because of the double exposure: tombeaux have a symbiotic, even phagic, relationship to dead thoughts and lost objects. In legend, the Roman matron Artesemia ate up the ashes of her dead husband so that she would become a living sepulchre for his remains, and he could be assimilated into her body. Lost things become introjections (as Freud might have it), in Harold Bloom's words a "fantasy transposition of otherness to the self, as an identification that seeks to defend against time and space."[14] Singing a mourning song means standing apart from the person being apostrophized. Tombeaux, like their architectural cousin (and like Artesemia), contain the dead.

This is so strong an implication that there is no real way to translate *tombeau* into English. "Monument," which would capture the panegyric aspect, is inadequate, for as the *Encyclopédie* points out, monuments need not house a body, and a tombeau, even referring to a poem or lute dance, arrives with all its literal and mortuary connotations intact. Narrative descriptions attached to Denis Gaultier's lute tombeaux from *La Rhétorique des dieux* (1648–52) suggest this quite bluntly. In the description accompanying Gaultier's *Tombeau de Monsr. de Lenclos*, the Muses fashion a lute from a yew tree and put Lenclos's ashes inside: this lute, containing the mortal remains, is then given to Gaultier, who composes his piece on it.[15]

There is nonetheless one form of lament associated specifically with tombeaux in certain sixteenth-century poems that speak of tombs or stones that have come to life and begin to talk.[16] Rousseau's sarcophagus may well refer symbolically to this literary conceit. A thing, however, and not a person is doing the singing. Similar reanimated and vociferous objects haunt the Orpheus narratives that are also typical of tombeau poetry.[17] Gaultier's famous *Tombeau de Mademoiselle Gaultier* (ca. 1650), written for his dead wife, comes with an Orpheus parable attached. The situation clamors for the traditional myth of Orpheus and Eurydice. What is written is rather different:

> The illustrious Gaultier, favored by the gods with the supreme power of animating bodies without souls, makes his lute sing of the sad and lamentable parting from his better half; makes it describe the monument that he has raised to her in the noblest part of the half that remained to him, and has it recount how, in imitation of the phoenix, he has restored himself to life by immortalizing the half that has died.[18]

"Singing" and "recounting" are attributed to a dance piece with no overt vocal gestures. Even a stock phrase like "the monument that he has raised to her" ("le Tombeau qu'il luy a elevé") is a double entendre. The ordinary meaning of "raising a monument" is jostled by the underlying inheritance from tombeau poetry: tombstones that come alive. More to the point, though a number of dead things have been resurrected, none of them is a dead woman. Gaultier does not rescue Eurydice; he is said instead to have the power to animate soulless "bodies." An instrument has been raised from the dead and sings. In another narrative from *La Rhétorique des dieux*, the "great Gaultier" similarly extracts "words that express so strongly the grief of his loss" from the instrument.[19]

The lament metaphor is thus no *Geheimnis der Form* but rather a figure of speech, converting a lifeless instrument into a live "singer," a dead object raised into motion and noise. The "double exposure" is recouped when inert matter laments, animated "from within" by an invisible hand. And this *objet animé* can accomplish another resurrection: here, "dead" Gaultier is reanimated by his own musical utterances. A piece is moved from within by the work of its own author; reproduction brings back oneself.

This solipsistic moment seems an appropriate bridge to another century. The opera *L'Enfant et les sortilèges* is a tombeau, even though it does not declare this by name. In an opera that concerns lifeless objects and their animation, music reflects the idea of mechanical reproduction. Baroque tombeaux engender a "mélancholie rêveuse" not unlike the melancholic nostalgia inspired by Arcadia, because the lost object they contain is heard as if at a distance, unchanging even as we move away from it.[20] In modernist musical tombs, the lost objects are many, and their distance from us becomes very great. Ravel's *Tombeau de Couperin*, for instance, is a neoclassical work written in an old genre (the dance suite), borrowing obligatory features from François Couperin's keyboard dances (rhythms and forms, characteristic ornaments) and clothing them in strange harmonies.[21] Meanwhile, *L'Enfant et les sortilèges* feasts on various musical objects—ragtime dances, fugues, waltzes, musettes, *bel canto* coloratura—as if the composer had found his study littered with broken but useful things, much as the Child does his room *après le déluge*. Such works reproduce dead sound-objects even as they are the inverse: dead objects animated from within by past sounds. As with baroque tombeaux, Gothic motifs cluster around them. Baroque tombeaux, finally, might be understood as artistic reveries about mechanisms for bringing back sound, technologies that were nonexistent in 1700, while Ravel's works might be understood as both recognizing baroque tombeaux as fellow dreamers and reacting to technologies fully in place by 1900. Separating 1700 from 1900 were two centuries in which mechanically reproduced music passed from an infant genius phase of musical automata, through various forms of music box, to reproducing pianos as well as something new and of a fundamentally different order: the phonograph itself.

These works, and perhaps others categorized as neoclassic, are thus *not only* nostalgic, or melancholic, sardonic, anxious, awed, reverent, or painful stolen glances at antiques from music's attic. The litany is not entirely ironic. Neoclassicism as an idea is protean, as Richard Taruskin has shown in witty commentaries on the phenomenon and the scholarship it has engendered.[22] What does it mean to invoke the past? What past? How? When? Here neoclassicism is a Parisian cordon sanitaire against Wagnerian encroachments; there (Stravinsky) an aesthetic of inexpressiveness, a sinister compositional cool; somewhere else Teutonic chauvinism mixed with psychopathologies of influence (Schoenberg and friends); somewhere else again, nostalgic kitsch (Richard Strauss). Anxious influence and psychology, or politics and sociology, have become classic grounds for debates about twentieth-century works in which we sense the presence of an old and alien voice.

But suppose the alien is something else: not the past, but the machine?

Ravel's affinity for the mechanistic is no secret. Jankélévitch celebrated this quality, declaring that "even where there are no machines, pianolas or musical snuff-boxes, Ravel's writing preserves the trace of cogwheels [*roues dentées*]."[23] Musical symptoms of this trace take several forms, some of which Jankélévitch has defined. For him, these symptoms transcend history and are simply part of Ravel's oxymoronic genius, which blends mechanism with enchantment, artisanship with charlatanism, since "Ravel is profound precisely because he is superficial."[24] Yet, put musical mechanism in historical context, and the thing that Jankélévitch left almost unsaid seems unusually self-evident: the phenomenon is disquieting. Thus a classic pair, the early twentieth and the eighteenth centuries, not only reflects how Debussy looked back to Rameau, or Stravinsky to Pergolesi, but also defines the boundaries in a history of music machines that begins with delight and ends with something like terror.

II

Earlier visions of music machines and animated objects are mostly unclouded: only in the 1790s did such objects become nocturnal. The eighteenth, the great century of automata, saw genius in invention and the production of astonishing toys suddenly collide with mechanist thinking on the nature of body and soul. This collision was documented in classics such as La Mettrie's *L'Homme machine*.[25] The history of automata is almost too rich, and language itself was drawn into the web, since speculation on its origins and production intersected precisely with the invention of machines that could reproduce human speech.[26] Even the famous music-theoretical debates of the Enlightenment, such as those on the merits of French and Italian music, refract the light from this collision. D'Alembert (who wrote the articles "Androide" and "Automate" for the *Encyclopédie*) was as strict a materialist as Diderot and shared his fondness for automata as analogues of humans. This marked their unusually phenomenological thinking about opera as that which actors or musicians produce, not merely as an abstract text that imitates the natural world.[27] The toy theater, the little marionettes and their tinkling music: they are the opera.

The Gothic moment represented by Rousseau's tomb in 1797, like *The Magic Flute* in 1791, marks a caesura in the literary and philosophical reception of animated objects. Why have they become terrible? That question is immense, but Stanley Cavell's Hoffmannesque vision of automata offers one answer. The animated figure we confront, astonishingly talented at assuming human functions, suggests that we could look down to find our own chests covered by brass plates, ripped open to expose "an elegant clockwork" within.[28] The perfected mechanical man injures human individuality and consciousness. He erases the transcendent, as a mirror form of the self that can only mechanically sense objects as they appear, having no capacity to go beyond, to the inconceivable.

Speculations on the perfected automaton fully acknowledged this insight by the time of Hoffmann's "Die Automate" (1814) and "Der Sandmann" (1816), but it was stirring already in Jean-Paul's "Menschen sind Maschinen der Engeln" (ca. 1786) or his "Der Maschinenmann nebst seinen Eigenschaften" (1789), representing an earlier literary phase. Both men possessed an entirely sardonic and everyday familiarity with such machines and the polemics they had engendered.[29] One can best measure the immense distance between Hoffmannesque terror and Enlightenment glee by recalling Diderot's animated clavichord (see pages 76–77). But one can also trace the prehistory of the nightmare in the eighteenth century, in warning tremors associated not with speaking machines—the automata imitating human speech—but specifically with music machines.

Nowhere is the machinelike status of human beings more clear than in a musical performance in which someone plays (is played by) someone else's work. The performance network can suggest a master voice animating a medium, a human performer: this is the dead object problem described in chapter 1. There is a puppet master, and thus a marionette. For Jean Paul, human pianists are de facto mechanical. Angels build human meteorologists to be their barometrographs. So, too, they build human pianists to be their playing machines: "That female automaton, for instance, who plays the piano, is at best merely a successful copy of all the female machines pounding on pianos, and accompanying the notes by swaying back in forth, in efforts to suggest passion."[30] In 1777, Ange

Goudar wrote of Italian keyboard players ("professeurs du clavessin") in similar terms:

> Deprive these professors of the harpsichord, take away their staff paper and the use of musical notation, and you make them into bodies without souls, inanimate beings who occupy a place in society only by means of their human form. Since they derive their movements from the musical beat, one cannot talk to them except by means of that beat. When I saw the celebrated virtuoso Anf[.] for the first time in Venice . . . I believed myself to be witnessing an automaton, a machine mounted on brass wires. One has to imagine a man from another world who ignores everything that happens in this one, who says nothing, does nothing, knows nothing, with whom one can have no conversation, who has no expression except that drawn from quarter notes, eighth notes, and sixteenth notes. Since he had left his soul on the lid of his clavichord, I begged him to retrieve it, that is, to play an arietta of his own composition, that I might know that he existed; but he didn't want to exist: so on that day, I had a conversation with his cadaver.[31]

What Goudar describes is the performance network with all its parts connected physically to one another. His virtuoso, wired to a higher will, is a machine or corpse whose soul can be recovered only if he should *compose* and play his own piece, thus speaking in his own voice. Such a recovery would be tantamount to a corpse returning from the dead, to a puppet that, like Pinocchio, becomes flesh and blood. Those brass filaments postulate a connection to a hand attached to a body with a soul, that of the composer who wrote the work.

Such associations between soulless playing and music machines have remained common, so much so that they now seem mere clichés from late-twentieth-century music reviews.[32] Yet it is useful to recall that in the latter half of the eighteenth century, automata were celebrated inventions and familiar art objects. Both Goudar and Jean Paul were writing not many years after a famous real automaton (Henri-Louis Jaquet-Droz's "La Musicienne") first put her leather-covered fingers to her keyboard. Jean Paul's "female automaton who plays the piano" is a direct reference to Droz's creation. Not surprisingly, the critical discourse associating musical performers with automata evolved historically alongside the automata themselves.[33]

Even by the 1820s, when such automata were outmoded playthings of the Enlightenment, the reproach of mechanism remembered the toys. Goudar's terms are, for instance, echoed in Hegel's *Aesthetics,* where the performance network, with its whiff of the marionette, is confronted more systematically. Hegel distinguishes between two kinds of musical execution. One "does not wish to render anything beyond what the work in hand already contains." The other, however, "does not merely reproduce but draws expression, interpretation, the real animation in short, principally from its own resources and not only from the composition as it exists."[34] The first, in which the performer is an "obedient instrument" played by the work, is appropriate to certain pieces yet must never "sink to the merely mechanical":

> If, on the contrary, art is still to be in question, the executant has a duty to give life and soul to the work in the same sense the composer did, and not to give the impression of being a musical automaton who recites a mere lesson and repeats mechanically what has been dictated to him. The *virtuosity* of such animation, however, is limited to solving correctly the difficult problems of the composition on its technical side.[35]

Even though Hegel speaks of giving "life and soul" to the *work,* the framing metaphor of performer as instrument declares the human being to be a lifeless thing animated *by* the work. Hegel anticipates Leibowitz and his "reversal" by more than a hundred years. And the attempt to restore life to the faithful executor seems contradictory, as if those implications of corpses and puppetry had caused a short circuit.[36] More than a century later, Hegel's obedient medium also becomes Stravinsky's mechanical "transmitter" in a harsh performance philosophy in which automatism and lack of will were positive virtues.[37] No equivocation for him.

Hegel departs from the question of the medium to a less fraught topic, Italian opera arias. These pieces, themselves soulless, must be "ensouled" by the improvisations of a performer who "composes in his interpretation" so that "we have present before us not merely a work of art but the actual production of one." Through improvisation, the puppet performer thus becomes the human composer. A discourse of lifelessness and ensoulment is subsequently extended to musical instruments themselves as "dead things" whose external reality (deadness) must be animated by music's internal reality of movement and activity.[38] Thus, what baroque tombeaux did by poetic implication, as instruments come to life, becomes a prescriptive metaphor for all instrumental performance.

A sense of performance as mechanism is most keen when something—a memory lapse, perhaps—goes awry in a solo instrumental performance. One might assume that the failure marks the performer's liberation from the instructions that control him, yet in practice it simply reinforces his mechanical status. Remember concerts in which the pianist stops, unable to continue. He seems blank, at a loss. He does not try to improvise. Instead, he replays this or that passage in an attempt to reenter the piece, until he locates some node in his unspooling movements where the mechanism can be reengaged, leaving the impression that a machine has given a few coughs before moving on.

This sense of the mechanical is conveyed most strongly by child prodigies, who embody a spectacle of adult thought perfectly reproduced by a small laborer who cannot be expected to have experienced the emotions he or she is mimicking. Goudar linked memorization and child performers, claiming that Italian child virtuosos, unable to *improvise* accompaniment, simply memorize all possible accompaniments for figured bass patterns through "painful and hard labor. Are they then musicians? No: they are musical automata, whose only merit is that they strike little bits of wood or ebony, thus producing sounds."[39] Children, as little homunculi, are thus easily reduced in imagination to animated toys, miniatures, and machines. Adorno flirted with this thought without directly citing the automaton in his aphorisms on musical *Wunderkinder.* Child prodigies, he writes, reveal how musical performance obeys different laws, not the "pseudoreligious" function of "experience and struggle" generally projected by adult performance. Prodigies make us uncomfortable, and we tend to wish that they would die or grow up: "We are right in comparing child prodigies to comets. Each one born destroys musical (and not merely musical) order and its consciousness of worth, autonomy, and freedom."[40] By their unalloyed resemblance to puppets, these children suggest the illusory quality of our own autonomy. Perhaps one reason the child Mozart so astonished his audiences was that by improvising or playing his own compositions he managed to retrieve his soul from the clavichord's lid.[41]

A moment when something fails, which in performance exposes the machine in the human being, can conversely mark the humanity of the machine. One obligatory ingredient in musical works written to mimic mechanical music and automata is the hint that the machine has gone awry. This moment of failure may represent either wit or horror. One sees a familiar form in the third movement of Mahler's Symphony No. 2 (the *perpetuum mobile*), where the dance-machine is halted under pressure from a highly subjective voice screaming out its ennui. When the silenced *Ländler* rises again and propels itself back into motion, that is horrible, a "back from the dead" effect.

Mechanism is a defining topos in an earlier work, the Allegretto of Beethoven's Symphony No. 7, which is switched on by its opening woodwind chord.[42] Several effects—the click that sets something in motion, the pervasive rhythmic ostinato, the twenty-four-measure period repeated fourfold—suggest a slow and subtle music box. This, however, is no ordinary box. Capable of adding counterpoint, new timbres, and some Sturm und Drang to the repetitions of its melodic period, it even discovers a contrasting idea and later a fugue. What would we see if we could get a peek at the internal mechanism? The Allegretto's initial twenty-four measures are inscribed on a cylinder. And something impossible is happening with each complete rotation and repetition. The cylinder is sprouting new pins, as if it were Diderot's clavichord thinking about what it plays and reacting with musical embellishments. This movement has the intense voicelessness peculiar to mechanical music, but there is no silly toy at play, as evinced not only by solemnity of affect, but also by how the piece ends. The mechanical failure arrives in the final measures with the rhythmically skewed and overlapping statements of the initial melody's four final notes. Something goes wrong. The music returns to the same chord that opened the movement, which turns off the mechanism, yet avoids the dead stop that betrays an empty machine. Those woodwind chords at the beginning and end, so unique in their timbre, are strangely like sudden apparitions from somewhere else. Lying outside everything otherwise heard, they are the only music not made by the box. But then, by what?

III

Olympia's many breakdowns in Offenbach's *Les Contes d'Hoffmann* teach another lesson: that an android embodied in opera is quite different from a music machine producing symptoms in an instrumental work. The *vox humana* has special imperatives. Olympia breaks down in two different ways. She runs down during the verse of her song and has to be wound up in a bit of slapstick serving to underline Hoffmann's comic obliviousness to her true nature. But she also goes haywire at the end of the act, not by winding down but by breaking into flights of coloratura. In Hegel's terms, her improvisation is a sure sign of the human imagination at work. Heather Hadlock offers this postlapsarian reading of Olympia's free flight, seeing in it a commentary on female singers' capacity to transcend their mechanical status as media for a male-authored text.[43]

Olympia's presence as a character in an opera—where she is a performed character played by a real singer—means that her autonomy has been proven another way as well. It is not just the written-out improvisation within the finale to act 1, but the fact of life, the very fact that someone is singing. Like speaking, singing plays against implications of puppetry. This is one reason why Orpheus's postmortem singing or Callas's Violetta are so very disquieting: because they suggest that singing can originate in the manipulation of dead matter, and they make this so brutally evident. When Orpheus's mouth continues to sing after his head has been separated from his body, this forces a reexamination of all singing, introducing an instance of doubt. If singing were not a paradigmatic instance of presence, if its implications of life were not so strong, the challenge would not need to be so violent.

That live voice suggests the individuality and autonomy of the singer is a phenomenon that cannot be dismissed, not even by the most forceful postmodern critique of voice as presence in Western thought.[44] Unlike instrumentalists, singers are not mutely clutching wood or metal objects that "make music"—things in the shape of boxes and pipes, festooned with wires, morphologically related to music machines or marionettes. Thus Papageno's muteness, the suppression of his voice by the magic bells, represents a troubling moment within Mozart's opera. When the prop bells crawl up toward Papageno's face, they assume shapes that resemble the human head that they have replaced, as a reminder. Yet it is not easy to construe singers as lifeless media, as the case of Orpheus shows: you need dramatic means.

While human voice conveys the strong sense that the speaker "speaks his own words," all instrumental versions of voice are by contrast suspect with regard to the origin of sound. They construe the medium as dead. This belief determined Bloch's suspicions of stage instruments in "Magic Rattle, Human Harp" (see page 57), as it did Plato's prohibitions against flute playing in *The Republic*. In a discussion of Plato, Dolar points out that the "compelling reason" for the proscription is the fact that flutes (and all wind instruments) make the human voice mute. You cannot speak while playing them; they have taken away your voice. What is more, "the wind instruments have the vicious property that they emancipate themselves from the text, they are substitutes for the voice as the voice without words."[45] Human voice appears to speak without ventriloquism. Instrumental music degrades, in imagination, into mechanism. If operatic works can engender a miraculous sense that characters have authored what they sing, this depends fundamentally on the difference between the human voice and all other musical sound.

Allowing a utopian moment in Olympia's improvisation nonetheless goes beyond reasserting a defiant ontology of operatic performance. Olympia herself as an inhabitant of her historical era—the nineteenth century—was fundamentally implausible. She was a fake or an obvious trick in a way that an android pianist was not, because a *singing* voice in fact could not be generated mechanically. The greatest of eighteenth-century speaking automata—Abbé Mical's Têtes parlantes (1783) and Wolfgang von Kempelen's Sprachmaschine (1784)—could talk only in strange monotones. In 1840, inventor Joseph Faber, building on von Kempelen's mechanics, devised a speaking machine called the Euphonia, which was by some accounts capable of reproducing melodious speech with intonational ups and downs. Its noise went beyond the buzzing of the Enlightenment automata, whose artificial sounds were noted by earlier wits.[46]

A true singing automaton was never perfected. After the 1850s, the quest seemed quixotic and historically belated, since gramophonic devices and early experiments in sound recording replaced speaking machines and the work of automaton builders. As one early historian wrote concerning this turning point, "The automata . . . were contrivances designed to produce speech, whereas the newer school of experimentalists were content to devote themselves to the far more profitable and interesting technique of sound reproduction."[47] Once these experiments culminated in Edison's phonograph (1877), the creation of machine speech would have to wait for the computer. Ironically, the triumph of recording over mechanical sound generation had been prefigured in the golden age of automata. In 1787, Ernst Florens Friedrich Chladni's experiments with quartz dust on vibrating plates had led to his celebrated discovery that acoustic forces left material traces: *Klangfiguren*.[48]

IV

Experiments that led to the phonograph were one by-product of a quest to reproduce the human singing voice; the problem of "reproduction" became the search for a "recording" almost simultaneously with the realization that singing could never be generated by machine. Yet the problem of mechanically "reproducing" instrumental performance, solved so well on the technical level in the eighteenth century, continued to constitute a trauma on another plane. Consider the morphological twinships that join music boxes, mechanical musical instruments, and musical automata on the one hand, instruments and performers on the other. If Beethoven's Allegretto reacts seismically to relatively new devices—music boxes and their large cousins like Orchestrions—then there is a parallel phenomenon at the beginning of the twentieth century in the instrumental works that refer to newer models. Even by Beethoven's later years, android automata had largely given way to music machines that conceal or distort the human form.

Musical automata, music boxes, and their elaborate relatives like the fin de siècle player pianos—indeed, all mechanical musical devices—have three parts. The first is the sounding instrument: the comb, the strings or organ pipes with keys and hammers, and so forth. The second is something that touches the instrument: the pins on the cylinder, the player mechanism that depresses the keys, the fingers and mouth of an android (as in the eighteenth-century musical automata). The third is an inscription of the musical work, which determines rhythm and pitch as well as other nuances by the specific arrangement of pins on the cylinder, or punches in disks, or in rolls of paper or brass. Some of these correspond to elements of human music making. The first is analogous, say, to the piano, the second to the hands and fingers of the pianist.

But the third part—a material trace of the musical work, yet not a score (a symbolic prescription for the work's realization) and not a gramophonic impression of the work's sound (a recording)—has no double in a familiar musical object. Neither score nor recording device touches the human performer physically, yet the mechanical inscription must be in contact with the player mechanism, in some cases even melding with the performer's mechanical double. In the case of the music box, both are embodied in the same physical object, the pinned and bridged cylinder, which is simultaneously notation and fingers. In the case of the piano player or the android, the roll or cylinder is the hand *inside* the puppet, the hand *on* the strings of the marionette.

There is a dark quality to this form of inscription. A score causes a performer to play from a distance; between the score and player there is a significant physical space, a gap filled with air and light. Just as the symbolic nature of musical notation indicates that human perception and intelligence are in play, this gap speaks for the humanity of the performer. Thus whatever dead-object problems musical performance otherwise might suggest, the performer is located far in time and space from the compositional voice whose utterance is symbolically encoded in the score. This distance assuages signs of the mechanical and suggests their inverse: the performer's autonomy. There is no such space in a player mechanism, where mechanical body parts are shut close inside a box with a notation machine.

One might nonetheless be tempted to see the writing on the cylinder as embodying some sort of inscriptive utopia, wherein a material prescription for recreating the work is also a physically direct and unmediated trace of its being. Such was Adorno's view of the matter, as Thomas Y. Levin points out.[49] Adorno saw cylinder and pins as precursors of a machine that interested him more directly, the phonograph. The form in which music is inscribed on the recording medium constitutes an ideal; "The notational system for music prior to the invention of the gramophone, Adorno explains, was an arbitrary signifying system, a structured collection of 'mere signs.' Through the gramophone, however, music liberates itself from the shackles of such notation, from its long subordination to the dictates of marks on paper, and *itself* becomes writing."[50] Gramophonic sound traces, in Adorno's writings, become magnetically aligned with a cluster of German Romantic and idealist notions; they are an *Ursprache,* a hieroglyph that, like music itself, is mysterious and perfect because "sign and referent . . . [are] the same."[51] Levin reveals how Adorno, with his affection for such utopian inscriptive forms, must struggle to minimize their negative implications—foremost among them the loss of aura and immediacy implicit in gramophonic reproduction—and thus neutralize their acidity.[52]

Equally acid is the fact that the directness of cylinder notation marks the dystopia in which this notation exists: the lightless, claustrophobic space within the machine where notation and fingers can become one. In any human sphere, notation requires mediation. Touch it as if it were Braille or read it as a visual pattern, and you would need to treat it as symbolic or arbitrary, to translate it so that it can tell you what your fingers should play. Thousands of pins frozen in enigmatic cascades are as unsettling and as secretly resonant as organ pipes silent in the dark: this notation is "the cipher of the cylinders" ("die Geheimschrift der Walzen"), and whenever Adorno contemplates these hieroglyphs, his suddenly umbral vocabulary suggests subconscious misgivings.[53]

The two most famous musical automata of the eighteenth century—Jacques de Vaucanson's "Flûteur automate," built in 1737,[54] and Droz's Musicienne, from 1774—operated by means of elaborate physical contacts between inscription and human stand-in. These are androids that really do play instruments by touching, blowing, and moving their tongues, arms, and hands. Vaucanson's description of his invention, *Le Méchanisme du flûteur automate* (1738), is a classic in eighteenth-century automaton philosophy. Both the Flûteur automate and the Musicienne have been exhaustively analyzed and frequently illustrated in histories of automata, which stress how their cylinders had to control complex motions.[55] As Alfred Chapuis writes of the Flûteur automate:

> The cylinder is divided into fifteen equal parts and laid out in bridges and individual pins in the manner of organ barrels. Over the cylinder is mounted a frame of fifteen keys, which the pins [and bridges] lift as the cylinder revolves; by means of wires, each key controls a different function. The first seven keys activate the fingers; the next three control the valves in the air reservoirs; four keys correspond to the movements which the lips make: opening, closing, retracting, or moving forward toward the edge of the mouth-hole of the flute. The fifteenth key operates the valve in the throat.[56]

The hand inside this puppet has fifteen fingers, and the notation nailed into it is only faintly isomorphic with the melody that it plays. That is, the pins and bridges on the cylinder bear only a tenuous spatial relationship to the order and duration of the notes blown by the flute. One could not easily look at this cylinder and read or reconstruct the melody. And the whole mechanism—the polydactyl hand inside the flute player—is like a controlling will in material form, wired to the creature it moves. Something metaphysical and insubstantial—the musical utterance that animates a human performer—is thus transmuted into pins and strings in the mechanical double. A work has, at last, assumed a permanent material form that is not its performance, yet at what a price.

V

In mechanically reproduced music, the form of the inscription, the "cipher of the cylinders," itself may breed anxiety; but so should the gradual disappearance of originally android forms for automata after 1800, just as singing and dancing androids appeared as nightmares in literary form, most notoriously in Hoffmann's "The Sandman."[57] Perhaps machine makers discarded the human facsimile because, as a body pinned or wired to a mechanical device, it is a faintly revolting spectacle. That facsimile is a forceful reminder that musical performers may also be marionettes, a reminder suppressed by erasing gross human forms. The morphology of the boxes that resulted was nonetheless, in many ways, more disturbing still. Whole bodies were broken into parts.

In the eighteenth century, music machines regularly assumed android form whether or not the puppet actually played an instrument (true automata) or mimed performing while music was played by a hidden mechanism (false automata). By the time Rousseau's dead hand pushed out of his tomb in 1794, the requirement for a human form was less keenly felt, and over the course of the nineteenth century, musical player mechanisms and music boxes began to drop their android ornaments.[58] They were sometimes still fitted out with dummy musicians. Overwhelmingly, however, they became rectangular prisms, their mechanisms enclosed—as with most piano players—or even happily exposed.

With speaking machines, this metamorphosis never took place. Von Kempelen's famous Sprachmaschine—unlike the Flûteur automate and the Musicienne—was not an android but a box with levers. Its internal mechanism essentially duplicated human lungs, larynx, and tongue, but its outside resembled a sort of typewriter with bellows, which a human operator worked in plain sight. Yet, this form seemed inappropriate. Wieland, who expected an automaton resembling a human being, was disappointed in the visual aspect of this "Speech-Piano" with its box-and-keys appearance.[59] Other eighteenth-century speaking machines such as Mical's Têtes parlantes, as well as Faber's nineteenth-century Euphonia, internally similar to von Kempelen's, were decked out with human impedimenta (heads, bodies, clothing).[60]

Hence one might say that a separate path led from speaking machines, to their failure to reproduce singing and their abandonment, to the phonograph. On this separate path, the human form was a desired ornament to anything that talked, up to the moment the phonograph was invented. Phonographs, of course, were always boxes, and as far as I know, no one ever built a phonograph in the shape of a human being. Yet because phonographs could talk and sing, a human presence was recouped separately in fabulous gestures that imagined them as people. The "Song of Mister Phonograph," published by Schirmer in 1878 as music authored by the machine itself ("Words and Music by H. A. H. von Ograph"), is a real piece of grotesquerie. The cover illustration (see fig. 5.2) shows a bizarre manikin with a cylinder for a head, eyes but no mouth, and a voice emitted from a horn held in its left hand.

Figure 5.2. Title page, The Song of Mr. Phonograph.

Figure 5.3. The Needham piano player.

Unlike talking machines, music boxes in time became even more box-like and were not abandoned when phonographs appeared—far from it. They grew and grew, and took over the functions of human instrumentalists with playful ease. If a cylinder with pins could play a metal comb in a little painted box, the same principles could be applied to massive machines that played violins, pianos, harps, organ pipes, and percussion instruments, imitating full orchestras. Photographic galleries of fin de siècle music machines illustrate monumental inventions from the late nineteenth and early twentieth centuries, mainly of German or American manufacture. They have sonorous names—Phonoliszt-Violina, Symphonion, Flute-Pianino, Violano, and Orchestrion—and they are nightmares, immense coffins in which deformed instruments entrapped by infernal player mechanisms are kept behind glass doors.[61]

But even after androids disappear from mechanically generated music, the human body lingers in debased forms. The mechanisms of instru-

Figure 5.4. The Telektra piano player.

ment-players invariably replicate fragments of human morphology, as do so many machines designed to duplicate human labor. Simulacra of fingers, for instance, inhabit every mechanical music instrument, and their presence suggests the ghosts of human hands. The late-nineteenth-century piano-player was a box that "plays the keys with tiny, felt-tipped fingers."[62] It was positioned over the keyboard of an ordinary piano, with the operator sitting in front of the box: "The [human] player's only task is to decide how slow or fast the notes shall sound, how loud or how soft he wants them. Also he uses the sustaining pedal. Three little levers serve to impart the player's wishes to the Pianola. On these his fingers rest." Later the playing mechanism would be incorporated within a specially built instrument as a player piano. Some piano-players had a constraining, cyborg aspect to them, for the human operator did not simply pedal or switch on the electricity: she was closely tied to the device, operating keys that controlled volume and speed (see fig. 5.3). Others distinctly cast the operator as a puppet master. An early advertisement for the "Telektra" (see fig. 5.4) shows two couples sitting in a darkened dining room as the host extends one pale hand toward a discreet black box. A wire trails from this box into the brightly lit salon, connecting to banks of electromagnets in a player piano; the magnetic mechanism depresses the piano's keys. One could choose to let the box engage the player mechanism without human intervention. Or one could adjust volume, bring out a melody, subdue the bass, and change the speed, rather the way we adjust such things on playback equipment today.[63]

VI

Some mechanical players, however, aspired to capture the playing of great pianists and reproduce it without human intervention. They were more than fancy music boxes: they were recording devices, and their fidelity, subtlety, and perfection in reproducing a performance was loudly proclaimed by their manufacturers. Toward the turn of the century, the German companies M. Welte und Söhne and Hupfeld began marketing reproducing piano-players and reproducing pianos whose inscription technologies could record dynamics, attack, pedaling, and nuances of phrasing.[64] Welte especially—as is well known—courted many famous composers and pianists, including Skryabin, Debussy, and Ravel, who had rolls of their playing made for "Welte Mignon" reproducing players and pianos.[65] Such reproducing instruments were not acoustic recording devices that captured the sound of Ravel's playing. They instead encoded every movement of Ravel's hands and feet as they touched the instrument, movements that were rematerialized every time the player was put into action.

This distinction is not trivial. Gramophonic impressions record sound's impact on air and membrane, so if they conjure up a body or body part, it is a fictional listener and his or her ear, someone sitting in a specific space and hearing a live performance, recreated within the real listener hearing the recording. Their suggestion of the listening ear shaped the most famous advertising icon for acoustic recording: "Nipper," the

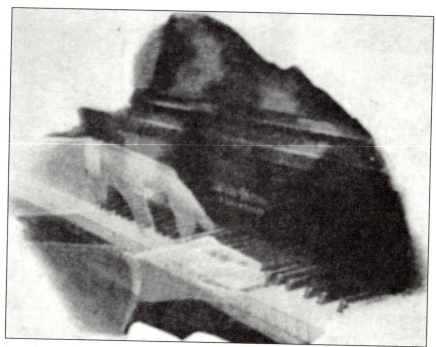

Figure 5.5. Phantom hands (from a Welte advertisement).

attentive dog who hears "His Master's Voice." Reproducing pianos, on the other hand, bring back the performer's body in rather concrete ways. Thus Welte's advertisements featured "Phantom Hands" detached at the wrist (see fig. 5.5) or phantom bodies that were incorporeal and dead. The "unseen touch" of their fingers was imagined to hover over the keyboard as the machine worked.[66]

Phantom hands play the instrument from within: such devices recapitulate the fantasy carved into Rousseau's tomb. There is a box with something unexpectedly lively inside. Rousseau's hand bears a torch signifying the continued resonance of his voice; the hands in the Welte advertisement also convey the sense of something that is past but nonetheless endures, a past musical performance. If Rousseau's tomb also suggests art brought alive by the ghostly introject it has consumed, a machine like a reproducing piano has no obvious symbolic relationship to modernist neoclassicism, since the pianos aspired to recapitulate the past without flaw or variation, while the music constantly announces a separation.

Yet much was lost in the technology of reproduction, even though the product one heard via reproducing piano was superior for many decades to the tinny facsimiles produced by early acoustic recordings. This loss was not a matter of sound quality, accuracy of tempo, or other technical details. It was the performer, his or her present physical being, that was lost. The force of this loss is patent in early advertisements for reproducing pianos, which show instruments playing concertos by themselves while human orchestras labor behind them, or pianos without players performing for rapt Edwardian audiences. There is in a profound sense "something wrong with this picture," and the advertisements are still astonishing after a hundred years.

Such losses can be projected in one form as a musical object from the past whose reanimation can be glimpsed through the walls of its modernist tombeau. But the alien in modernist music is also "something else": not just the past, but the machine, and thus what is gone must be expressed even more strongly. Sound reproduction strangely implies a missing man. So do many modernist works that deal with animated objects: toys, puppets, children's books, things that come to life, the *Boîtes à joujoux,* the *Noëls des jouets,* and *Mères l'oye.* Their mechanistic symptoms are clearly appropriate to their fairy-tale narratives, but those symptoms refer not to *a* machine, but to *the* machine—the one that reproduces dead music—and to what happens when it is engaged. Perhaps this explains their air of serene devastation, as in *Ma mère l'oye.* Restrained, full of beautiful sounds, such pieces nonetheless convey an undertone of desolation. As spectacles portraying the clockwork we may harbor inside ourselves, they interrogate the meaning of reproduction, asking what has been stolen by the machine. By extension, they interrogate the humanity in any human musical performance.

In 1913, a fabled year that ushered in an efflorescence of neoclassic works by Ravel, the composer made two recordings for the Welte Mignon: the *Sonatine* and the *Valses nobles et sentimentales.* An account of his behavior contrasts him favorably with other pianists:

They had quite a time with Debussy, an egomaniac who once stood up and said "There have only been produced so far in the world two great musicians, Beethoven and me." . . . In sharp contrast to Debussy and Paderewski, Ravel was very quiet, very tractable, and very easy to get along with. He came, performed at a recording session and that was that.[67]

This story, originating with Welte impresario Karl Bockisch, may be excessively uncomplimentary to Debussy. Yet Ravel was evidently obedient and untemperamental in recording sessions: a well-programmed machine.

VII

Ravel is a machine, and happily so. This précis, seeming to recapture an old materialist glee, also measures the distance between Hegel's idealist assumptions and an alternative adumbrated in French modernism well before 1913. Jankélévitch describes this alternative, observing how an apparently paradoxical synthesis of enchantment and mechanism pervades Ravel's work, and placing that synthesis in a general context of Parisian musical modernism around 1913. Some modernist composers, by "setting automata in motion, arranging their *pas d'acier* [Prokofiev] and *danses cuirassées* [Satie], imagine . . . that they are being ironical about romantic tender-heartedness." These ironic gestures encompass "Eric Satie's Bottle-Imps, Puppets, Little Wooden Men and Bronze Statues, Maître Pierre's Punch and Judy figures in de Falla, the dolls in *Petrouchka* and even the lead soldiers in Debussy and Séverac." Ravel, on the other hand, is not sardonic. He has the wisdom to see artifice as a "profound philosophy," a vision that Jankélévitch associates with his "Baudelairian side."[68]

This covert reference to Baudelaire's essay *The Philosophy of Toys* (1853) recalls for us Madame Panckouke's toy room, "a chamber where . . . the walls were invisible, so deeply were they lined with toys; the ceiling had vanished behind a great flowering bouquet of toys, which hung down like wonderful stalactites."[69] Jankélévitch envisions Ravel's oeuvre as a cornucopia in terms that echo the abundance of that room, composing an extraordinary three-page rhapsody where those works are characterized as a catalogue of artifice. Ravel offers a "profusion of patent toys, puppets and animated automata that are created and set in motion everywhere in his music by a mind occupied with a mimed version of life." There are "fabric dolls in *Adélaïde;* a fairytale of steel in *L'Heure espagnol;* and in *L'Enfant et les Sortilèges* a fairyland of porcelain, paper and furniture." As in Chausson, or Louis Aubert, or Roussel, where forests "seethe" with mechanized animals and bird devices, the garden in *L'Enfant* sounds like a "great humming aviary where the squeaking of insects mingles with the music of the toads and the creaking of the branches."[70] Even his domestic animals are artificial. In *L'Enfant,* lambs come in shades of rose, and goats in amaranthine violet.

Jankélévitch points to a predilection for derailed mechanisms like out-of-tune pianos and "bleating gramophones" that Ravel shares with Satie, and to music box and mechanical piano sounds he favors along with Séverac, Milhaud, and Debussy.[71] Finally, he describes "symptoms of . . . automatism"[72] in works that have no text, title, or narrative aligning them with machines or toys. He reminds us how *Boléro* swerves into E major before ending, alluding to that *topos obligé* of mechanical music, a breakdown that is both a termination and a hint at freedom from automation: "This is how we should interpret the famous modulation into E, the arbitrary 'clinamen' which all of a sudden shatters the spell of the *Boléro,* spurring the music on toward its liberation in the coda, without which the mechanical bolero would constantly be born again from its own self and would dance round in circles until the end of time."[73] Yet how different this is from Beethoven's Allegretto. Foremost among these musical symptoms are "notes which are reiterated until they lose their breath, imitating the beating of a cembalo," *perpetuum mobile,* and a "phobia for *ritardando*"— since, he claims, "automata stop all at once when their spring has run down." *Ralentir,* like improvisation, is a musical sign betraying human presence in the performance machine. Slowing down bespeaks weakness, and the "continuity of *rallentando,* like that of crescendo, corresponds well to the eloquent depressions and exaltations of the romantic soul."[74] Ravel explores a spasmodic alternative, the hesitation of an unsprung and inhuman pianist who searches for a way back into the piece he or she has forgotten.

But most extraordinarily, Ravel even finds it necessary to shout out a prohibition *against* rallentando in a performance direction that recurs in several piano works, "ne pas ralentir" or "sans ralentir." In a marvelous insight, Jankélévitch observes that this is an outcry and constitutes a paradoxical moment. Within an oeuvre "entirely occupied with composing for itself the imperturbable, indifferent and perfectly inexpressive mask of the engineer," there is this unique sign of emotion. Ravel lets down his guard because he senses danger, that a marionette playing a soulless instrument might be betrayed (through rallentando) as an ordinary human creature in some quotidian theater of musical execution.[75] Reflecting on this conclusion, Jankélévitch proposes that Ravel's capacity to enchant his listeners is not defeated by an exposure of mechanism, but rather is founded in some fundamental way upon it.

In this way, Jankélévitch writes against the grain of German modernist philosophies of music in much the same way he wrote against German music itself. Modern demystification in Western culture is supposed to entail a gesture of unmasking, revealing the labor and technology that enable the illusory magic of performed arts. Adorno, in his writings on Wagner, imagines that the human subject's nostalgic dream of autonomy ends through a critical gesture that discovers deep-buried social mechanisms lying under a lush and misleading musical surface.[76] For Jankélévitch, disenchantment follows upon the discovery of what hides under a glittering machine: body and soul, nothing more interesting than a genuine human subject after all. Such intellectual playfulness nonetheless cannot erase the fact that Diderot's century is past. By 1900, marionettes and automata, vast music boxes, and music machines with their phantom hands are all Janus-faced, both magical and terrible. In Jankélévitch's essay on Ravel, certain pieces and their toy stories occupy a privileged niche for their ineffable purity. What remains unspoken is the degree to which magical mechanisms, even within such pieces, continue to suggest dystopias, and whether Ravel's music, with its fugitive melancholy, acknowledges both faces on Janus's head.

VIII

One work with the warning "sans ralentir" is the Forlane from *Le Tombeau de Couperin*. This movement is unique within the suite, being the only one associated with a real antique, an instrumental Forlane by François Couperin that Ravel had transcribed in 1914. Ravel's Forlane for this reason has a certain interpretive irresistibility and is a much analyzed piece. One might argue that by taking Couperin's Forlane as a ground, Ravel's Forlane as figure defines the compositional terms and conditions of neoclassical mimesis.[77] Such claims need not be reiterated.

I would like to dispense with the genuine antique, since tombeaux are uncanny not because they are modeled on some specific piece, but because they summon a more nebulous object that is heard despite having been entombed. There is a dead Forlane within Ravel's Forlane; its hand moves the piece from within, but it is not Couperin's Forlane. This Forlane is "unreal," to invoke Žižek's Lacanian term for an "absolutely inaudible" sound or "unrealizable sonority," something "around which, like a traumatic kernel, the musical sounds actually produced circulate."[78] Unlike the genuine antique, it is impossible to possess. But it seems to create symptoms.

One of these is pervasive distortion, a sense that every chord in the rondeau section has one or more wrong notes, and that the theme itself is somehow constantly appearing on the wrong beat of the measure (see music ex. 5.1). The first sonority in the piece, with E against an augmented triad with D♯, has been pushed out of shape. What goes awry from the outset ricochets through all those unvarying dotted rhythms, which in their turn seem oblivious to the odd sonorities. Such obliviousness is one fundamental mark of the grotesque. To understand this, we can imagine an elegant dinner party at which a man across from us chats with his neighbors, unaware that a woman's lips are painted large and red on his forehead. In the Forlane, the obliviousness with which a dance rhythm wears its harmonic distortion is a grotesque mark, one that recurs in other works such as the duet for furniture from L'Enfant et les sortilèges.

The contrasting episodes in the Forlane are full of ornaments, which are significantly absent from the rondeau. Their harmonic motion is often transfixed by repeated single pitches in the bass or treble (mm. 29–55, 63–96). And the episodes are not much plagued by dissonance, with one interesting exception (see music ex. 5.2). A phrase in the first contrasting episode rests on a D♯ pedal point in the bass; in the midst of it, an accented E is struck just once in a middle voice by the left hand (m. 44). Thus the

Example 5.1. *Le Tombeau de Couperin*, Forlane (opening rondeau)

I

Example 5.1. (*continued*)

II

pitch that was a figure in the rondeau becomes a ground in the episode, but its adversarial twin becomes the twisted figure as their roles are inverted. And as serene as the contrasting sections may be, they always end by becoming the rondeau's odd beginning (as in music ex. 5.3), as if they are absorbed by force majeur. Thus the unreal Forlane is not something nice in E minor that Ravel modernized with some funny notes. Rather, it is something that pushes, that distorts and twists, propelling a rondeau that tolerates departures only to consume them. There is something internal to the piece that is not the piece, but that animates it: the hand in the box.

Example 5.2. Forlane, mm 42–46

Example 5.3. Forlane, end of the second contrasting episode

IX

A hand and a box: Rousseau's tomb, the rectangular prism containing something alive and noisy, the music machine. For Jankélévitch, the mechanistic symptom in the Forlane resides in the prohibition against slowing to a stop. Other mechanistic symptoms abound: several contrasting episodes in the Forlane sound like musettes.

In 1700, a "musette" was either an instrument resembling a small bagpipe, or a genre piece, a pastoral dance with a drone bass. François Couperin wrote a number of keyboard musettes, faux-naive peasant dances that suggest Watteau's canvases with their aristocrats playing at being shepherdesses.[79] Couperin's musettes thus harbor the ultimate lost sound-object: music made in Arcadia. Between 1700 and 1900, however, the meaning of "musette" underwent a mutation, for its connotative extremes now span the distance from Couperin's mock-shepherd works to Schoenberg's Musette from the Opus 25 piano suite.

What remained constant was a musical feature, the single note sustained in almost every measure. What shifted was the meaning of the style: keyboard musettes came to represent not pastoral music per se, but music boxes. Music boxes played little shepherd dances, and musettes came to imitate not the dance, but its automated medium. Once that had happened, Arcadia could easily leach away. The metamorphosis into mechanism was implicit from the outset, however, since musettes representing pastoral sounds already imitated something constructed, not real. Just as Couperin's bird pieces invoke mechanical birds, so his musettes invoke the artificiality of the aristocrat-peasant, no more natural than a bird-machine.[80] By 1862, the transformation in mimetic implications was complete, and Variation 22 in Brahms's "Handel Variations"—the music box variation often seen as a salute to Couperin—is a musette that lacks only a subtitle. By 1935, this sense of musette as music box could be used to sinister effect, as Alban Berg does in *Lulu* for the confrontations between Lulu and Dr. Schön. The Gavotte we hear during their first scene together (act 1 scene 2) contains one prominent melody played and sung, according to Berg's directions, "à la Musette" (for example, at Lulu's "trotzdem können wir uns treffen, wo es Ihnen angemessen scheint"). When the Gavotte returns in act 1 scene 3, Lulu is dictating a letter to Dr. Schön; he repeats her words mechanically as he copies them out. The melody "à la Musette" pervades this dictation scene, but the actual direction "à la Musette" has disappeared, having become superfluous. The thing that reproduces a musical work, the "box" implicit in "musette," is now put before our eyes in the form of a debased human figure robbed of his own voice, who parrots what he hears.

While the genre piece morphed from pastoral to mechanical, the instrument was undergoing a similar if slower transformation. In Paris around 1900, musettes were bagpipes or accordions that accompanied so-called *bals-musettes* or *danses-musettes*, popular lower- and middle-class dance fêtes. At the same time, just as an imitated pastoral dance had become an imitated music box, the shepherd's instrument became a machine. In the 1880s, an organette (a small player organ) manufactured by Autophone was baptized "Musette"and marketed to the working class as a cheap cousin to very expensive devices, the elaborate music boxes or piano-players the lower classes could not afford.[81] This seems logical: bagpipe or accordion timbres resemble that of a mechanical barrel organ, and their social connotations of peasantry and proletariat are reproduced in the object's function as a poor person's toy. But a final metamorphosis came in 1909 when the name jumped across a fundamental timbral gulf, from bellows and pipes to strings and hammers. In that year, Buff-Hedinger in Leipzig created widely marketed piano-players and player pianos named the "Musetta."[82]

This is the endgame in the play of metamorphoses, where even a family timbre and its social implications drained away from the instrument, leaving only a machine. As a box that sidles up to and covers the keys of a piano, the piano-player recalls music boxes morphologically, just as piano timbre recalls them acoustically. Hence by the year 1909 the instrument comes face to face again with the musical genre, and after the historical mutations that had separated them, the two are joined once more. Now, however, the instrument is no pleasant Arcadian prop. It is a massive box with "phantom hands."

In *Le Tombeau de Couperin,* both the Forlane and the Minuet replay this meeting. In the Forlane, musette sounds are heard here and there, as in the berceuse bass E–B–G–B–E (mm. 29–31 and following), resembling the bass on G–D–D–D–G in the contrasting section of the Minuet movement, labeled "Musette." The episode in measures 63–96 of the Forlane epitomizes Jankélévitch's observation that funeral marches are unnecessary when one can write devastating dances.[83] This episode flees to the piano's upper registers, where musette traces appear as the pedal points on repeated notes, in the way those notes are quietly hammered and accented by ornament, repeated perhaps a few too many times. The shift upward suggests the miniaturization of sound; the hammer springs to the ear, bringing along the little box and its internal works. While the rondeau may seem to consume such contrasting episodes and their musette automatisms, if it could step back, it would understand itself as part of a music machine, a much larger one. Such Forlanes end by breaking down. The rondeau melody chokes and can go no further; it attempts to restart, comes in on the wrong beat, and closes down like Beethoven's Allegretto, with fragments of the theme overlapping into

Example 5.4. End of the Forlane

higher registers (see music ex. 5.4), *sans ralentir.* Then the G-minor Musette in the Minuet (see music ex. 5.5) represents mechanism gone awry, now at once ironic and terrifying.

First, there is the joke. In measure 49, the soft pedal comes off, the volume increases, and the box loses a few cogwheels, developing Romantic piano concerto *angoisse* and some tolling bells, which swell and recede only to be cut off. In measure 65 the original Musette theme is restored. But the point of return—the cut from a C♭-major to a B♭-major chord in the right hand—instantaneously bridges an infinite divide. Ravel implies— perhaps even cruelly—that Romantic musical rhetoric, symbolically representing human subjectivity, is just the by-product of a broken machine. But the joke has an afterburn that is more serious. Even as the joke is made, the sound is neither amusing nor parodistic. For a few seconds it seems to consume the world, as if the object gone haywire were not a little gilt *boîte* but a looming Orchestrion whose disorder is lethal.

Does this anguish really originate with a machine imitating human passion? Or is it Ravel's outcry—"Ne pas ralentir!"—that has taken musical form? As a rare subjective emotion, displayed only in extremis, this outcry is usually banished to the expressive directions and left silently on

Example 5.5. The Musette in the Minuet

I

the page. Paradoxically, the unsprung moment could simultaneously give voice to the "cry" *and* betray a human presence in the machine, the very thing that cry so bitterly protests.

This Musette does not end mechanically when something breaks. Instead, the cylinder seems to sprout new pins. The original theme

Example 5.5. (*continued*)

II

returns and circles around to repeat as it had before, now in G major, as a left-hand counterpoint to the Minuet's recapitulation in the right hand. Following the Minuet into far harmonic fields, it is absorbed by that Minuet without actually ending at all. With this extraordinary transfigured turn, Ravel suggests that the Musette keeps on playing but has withdrawn beyond range, out of earshot, hidden behind the Minuet, which magically slows down before it stops: "ralentir beaucoup." Thus there *is* a rallentando in the machine, but this dread revelation is made where no human ear remains to contemplate its meaning.

This fade-out ending beyond the range of human hearing is repeated in *L'Enfant et les sortilèges,* appropriately enough in a pastoral interlude. Ravel's wicked Child destroys almost everything he can reach within the first few minutes of the opera, and one of the things he tears is his wallpaper. Like much nursery décor since, this wallpaper features lambs and other bucolic figures. In their turn, these torn figures—delicate sheep, shepherds and shepherdesses, a dog, and a goat in melancholy procession—come to life, singing of their plight. Ravel's librettist Colette specified their sound as "naive music of pipes and tambourines," and Ravel, following this cue, composed an orchestral musette.[84] These Arcadians are succinct in summarizing their loss—"our loves seemed eternal, eternal our piping"—and where pastoral poetry becomes an essence so reduced, *musette* also reverts to its root meaning as a drone and piping of the *cor anglais,* the naive music pastoral people play. In fact, they bring it along in the only scene where music making is meant to *seem* as if it emanates from the stage, as Colette's note suggests. This is not merely an incidental point. On this ontological level, the musette must be declared original and natural, not subsumed in an overarching artifice characteristic of operatic music per se, in order that its mechanistic signs properly represent the blue dog and the people made of paper. This is the music natural to artificial objects.

Hence the music box returns by a back door. A fictional original musette is recalled by frequent reversion to pastoral wind instruments like the clarinet or *cor anglais.* Yet the musette genre's keyboard past, and the mechanical box implicit in that timbre, lurks underneath this pastoral illusion (see music ex. 5.6). Below it all, a pianist softly strikes the obligatory pastoral drone on open fifths. This piano provides a significant instrumental counterpoint, one that suggests how the Arcadias promised by woodwinds are irretrievable, instantly recreating the history erased by prelapsarian wind timbres, and the mechanical endgame those winds would deny.

Even more radically, some shepherds and shepherdesses (altos and basses) are taken prisoner in the piano's realm, transformed into drone

Example 5.6. *L'Enfant et les sortilèges,* the pastoral lament

I

Example 5.6. (*continued*)

Example 5.6. (*continued*)

III

instruments that buzz strange phonemes, *Zzzzz*. Others (some tenors and sopranos) are turned into pipes that hum *Annnn*. These instrumentalized voices are the music made by human bodies being converted into animated devices, the sound of automata coming into being. Here, the "enchantment of animation" implicit in the opera's name is at once allied with mechanism and revealed as mechanistic through a musical sign. When this happens, the little figures depart, and with them their music of cornemuse and tambourine, disappearing into silence.

X

André Hellé, the artist who provided the scenario for Debussy's *Boîte à joujoux*, designed the cover for the piano-vocal score of *L'Enfant et les sortilèges* (see fig. 5.6). A child sits in a messy room that is also

Figure 5.6. André Hellé, watercolor for the frontispiece to *L'Enfant et les sortilèges* (private collection).

a necropolis: the broad back of the armchair, supplied with hollow eyes and mouth, resembles a ponderous tombstone, and the clock could be an elongated, more elegant version of the same object. Things are crowded together, leaning this way and that like the gravestones in Prague's Jewish cemetery, as if jostled by unquiet geology, from below. Then there is the shadow. The figures seem poised against some shrubbery, or against a black cloud, or even the edge of the world. The frontispiece is a double exposure, expressing ambivalence toward animation that is at once magical and disturbing.

How does this double exposure play out? On one level, the opera's music is calculated to supply an aura, bringing the listener *into* the Child's enchanted world, into the belief in magical toys. Children cross a barrier impermeable to adults:

Objects do not meet the picturing gaze of the child from the pages of the book; instead, the gazing child enters into those pages, becoming suffused, like a cloud, with the riotous colors of the world of pictures. Sitting before his painted book, he makes the Taoist vision of perfection come true: he overcomes the illusory barrier of the book's surface and passes through the colored textures and brightly painted partitions to enter a stage on which fairy tales spring to life.[85]

Benjamin's "barrier of the book's surface" is the operatic barrier of the proscenium, the fantastic narrative, and the material phenomenon of performance. In opera, this barrier is overcome by music; certainly classic debates about operatic *vraisemblance* tend to assign music this role. In *L'Enfant et les sortilèges,* however, this is spelled out in terms a child could understand: music is the audible trace of the gazing Child's passage into the fictional world, into its textures. Music puts the listener there too.

This point is fully evident only at the end. The Child goes outside to his garden to discover that trees and animals can now talk as well, berating him for his cruelty. Finally, the Animals attack him en masse and he loses consciousness. At this precise moment all music ceases in a long "profound silence" that one Animal, suddenly unmasked as all but mute, will break with halting *Sprechgesang,* "plaintive and supple declamation, almost without timbre" (see music ex. 5.7). The orchestra spasmodically rewinds itself into motion in an effect that strongly recalls *The Sorcerer's Apprentice.* At the same time the Animals slowly teach themselves to speak and finally to cry out "Mama" in a tumult of overlapping voices.

Their acquisition of speech is played out step by step as a critical point about enchantment. The Animals, the trees, the teapot, the wallpaper, the book: none of these things could speak, dance, or sing. They had *seemed* to, but their animation and voices are now understood as an illusion engendered by a gaze that had broken into a secret world but had then fallen away. At the exact point where the Child regains consciousness, everything changes once again. The auratic gaze-music returns and instantly cuts off the Animals' groundswell of self-made speech. The Child's open eyes mark a transfigured moment—set off with harp glissandos—which ushers in the final fugue sung by Animals who—"pictured" once more—sing again as they had before.

This finale has brought back tone colors from an earlier scene, one that represents the heart of the opera and resonates sympathetically with Benjamin's aperçu about the child and his book. After the paper shepherds

Example 5.7. Orchestra and Animals learn to speak

depart, Colette's stage directions tell us about a strange apparition. A torn page from a book, "on which the child is stretched out, raises itself like a stone slab, in order to allow first a languorous hand, then a blond head, then finally a whole and beautiful Fairy-Tale Princess to emerge." A stage image depicts the book's surface being breached, and a page that becomes an open door to an unseen interior. As the door opens, harp arpeggios mark the Princess's passage; they come back for her departure. If, how-

Example 5.7. *(continued)*

II

Example 5.7. (*continued*)

III

ever, music in general seems to double the Child's passage into hidden spaces—bringing the listener's ear inside the fairy-tale world—that effect is undone in small details in the Princess's scene. And it is critical that it be undone, that the passage be barred.

Once the harp glissandos fade, the Princess sings a long solo in which she reminds the Child of his secret love for her. Ravel's gift for minimalist scoring is fully on display in this passage with its flute accompaniment. He recalls many solo flute-and-sopranos of operas past, while he prefigures the even more austere a cappella texture of the Animals' final fugue. But along with the sparse scoring, the Princess's reminiscences end when she turns from the past to point out her tragedy: "Since you have torn the book, what will happen to me?" She speculates about her unknowable future: "Who knows if the evil enchanter will return me to Death's sleep, or transform me into a mist." The Child asks about each magical talisman, only to be told that it was destroyed when he destroyed the book. During all this, the orchestra returns (see music ex. 5.8).

But, as Jankélévitch points out, this orchestra has become mystifying.[86] Fast arpeggios are played by bass clarinets, bassoons, and clarinets, moving upward through the winds to reach flutes and piccolos. One nonetheless does not hear winds. These arpeggios belonged to the harp, moments before. Now there is an imaginary instrument that has taken the real harp's place, a harp-object engendered by a nameless sound, a trick of instrumentation that creates the sound of a harp heard through a filter, imperfectly reproduced, a real harp from the past whose voice is behind the present sounds that have walled it in.

This harp-object continues playing until the Child replies and imagines himself as the Fairy Tale Prince, at which point the real harp reclaims its stolen arpeggios. A crescendo accompanies the fantasy, but the Child's ecstatic vision ends, and the Princess reminds him that he is dreaming, and that she is doomed. Once the slab that had released her swallows her again, the real harp plays one last time. Real harps and impossible ones thus

Example 5.8. Unreal Harp Sounds

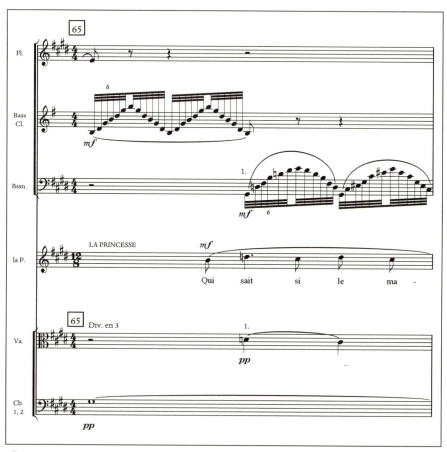

I

Example 5.8. (*continued*)

II

Example 5.8. (*continued*)

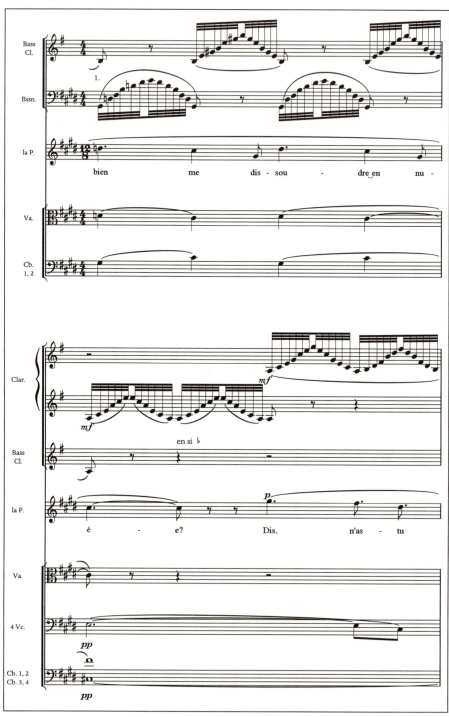

Example 5.8. (*continued*)

Clar.

la P.

pas   re - gret   d'i - gno - rer   à   ja - mais   Le

Vc.

Cb.
3, 4

poco cresc.

Clar.

la P.

sort   de   ta   pre - miè - re   bien - ai -

Va.

Vc.

Cb.
3, 4

pp

IV

Example 5.8. (*continued*)

V

disappear and reappear, in flights and returns that place the listeners outside a wall while nonetheless conveying what is hidden within, as something barred to the ear. If there were a listener who could become the gazing child, he or she could pass the barrier into the hidden space and would hear the sound kept inside. Those outside the tomb listen to a reproduction.

The Princess's disappearance is described in odd terms: the ground opens below her, and she is pulled back down by an invisible force, a staging that nods irreverently at another lady from the center of the earth, Princess Erda and her elevator. But where Erda is Cassandra, gloomy about a future clearly seen, Ravel's Princess is Mnemosyne. Like many animated objects in the opera, she sings about an ideal past, the time before disaster. Visually, she rises from and returns to a hollow place covered by a stone, a tomb in the very first sense described by the *Encyclopédie*: the place that swallows memory.

The unreal harp sounds thus produce an optical illusion. A harp voice propels woodwinds to unnatural gymnastics; a lost voice shimmers through the medium of its imperfect reproduction by winds. The necropolis is there, behind the messy playroom. If the unreal harp sounds represent a double exposure, however, they also suggest a fundamental paradox. What contains them, what engenders them, is an object whose lifelessness is animated from within, which is, simultaneously, something alive that remembers dead sound. This description recalls a "tomb," of course, the baroque tombeau as musico-reproductive apparatus.

In the abstract, however, the words describe musical performance itself, its oscillation between suggestions of deadness and life, the reversal that imagines works galvanizing inert human bodies at the same moment that living individuals bring sound that has existed in the past, and died there, back into being. *L'Enfant et les sortilèges,* one last opera, traces an image of musical performance as music whose complete devastation reflects the loss few of us want to bear: that what we are hearing is always in flight. It fades away.

What visual image best captures such music? The very first thing seen onstage is the Princess's hand, rising from the earth, pressing importunately against a door that would contain it. This stage picture should be fixed in an imaginary freeze frame as a living tableau that recreates Rousseau's last tomb, in a scene that has reimagined its meaning.

XI

Disenchantment: that is why it is so important that the passage be barred. Anyone who tries to look into the space behind the walls or to hear what is really there is making a grave mistake. Children—barbarian destroyers like the Child in Ravel's opera—have not yet learned this truth. As Baudelaire points out in *The Philosophy of Toys,* children have "an overriding desire . . . to get at and *see the soul* of their toys, either at the end of a certain period of use, or on occasion *straightaway*." Soon, he remarks, the toy has been banged, shaken, and finally pried open and destroyed, "but *where is its soul?* This moment marks the beginning of stupor and melancholy."[87]

What would be disclosed if the tomb were pried open, and the hidden sound became audible? In *The Romantic Generation,* Charles Rosen explores an odd phenomenon, the Romantics' affection for virtual melodies—musical ideas hidden within the piece but never articulated.[88] This Romantic conceit is precursor to the related Symbolist fondness for unrepresentable sound, one influenced as much by fin de siècle literature as by musico-historical precedent. Drawing on Rosen in writing on Schumann, Žižek refers to such music as "unreal" or "impossible-Real." His psychoanalytic interpretation of the phenomenon says something not only about prohibitions against looking beyond barriers, but about the doubts associated with mechanism.

The unreal/impossible-Real is not synonymous with the "imaginary," for it is conceived as an uncanny by-product of symbolization and subject formation; thus Žižek elides this unreal/impossible-Real into its more famous Lacanian twin, the Real. The Real, notoriously, is not real. It does not belong to the inchoate presymbolic hum postulated in some schools of psychoanalytic theory as prior to subjectivity. Rather, it is an ungraspable object that eludes capture, standing for "what is lost when [this] presymbolic substance is symbolized" and "sticking out" both by resisting symbolization and by constituting one of its residues.[89] For Žižek, the Sphinxes in *Carnaval* are an example of the Real in music. His most amusing comment about such music concerns what might happen if it actually could be or *is* heard, as is possible with *Carnaval,* during performances in which the Sphinxes are banged out by the pianist:

The effect is suitably uncanny, as if we had stepped "through the looking-glass" and entered some forbidden domain beyond (or, rather, beneath) the phantasmic frame—or, more properly, as if we had caught sight of some entity outside its proper element (like seeing a dead squid on a table, no longer alive and gracefully moving in the water). For this reason, the uncanny mystery of these notes can all of a sudden change into vulgarity, even obscenity—it is no wonder that the most outstanding proponent of performing the "Sphinxes" was none other than Rachmaninov, one of the exemplary kitsch composers of serious music.[90]

That certainly sums up "disenchantment" and at the same time pinpoints a quality of Ravel's music. That object inside the tomb—music that is unreal, or impossible-Real, or Real—is in constant play. But those who transgress a border to the hidden places where such sounds can be heard discover only vulgarity, melancholy, and stupor.

To experience these emotions in full, one need only look inside Rousseau's tomb. In 1897, responding to decades of rumors that Rousseau's body had been stolen during the Bourbon Restoration, the French government undertook a midnight exhumation, lifting the sarcophagus to see what lay within (see fig. 5.7). The lantern casts a harsh light, and the odd angle of the sarcophagus transforms the mysterious torch and hand into a flat picture, one that can be turned this way or that to contemplate its silly conceits. A gendarme observes everything with satisfaction, and the bones and skull of Jean-Jacques Rousseau, which should rightfully engender awe, are about as mysterious as a Halloween costume the day after.

Never break open the toy and look inside. This dictum is straightforwardly illustrated in the Wedgwood Pot–Tea Cup duet from *L'Enfant et les sortilèges,* which was also published in a piano solo version entitled "Five O'Clock." This duet combines a warped ragtime dance with stock orientalisms to represent the Pot as a black American boxer and the Cup as Chinese. Inside the broken barrier there is something "vulgar," real popular dance music, along with something stupefying for Western listeners, ethnographically correct Chinese music: dead squids, both of them. Perhaps this is why scholarship identifying a priori objects as authentic sources occasionally leaves one feeling glum—it is a dead-squid problem.

Figure 5.7. Uncovering Rousseau's tomb (lithograph, Bibliothèque Nationale, Paris).

Not surprisingly, the prohibition against breaching a barrier is a motif that recurs several times in Ravel's opera. The Fire explicitly warns the Child not to insult gods who "maintain a fragile barrier between you and unhappiness." Žižek echoes this sentiment, writing of a "fragile mask" placed over the Real, the "horrifying life-substance" in *Carnaval* whose music can exist only by excluding this horror in the form of the Sphinxes. Žižek points out that this horrifying Real is also represented within *Carnaval*'s dramatis personae, "mechanical dolls" and "undead Life" concealed behind the carnival masks.[91] Automata are fearful objects, rightly hidden from sight.

But in Ravel's music, the machine is both the hidden nightmare and the fragile mask. Realizing this to be impossible, Ravel himself freezes up. His impassiveness, which for Jankélévitch is projected in artifice and musical mechanism, is itself along with those mechanisms "an allegory, a significant figure, the exoteric appearance of a hidden intention."[92] But one should leave it alone, revere its elusiveness: denying the automaton to find a "horrifying life-substance" is cause for a panicked outcry.

In another context, however, Žižek associates a less horrifying and dramatically ugly Real with a musical phenomenon reminiscent of devices associated with neoclassicism: the manipulation of musical objects borrowed from earlier composers or even one's earlier self. This "little piece of the Real" is "an external, contingent, found element which simultaneously stands for the subject's innermost being" in a "paradox of extimacy":

> A foreign body is first intruded as a meaningless trace, a trauma interrupting the flow of the "proper" melodic line; gradually, however, this intruder is "perlaborated," fully integrated into the composition's main texture, so that at the end it loses its external character and is reproduced as something generated by the inner logic of the composition itself.[93]

This process, similar to the analysand's integration of meaningless traumatic intrusions, could also describe what a more orthodox Freudian called introjection, the "swallowing-up" of a past and alien presence that paradoxically becomes the self.[94] An unfolded musical work, with all its integration and structuring of absence, is the trace of an "infinite longing that is constitutive of [modern] subjectivity."[95] For Ravel, however, the association of music with human symbolization and consciousness is inadequate. The Toccata from *Le Tombeau de Couperin* has toccata-language as a "horrifying" propulsive hand within the tomb, as well as external, found objects: some Moorish color, as well as the Rigaudon movement. The second time the Rigaudon swims into the Toccata, it has come to resemble the Toccata's own first theme, more integrated, less of an intruder. Since the overarching presence in this movement is the machine—a piano that has come alive as a tireless performance device—such gestures cannot be mapped onto ordinary human subjectivity. How can a machine remember a sound from the past or weave that sound into the continuum it is programmed to execute? How can one psychoanalyze an automaton? This is what is unsettling in Ravel: he commands impossible thoughts.

XII

In George Miller's 1982 film *The Road Warrior*, Max (Mel Gibson) hangs on to only one object from his former existence, a tiny music box of the sort one puts on a key chain, with meager inner works. His music box becomes loaded with heavy symbolic freight when he uses it to communicate with the Feral Child, a sturdy five-year-old savage who can speak only in grunts, who adopts Max as his hero, and who grows up to become the narrative voice-over of the film. One implication of all this is that the Feral Child's first experience of delight—a delight in music—will lead him out of muteness to speech. To the Child, the box is magical. His is a shamanist universe, the box a fetish with great powers. He can hardly believe his luck when Max throws it at him, for keeps. Max discards the music box because he knows that magic, as well as the pre-apocalyptic bourgeois order that produced such toys, has vanished beyond recovery. The box is so small that it hardly seems threatening; it is never, qua mechanism, aligned with all the deformed machines that roar through the Australian outback. At most, the audience is encouraged to regard it with a sentimental melancholy that Max has renounced and that the Feral Child, with no knowledge of history, cannot experience.

If *The Road Warrior*'s postindustrial future is an endgame in Western civilization, then music machines have apparently survived in a radically simple form that nostalgically recalls their purer eighteenth-century incarnations as a wondrous sight. How appropriate, then, that the music box ends up with the Feral Child, another semiotic fragment from the Enlightenment. He recalls the famous Wild Boy of Aveyron, a mute child of the 1790s whose story was told in François Truffaut's film *L'Enfant sauvage* (1970). Like other wild children since, he was seen both as a soul to be rescued and as a living laboratory for investigations into language as a signifying system. In the end, he could learn neither to speak nor to work freely with written signs; later it would be accepted that any human being who does not acquire some form of language in infancy is largely incapable of learning ex post facto what language is.[96] Hence the Feral Child's metamorphosis into the articulate adult of the voice-over is wholly magical and affirms the magical powers of his music box.

His acquisition of speech, finally, constitutes the third and last scrap of Enlightenment mythology in *The Road Warrior*, referring to a curious but widely held belief that the principles of musical automata could be mustered to teach deaf-mute people to speak and even sing. As Pierre Bourdelet and Pierre Bonnet wrote in 1715:

> Jean de la Porte Napolitain, author of a treatise on natural magic and a great musician, tells us that by means of artificial music, one can teach the mute to speak and sing, even when deaf from birth; he had several experiences of this nature, as he informs us, saying that, in playing some musical instrument, one need only have the deaf person hold the neck between his teeth, and immediately one sees him tremble with joy, and one easily comprehends that he hears; he claims that the sounds reach the brain by means of two orifices that are located above the soft palate, and thus make themselves heard; . . . all these facts should not appear at all surprising to those who have some notion of the art of mechanics, since, by its principles, one can make inanimate figures sing, and instruments play themselves.[97]

The deaf man can hear, the mute man can sing. The deaf-mute man is not, however, being asked to analyze the machinery of a music box in order to cure his ills. Instead, he must be made *into* an android and trapped by clockwork, animated by something that touches him and inscribes music directly onto his body. Music and mechanism have come together with a magical result, but should anyone rejoice? These living automata with their gripping teeth, blandly cited as triumphs of science by Bourdelet and Bonnet, seem at the beginning of the twenty-first century both pitiful and terrible. If *The Road Warrior*'s Feral Child and his music box stand for the enchantment of music machines and animated objects, the living automaton can stand for an irrepressible obverse, the one that traveled alongside that enchantment through several centuries.

This obverse—recognized instantly by Friedrich Meyer when he saw Rousseau's tomb in 1797—never strayed far from musical reality. The cults that surrounded nineteenth-century virtuosos, for instance, were attempts to discard the marionette in the performer by attaching hyperbolic value to improvisation, the very thing traditionally said to betray the human being in the performance machine. Thus they resemble movie star cults, which Benjamin famously identified as a compensatory device, an attempt to recoup the aura lost when cinema mechanically reproduces the actor by transforming loss into a surplus that flourishes hypertrophically and apart in time and space from the original.[98] But I would go further still: to see how mechanical music has marked Ravel's opera and his piano suite is to see how an uncanny performance network is represented within music both as a nightmare, and as what is mourned.

What traces are left by the music machines? There is the Orchestrion blare of the instrumental *Menuet antique,* or the hammers that strike like phantasmic clock chimes as Dr. Schön dies and in the third movement of the *Music for Strings, Percussion, and Celesta.* But the musical clockwork is never Apollonian, never just the Enlightenment's sunlit toy. The shadowed obverse of that toy had been turned to the eye, and Ravel's impassive gestures mask and unmask what he had seen: the box, and the lifeless hand.

✵ ACKNOWLEDGMENTS

First, there are the institutions: the Guggenheim Foundation, the National Endowment for the Humanities, the Wissenschaftskolleg zu Berlin, and Princeton University. Their generous fellowships and sabbatical support enabled me to plan and to write this book. The staff of the Kolleg, particularly Reinhart Meyer-Kalkus, provided assistance that always transcended the merely mechanical. Udo Bermbach, Dieter Borchmeyer, Hermann Danuser, and Albrecht Riethmüller asked me to present colloquia in Bayreuth and Berlin in 1994–95, and I am grateful to them for their encouragement to lecture. The Music Departments at Yale, the University of Pennsylvania, and Brandeis; the German Department at Princeton; the Art History Department at Columbia; and the Critical Inquiry Lecture Series at the University of Chicago all invited presentations based on what remained for some time a book project and thus jump-started its completion.

Above all, my thanks go to Roger Parker, as always. He reviewed an early form of chapter 4 for the *Cambridge Opera Journal* and read every other chapter as well: echoes of his unmistakable voice are present throughout. I also owe a large debt to Thomas Levin. Our collaborative seminar on music and technology (which I recall with delight), along with his unfailing intellectual engagement, were critical to shaping and shading certain aspects of this book. David Levin, fellow Wagner critic, responded on many occasions to provocations as well as requests for advice, as did Arnold Davidson, fellow admirer of Jankélévitch, and Simon Morrison, fellow connoisseur of Symbolism. Those who contributed fine details deserve more elaborate praise than the litany that encompasses their names here: Scott Paulin, Dana Gooley, Wendy Heller, Ralph Hexter, Ruth Padel, Gabriela Cruz, Caroline Bynum, Michal Grover-Friedlander, Eli Friedlander, Robert Bailey, and Margaret Cobb. Thomas Grey refined a version of chapter 5 that appeared in the *Journal of the American Musicological Society.* Joseph Kerman, Stanley Cavell, and Paul Robinson reviewed the entire manuscript, suggesting several changes, and Walter Lippincott at Princeton University Press escorted the book through production, providing moral support through many stages of revisions and rewriting, as did my patient editor, Fred Appel.

I played out the material in this book in graduate seminars over many years: my former students at the Freie Universität in Berlin, and all my doctoral students at Princeton University during those years, have been invaluable as interlocutors. Two in particular, Stefanie Tcharos and Giorgio Biancorosso, were exemplary editorial assistants. Members of my NEH Summer Seminar on opera, for whom the book was a covert structuring presence, offered witty responses to eleventh-hour trials of its most eccentric claims. Marsha Siefert gave me her name for the role she sang many times in *Parsifal:* "Dome Girl."

My sons, Carl and Lucas Mitchell, are assiduous in blocking all maternal attempts to write anything whatsoever, sensing in this activity something inimical to their interest in reading stories and playing trains. To them and to Lee Mitchell—ideal reader for the impossible author—this book is dedicated, with great affection.

Tristan und Isolde
James Levine: Metropolitan Opera
Ben Heppner, Tristan
New York, 29 November 1999
Richard Wagner

Toccatina for Piano
Carl Mitchell, pianist
Pennington, 21 March 1999
Dimitri Kabalevsky

Orfeo und Eurydice
Hartmut Haenchen: Komische Oper Berlin
Jochen Kowalski, Orfeo
Berlin, 20 November, 1990
Christoph Willibald Gluck

Götterdämmerung
Wolfgang Sawallisch: Bayerische Staatsoper
Caterina Ligendza, Brünnhilde
Munich, 29 January 1980
Richard Wagner

Pelléas et Mélisande
Renald Giovaninetti: Bayerische Staatsoper
Wolfgang Brendel, Pelléas
Munich, 18 November 1979
Claude Debussy

L'Enfant et les Sortilèges
C. William Harwood: Yale Symphony Orchestra
New Haven, 14 February 1975
Maurice Ravel

∞ NOTES

Preface

1. See *Unsung Voices: Opera and Musical Narrative in the Nineteenth Century* (Princeton: Princeton University Press, 1991).

2. Charles Rosen has explored one nineteenth-century version of this conceit in *The Romantic Generation* (Cambridge: Harvard University Press, 1995).

3. Vladimir Jankélévitch, *Debussy et le mystère* (Neuchâtel: Baconnière, 1949), 9–10.

4. Vladimir Jankélévitch, *La musique et l'ineffable* (Paris: Seuil, 1982), 5.

5. Theodor W. Adorno, "The Form of the Phonograph Record," trans. Thomas Y. Levin, *October* 55 (winter 1990): 59.

6. Theodor W. Adorno, *Philosophy of Modern Music,* trans. Anne C. Mitchell and Wesley V. Blomster (New York: Seabury Press, 1973), 30.

7. *The Imaginary Museum of Musical Works* (Oxford: Clarendon Press, 1992), chapter 1.

8. Roman Ingarden, *The Work of Music and the Problem of Its Identity,* ed. Jean G. Harrell, trans. Adam Czerniawski (Berkeley and Los Angeles: University of California Press, 1986), 11–13.

9. Philosophers who have dealt with performance (and not always at temperatures below freezing) include, after Goehr's *Imaginary Museum,* Paul Thom, *For an Audience: A Philosophy of the Performing Arts* (Philadelphia: Temple University Press, 1993); Peter Kivy, *Authenticities: Philosophical Reflections on Musical Performance* (Ithaca: Cornell University Press, 1995); and Stan Godlovitch, *Musical Performance: A Philosophical Study* (London: Routledge, 1998).

10. This, for instance, is the possibility that haunts Adorno's essay on musical performance, "Neue Tempi" (see *Gesammelte Schriften,* vol. 17, ed. Rolf Tiedemann [Frankfurt am Main: Suhrkamp Verlag, 1984], 66–73.). Adorno has no quarrel with the evolution of performances over time (in this, adopting an attitude from Schoenberg; see chapter 1, page 41). What ignites his anxiety is a fear that true interpretations—those policed by intellectual engagement, which crushes frivolity—may over time be crowded out by false ones. The essay (from 1930)

anticipates debates over authenticity and early music that resurfaced in Anglo-American scholarship in the 1980s. Adorno knows that "modern" (fast, clinical) performances of Bach are modern and not "authentic," and he points out that nonetheless, for the 1930s, such performances may be a "true" way to perform early classical works. Such performances are true to what the work has become, precisely because they emphasize distance and loss of cultural meaning. In them, individual notes huddle together in their swiftness, to make up for disintegration on a larger level.

11. This stance is adopted (with some nuances) in Edward Cone, *Musical Form and Musical Performance* (New York: W.W. Norton, 1968), Jonathan Dunsby, *Performing Music: Shared Concerns* (Oxford: Clarendon Press, 1995), and John Rink, ed., *The Practice of Performance: Studies in Musical Interpretation* (Cambridge: Cambridge University Press, 1995).

12. Janet Knapp, "Beginning-Ending Ambiguity: Consequences of Performance Choices," in Rink, *The Practice of Performance*, 150.

13. See Lydia Goehr, *The Quest for Voice: Politics and the Limits of Philosophy* (Berkeley and Los Angeles: University of California Press, 1998).

14. Vladimir Jankélévitch, *La Rhapsodie, verve et improvisation musicales* (Flammarion: Paris, 1955), with some sections republished in *Liszt: rhapsodie et improvisation,* ed. Françoise Schwab (Flammarion: Paris, 1998), and *Liszt et la rhapsodie: Essai sur la virtuosité* (Paris: Plon, 1989); Rosen, "Liszt: On Creation as Performance," in *The Romantic Generation*, 472–541; Dana Gooley, *Liszt and his Audiences, 1834–1847: Virtuosity, Criticism, and Society in the Virtuosenzeit* (Ph.D. diss., Princeton University, 1999). Liszt orients an interrogation of work-performance oscillations in Romantic literature in Susan Bernstein's *Virtuosity of the Nineteenth Century: Performing Language in Heine, Liszt, and Baudelaire* (Stanford: Stanford University Press, 1998).

15. Richard Leppert, *The Sight of Sound: Music, Representation, and the History of the Body* (Berkeley and Los Angeles: University of California Press, 1993). From another disciplinary angle—sociology rather than art history—the focus on attitudes shapes Christopher Small's *Musicking: the Meanings of Performing and Listening* (Hanover, N.H.: University Press of New England, 1998).

16. John Rosselli, *The Singers of Italian Opera: The History of a Profession* (Cambridge: Cambridge University Press, 1992); "Opera as a Social Occasion," in Roger Parker, ed., *The Oxford History of Opera* (Oxford: Oxford University Press, 1994), 304–21; Mary Ann Smart, "The Lost Voice of Rosine Stolz," *Cambridge Opera Journal* 6, no. 1 (March 1994): 31–50, and "Verdi Sings Erminia Frezzolini," *Women and Music* 1 (1997): 33–45; and Karen Henson, "Victor Capoul, Marguerite Olagnier's *Le Saïs,* and the Arousing of Female Desire," *Journal of the American Musicological Society* 52, no. 3 (fall 1999): 419–64.

17. Richard Taruskin, *Text and Act: Essays on Music and Performance* (Oxford: Oxford University Press, 1995)

18. Recent philosophical texts devoted to issues of authenticity include Salim Kemal and Ivan Gaskell, eds., *Performance and Authenticity in the Arts* (Cambridge: Cambridge University Press, 1999). Giulia Sissa's *Greek Virginity* (dis-

cussed in chapter 1, pages 8–9) deals at length with problems of belief and doubt in a certain category of performance, that of divine oracles.

19. Terry Castle, "In Praise of Brigitte Fassbaender," *The Apparitional Lesbian: Female Homosexuality and Modern Culture* (New York: Columbia University Press, 1993); and Wayne Koestenbaum, *The Queen's Throat: Opera, Homosexuality, and the Mystery of Desire* (New York: Poseidon, 1993).

20. *La musique et l'ineffable*, 38, "l'homme se sert de chant, et ne veut pas que le chant se serve de l'homme." This idea has also been proposed by René Leibowitz, *Le compositeur et son double: Essais sur l'interpretation musicale* (Paris: Gallimard, 1971); see chapter 1, pages 41–43.

21. See "Conflicting Ideals of Performance," in Goehr, *The Quest for Voice*, 132–73; citation, 134.

Chapter 1

1. In Ovid's *Metamorphoses,* book 11, the savage women, having scared off some peasants in the field, steal their sharp farm implements in order to murder Orpheus efficiently. The stones the women have thrown, and their vine-covered spears, have proven too blunt (Ovid *Metamorphoses,* trans. F.J. Hiller, 11: 30ff., rev. ed., Loeb Classical Library [Cambridge: Harvard University Press, 1984]).

2. In Frederick William Sternfeld's volume on the "birth of opera," for instance, we read: "that the severed head should sing or speak, and that the lyre should sound without Orpheus playing it, is miraculous, and must, to the poetic and allegorical mind, be another token of the permanence, the immortality, of music" (F. W. Sternfeld, *The Birth of Opera* [Oxford: Oxford University Press, 1993], 134).

3. The "birth of opera" controversy, a foundational controversy of modern musicology, centers on the degrees to which the genre "opera" is anticipated in late Renaissance music and theater, and what was so radically different about the "first operas" of Peri, Caccini, and Monteverdi. The classic statement of the problem—Nino Pirotta and Elena Povoledo, *Music and Theater from Poliziano to Monteverdi,* trans. Karen Eales (Cambridge: Cambridge University Press, 1981)—summarized and shaped the twentieth-century forms of the debate. But Gary Tomlinson's work on mimesis and magic, and on operatic metaphysics, has gone back to foundations and shaken them up significantly. His writings are a sustained inquiry into the issue of difference: what it was that created, and continually redefined, opera as a form of access to the supersensory. See in particular Tomlinson, "Pastoral and Musical Magic in the Birth of Opera," in Thomas Bauman and Marita McClymonds, eds., *Opera and the Enlightenment* (Cambridge: Cambridge University Press, 1995), as well as *Music in Renaissance Magic* (Chicago: University of Chicago Press, 1994) and *Metaphysical Song: An Essay on Opera* (Princeton: Princeton University Press, 1999).

4. Sternfeld explores the classical versions of Orpheus's legend and their adaptations in opera (*The Birth of Opera,* 1–30).

5. In musical settings of poetry about Orpheus, the episode can be kept in the form of narrative description, as it is in Berlioz's *La Mort d'Orphée* (1827), but—at this narrative distance—the head itself does not sing; rather, it is sung about. The same is true of Tippett's "Severed Head" episode from *The Mask of Time* (1984), which is based on Rilke's poetry. Sternfeld cites a single operatic instance, an *Orpheus* by Reinhard Keiser, performed in Braunschweig in 1698, in which the floating head and lyre were actually represented on stage (*The Birth of Opera*, 134–35). But they seem to have been silent props; see Klaus Zehn, *Die Opern Reinhard Keisers* (Munich and Salzburg: Katzbichler, 1975), 44–46.

6. For a transcription of the alternative ending from a surviving print copy of the 1607 libretto, as well as an English translation, see John Whenham, ed., *Claudio Monteverdi: Orfeo* (Cambridge: Cambridge University Press, 1986), 36–41.

7. This proliferation of dying Orpheuses is described in Dorothy M. Kosinski, *Orpheus in Nineteenth-Century Symbolism* (Ann Arbor and London: UMI Research Press, 1989).

8. Ovid, *Metamorphoses* 11:51–53 (trans. 123, 125).

9. See Whenham, *Claudio Monteverdi*, 29.

10. Put this way, of course, the dream sounds classically Neoplatonist, reflecting—as Gary Tomlinson has said—an assumption that "musical imitation . . . was a provocative force," with the capacity to move the spirit by setting up a kind of sympathetic vibration in the listener. See *Music in Renaissance Magic*, 110–15. The theoretical expansion of this association between physical force and persuasion is documented with great imagination in Downing Thomas's "Sensible Sounds: Music and Theories of the Passions," in his *Music and the Origins of Language* (Cambridge: Cambridge University Press, 1995), 143–76.

11. See chapter 4 in this volume.

12. Ingarden, *The Work of Music*, 10–13.

13. On the woman as instrument problem, see Heather Hadlock, *Mad Loves: Women and Music in Offenbach's "Les Contes d'Hoffmann"* (Princeton: Princeton University Press, 2000), 57–64.

14. Giulia Sissa, *Greek Virginity*, trans. Arthur Goldhammer (Cambridge: Harvard University Press, 1990), 3–4.

15. Ibid., 11.

16. Ibid., 24. Sissa describes iconographic evidence on vases that depict Apollo speaking directly to Orestes, with the priestess seated to one side: visually, she is there, but the implication is that the god speaks directly to the man (18–19). At the beginning of Aeschelus's *Eumenides*, the Delphic priestess sees a vision of Orestes and the furies before she can be properly "inspired" by Apollo, and she runs from the temple without being able to articulate her vision: she cannot speak. Thenceforth Apollo appears and talks directly to Orestes.

17. Ibid., 27. Sissa points out that two important treatises on the Delphic priestesses—Plutarch's and Lamprias's—revert frequently to musical imagery. Thus in Plutarch, "Everything in this treatise centers on the notion of an *instrument*. An instrument, 'must, in keeping with its intrinsic qualities, conform as closely as possible to the agent who uses it, and must accomplish the work of thought

that is expressed through it by exhibiting it not as it is found in the artisan, pure, intact, and irreproachable, but mingled with many elements intrinsic to it.'" (28). In summarizing Plutarch, she writes: "Here, then, is the mechanism of divinatory *enthousiasmos* as it appears in Plutarch: harmony between a woman's soul and a musician god, lunar attenuation of a searing brilliance, navigation of mountainous seas. The Pythia stands delicately balanced . . . on the ridge where the male god married the female voice, where the truth veiled itself as a sign" (32). And "Lamprias, too, sees the Pythia as a kind of musical instrument. Her soul is no longer a piece of wood but already a fragile—and very sensitive—instrument" (31).

18. These extremes—the dangerous diva and the mesmerized soprano—are explored at length in a number of recent studies. See, for instance, Susan Rutherford, "The Voices of Freedom: Images of the Prima Donna," in Vivien Gardner and Susan Rutherford, eds., *The New Woman and Her Sisters: Feminism and Theater, 1850–1914* (Ann Arbor: University of Michigan Press, 1992), 95–114, as well as the essays collected in Leslie C. Dunn and Nancy A. Jones, eds., *Embodied Voices* (Cambridge and New York: Cambridge University Press, 1994). Susan J. Leonardi and Rebecca A. Pope survey literature in English and French from the nineteenth and early twentieth centuries in *The Diva's Mouth: Body, Voice, Prima Donna Politics* (New Brunswick, N.J.: Rutgers University Press, 1996). German Romantic versions are anthologized and analyzed by Jörg Theilacker, *Der hohe Ton der Sängerin: Musik-Erzählungen des 19. Jahrhunderts* (Frankfurt am Main: Luchterhand Literaturverlag, 1989). What is striking is how fully most writers take the fictions to be realistic representations of female singers (or of performance), as well as generally shared assumptions that such fictions, and the attitudes they represent, must have shaped the careers of women who actually worked in this business.

19. See chapter 5 in this volume.

20. Heinrich von Kleist, *The Marquise of O— and Other Stories,* trans. David Luke and Nigel Reeves (Harmondsworth, N.Y.: Penguin, 1978), 220.

21. Kleist's phrase is "Absingung der *Gloria*"; the noun "Absingung" is translated by Luke and Reeves as "intone." But the word means a kind of "secondary" singing that is a distant copy of an original performance. "Absingung" hints at degradation: Kleist plays on the aural resemblance between "Absingung" and "Absinkung" (descent, decline).

22. One discussion stands out: Alice Kuzniar's essay on German Romantic texts and the female voice. See her "Hearing Women's Voices in *Heinrich von Ofterdingen*," *PMLA* 107 (October 1992): 1196–1207. Kuzniar reads Kleist's "legend" as a cautionary tale, one showing how easily a travesty can occur when a cultural assumption arises that "woman occupies the preferred signatory paradigm to which man must adapt." She points out that German Romantic writings consistently play out a suggestion that, in becoming poets, men accept an Orpheus-like "exchangeability of the self into the point of dissolution into the realm of nature-voice-woman" (1202).

23. Stephen King, "The Breathing Method," in *Different Seasons* (New York: Viking Press, 1982), 455–518.

24. Ibid., 514.

25. See Friedrich Kittler, "The Mother's Mouth" in his *Discourse Networks 1800/1900*, trans. Michael Metteer with Chris Cullens (Stanford: Stanford University Press, 1990), 40. He points out that "the maternal gift is language in a nascent state, pure breath as a limit value from which the articulated speech of others begins" (27).

26. In the rare iconographic representations of both body and head, this is made clear, as in Henri Léopold Lévy's *Death of Orpheus* (1870).

27. Heinrich Stefani, cited in Kittler, *Discourse Networks*, 34.

28. *Sonette an Orpheus*, part 1, sonnet 26 (Rainer Maria Rilke, *Sämtliche Werke* [Frankfurt am Main: Insel Verlag, 1987], 1: 748).

29. On the reception history of the aria's problematic cheeriness, see Ludwig Finscher, "Che faro senza Euridice? Ein Beitrag zur Gluck-Interpretation," *Festschrift Hans Engel* (Kassel and New York: Bärenreiter-Verlag, 1964), 96–110.

30. The most straightforward version of this argument in given in Joseph Kerman's *Opera as Drama* (rev. ed., Berkeley: University of California Press, 1988); it had appeared as well in Leo Schrade, *Monteverdi: Creator of Modern Music* (London: Gollancz, 1951), 229, 233–35. Denis Arnold, *Monteverdi* (London: Dent, 1963), 112–13; and Eric Chafe, *Monteverdi's Tonal Language* (New York: Schirmer, 1992), 148–50, are variations on Kerman's theme, though Chafe goes on to wonder whether Orfeo's singing, or the instrumental sinfonia that follows it, in fact has the desired magical effect. Silke Leopold, on the other hand, sees no reason to privilege the simpler declamation of the aria's final strophes (see *Monteverdi: Music in Transition,* trans. A. Smith [Oxford and New York: Oxford University Press, 1991]). Klaus Theweleit replays the traditional musico-dramatic argument in which Orfeo is said to run out of "'bel canto,' tricks, effects, and all" and "switches to a very direct, emotionally laden song" ("Monteverdi's *L'Orfeo:* The Technology of Reconstruction," in David Levin, ed., *Opera Through Other Eyes* [Stanford: Stanford University Press, 1993], 156).

31. Ovid *Metamorphoses* 10:14ff (trans. 65).

32. John Whenham for instance refers to an "apparent weakness in the opera" assuaged by the "unity of action that Striggio intended between Act III and Act IV" and the certainty that "both she [Proserpina] and Pluto have heard Orpheus's aria" (*Claudio Monteverdi,* 70–71). Jean-Pierre Ponelle's 1975 Zürich staging of the opera made this perfectly clear: Pluto and Proserpina are present on opposite sides of the stage and influence Charon's actions by waving their hands at several critical junctures.

33. Orfeo seems not to foresee this result, though several early accounts of the opera assume intent; Henri Prunières refers to Orfeo having "lulled the savage pilot to sleep by his melodious song," as if the faintly comic situation of having your audience fall asleep were too much for an operatic myth to bear. See *Monteverdi: His Life and Work,* trans. Marie Hackie (London: Dent, 1926), 59.

34. Jules Combarieu, *La musique et la magie* (1909; reprint, Geneva: Minkoff, 1972), 13.

35. Theweleit, "Monteverdi's *L'Orfeo*," 156.

36. Adorno, "Bourgeois Opera," in Levin, *Opera Through Other Eyes*, 40.

37. Ellen Rosand, *Opera in Seventeenth-Century Venice: The Creation of a Genre* (Berkeley: University of California Press, 1991), 387–91.

38. Theweleit, "Monteverdi's *L'Orfeo*," 172.

39. Ibid., 169.

40. Cited in Combarieu, *La musique et la magie*, 100.

41. Catherine Kinzler, *Poétique de l'opéra français de Corneille à Rameau* (Paris: Minerve, 1991), 368–71. This belief is discussed by Tomlinson, *Metaphysical Song*, 40–41, and Thomas, *Music and the Origins of Language*, 146–50.

42. Theodor W. Adorno, *In Search of Wagner*, trans. Rodney Livingstone (London: Verso, 1991), 86–87.

43. Friedrich Kittler, "World-Breath: On Wagner's Media Technology," in Levin, *Opera Through Other Eyes*, 215–35.

44. The telephone, and not—as Kittler suggests—the loudspeaker, with Elsa "the first resident of Electric Ladyland" ("World-Breath," 224). Even the most amplified rock concert does not travel four hundred miles.

45. Kittler, "World-Breath," 224.

46. Both the Latin (1673) and German (1684) versions of the treatise have been issued in facsimile: *Athanasii Kircheri Phonurgia nova sive Conjugium Mechanophysicum Artis & Naturae paranympha phonosophia concinnatum* (facsimile, New York: Broude Brothers, 1966); *Athanasii Kirchers Neue Hall- und Thonkunst oder mechanische Geheimverbindung der Kunst und Natur durch Stimm- und Hall-wissenshaft gestiftet* (facsimile, Hannover: Th. Schäfer, 1983).

47. See Ulf Scharlau, *Athanasius Kircher als Musikschriftsteller* (Kassel: Bärenreiter Verlag, 1969).

48. In the much simplified version of this woodcut that appears in *Neue Hall- und Thonkunst*, much of the visual detail has disappeared, and with it most of the classical allusions, including Orpheus's head.

49. Kircher, *Phonurgia nova*, 229.

50. On the technicalities of resurrection, see Caroline Walker Bynum, *The Resurrection of the Body in Western Christianity, 200–1336* (New York: Columbia University Press, 1995).

51. The use of corpses and body parts in scientific experiments on hearing and sound production is discussed in Wolfgang Scherer, "Klaviaturen, Visible Speech und Phonographie: Marginalien zur technischen Entstellung der Sinne im 19. Jahrhundert," in Friedrich Kittler, Manfred Schneider, and Samuel Weber, eds., *Diskursanalysen I: Medien* (Opladen: Westdeutscher Verlag, 1987): 37–54.

52. Goehr, *The Quest for Voice*, 144.

53. Hans Heinz Stuckenschmidt, "Die Mechanisierung der Musik," *Pult und Taktstock* 2, no. 1 (1925): 1–8, reprinted in Stuckenschmidt, *Die Musik eines halben Jahrhunderts: 1925–1975* (Munich and Zurich: Piper, 1976), 9–15; and Stuckenschmidt, "Mechanische Musik," *Der Kreis* 3, no. 11 (November 1926): 506–8, translated as "Mechanical Music" in Anton Kaes, Martin Jay, and Edward

Dimendberg, eds., *The Weimar Republic Sourcebook* (Berkeley: University of California Press, 1994), 597.

54. Richard Taruskin, "The Pastness of the Present and the Presence of the Past," in *Text and Act,* 114.

55. Arnold Schoenberg, "Mechanical Musical Instruments," in *Style and Idea,* 3d. ed. (Berkeley: University of California Press, 1985), 328.

56. Rene Leibowitz, *Le compositeur et son double: Essais sur l'interprétation musicale* (Paris: Gallimard, 1971), 25–26. Ingarden (as well as Sartre) was among those who fed Leibowitz's definition of the work as an intentional object; for an array of similar descriptions, see Jean-Jacques Nattiez, "The Concept of the Musical Work," in *Music and Discourse,* trans. Carolyn Abbate (Princeton: Princeton University Press, 1990), 69–90.

57. Leibowitz, *Le compositeur et son double,* 29–30.

58. "Über Schauspieler und Sänger," trans. William Ashton Ellis, in *Richard Wagner's Prose Works,* vol. 5 (reprint, New York: Broude Brothers, 1966), 157–28.

59. Ibid., 182.

60. Ibid., 201.

61. Ibid., 211.

62. See Fabrizio Della Seta, ed., *La traviata. Giuseppe Verdi: Operas,* vol. 19 (Chicago: University of Chicago Press, and Milan: Ricordi, 1996), xix–xxii. Catherine Clément, writing of *Traviata,* prefers the Violetta who "really sang," by this meaning not a specific performer but the character in act 1. Thus the fusion of fiction with performance is maintained in the case of this one opera, even by a writer who is otherwise completely aware that the two are distinct. See *Opera, or the Undoing of Women,* trans. Betsy Wing (Minneapolis: University of Minnesota Press, 1988), 65.

63. Theweleit, "Monteverdi's *L'Orfeo,*" 166–74.

64. Ibid., 171.

65. Kerman, *Opera as Drama,* 28.

66. Sissa, *Greek Virginity;* Sissa discusses at length vapors, metaphors of inspiration as wind, breath, and the *pneuma,* and she points out the difference between *epipnoia* (the breeze from above, which acts on male poets and enters through the ears and mouth) and *anathymia,* the vapor acting on the priestess from below, entering the body by the subterranean route.

67. See her "Gender, Musicology, and Feminism," in Nicholas Cook and Mark Everist, eds., *Rethinking Music* (Oxford: Oxford University Press, 1999), 491–92.

68. Christine Battersby, *The Phenomenal Woman: Feminist Metaphysics and the Patterns of Identity* (Cambridge: Polity Press, 1998).

69. Ruth Solie reproaches claims for transcendence in these terms, in "What Do Feminists Want: A Reply to Pieter van den Toorn," *Journal of Musicology* 9, no. 4 (fall 1991): 399–410. This point is made in a different context by Jean Starobinski, who sees the human body, as well as essential differences between the sexes, exploited as nostalgic objects, something mustered in arguments against the encroachments of technology. See "The Natural and Literary History of Bodily Sensation," in Michel Feher, Ramona Nadaff, and Nadia Tazi, eds., *Frag-*

ments for a History of the Human Body (New York: Urzone, and Cambridge: MIT Press, 1989), 360–70.

70. See chapter 4 in this volume, 156–59.

71. Carol Clover, *Men, Women, and Chain Saws: Gender in the Modern Horror Film* (Princeton: Princeton University Press, 1992.)

Chapter 2

1. Melanie Heinz and Rudolf Heinz, *Silberglöckchen, Zauberflöten sind zu eurem Schutz vonnöten* (Vienna: Passagen Verlag, 1992).

2. Ibid., 30.

3. Ibid., 77–78.

4. "[E]r [Papageno] lässt sich überaus rasch mit dem Glockenspiel ködern; dahin seine Furcht, nicht unberechtigerweise, denn immerhim kann man Klänge nicht eigentlich auffressen . . . für den Inhalt der Vogelsteige; ja für diese ganz mit Inhalt, das Glockenspiel; Vogelrückgabe der toten Vögel, Technik für Körper. Bei Nacht ist der Vogelkäfig mit einem Tuch verhangen—das Glockenspiel wie entsprechend verhüllt." Ibid., 90.

5. "Barockeinschuss in Klassik als Rokoko-Automatismus, Spieldosenmusik, folgerichtig west so die Königin der Nacht (immer noch) an. . . . mit der besagten Natürlichkeit ist freilich nichts, das Naturkind als die reinste Travestie." Ibid., 148–49.

6. "Angsttraum . . . dass nicht nur alle Glocken der Welt, vielmehr alle Dinge wie Glocken zu klingen begännen. Mozart, am Glockenspiel im Orchester, der nicht mehr aufhörte, das Glockenspiel zu spielen. Und also wird Papageno auf dieser Kultursühnelinie selber zum Musikinstrument: der mit einem Sack umhüllte Körper, Kopf zumal, Lärmsack, Quietschkasten." Ibid., 131.

7. "Selbst in der Fusion von Natur und technologischem Kunstlaut, ja gerade in dieser, erfüllt sich pseudologisch exkulpativ der humanistische Machenanspruch und also die rasende Prärogative der Technik, kurzum der Aufklärung." Ibid., 91.

8. See Renée Cox, "A History of Music," *Journal of Aesthetics and Art Criticism* 48, no. 2 (1990): 395–409. Cybele's more appalling attributes (she was also mothergoddess of castration and filicide) are, however, seldom mentioned.

9. Igor Stravinsky, *Themes and Conclusions* (Berkeley: University of California Press, 1982), 148. See the discussion of this remark in Daniel Albright, *Stravinsky: The Music Box and the Nightingale* (New York: Gordon and Breach, 1988), 21–22.

10. Aleksandr Ulybyshev, *Nouvelle biographie de Mozart suivie d'un aperçu sur l'histoire générale de la musique et de l'analyse des principales oeuvres de Mozart* (Moscow: Imprimerie A. Semen, 1843). Translated into German, the book was republished as *Mozarts Leben und Werke* (Stuttgart: Ad. Becker's Verlag [Gustav Hoffmann], 1859–64). Citations here are from the German edition.

11. Ulybyshev, *Mozarts Leben und Werke*, 49. In his phrase "dem Pfeifen des Maschinisten gehorchen," "Maschinist" is rightly translated as "puppeteer." The same word was used in that specific sense in the most famous early Romantic essay on puppets, Kleist's "Über das Marionettentheater" of 1810.

12. Ernst Bloch, "Magic Rattle, Human Harp," in Peter Palmer, trans., *Essays on the Philosophy of Music* (Cambridge: Cambridge University Press, 1985), 140–45. "Zauberrassel und Menschenharfe," in *Ernst Bloch Gesamtausgabe,* vol. 9 (Frankfurt am Main: Suhrkamp Verlag, 1965), 332–38.

13. Ibid., 140.

14. Ibid., 143.

15. Jankélévitch, *Debussy et le mystère,* 76.

16. The classic biography in this regard is Maynard Solomon's *Mozart: A Life* (New York: Harper Collins, 1995).

17. The story was originally published in *Les illustres Fées. Contes galans. Dedié* [sic] *aux Dames* (Paris, 1698) and was republished several times in French up to 1749. Details of the early publications, as well as arguments for attributing the story to Mailly, are found in Mary Elizabeth Storer, *Un épisode littéraire de la fin du XVIIe siècle. La mode des contes de fées 1685–1700* (Paris: Champion, 1928), 160–72. *Les illustres Fées* was first translated into German in Emmanuel Bierling, ed., *Das Cabinett der Feen,* vol. 7 (Nürnberg, 1764). The stories from *Les illustres Fées* were subsequently included in *Le cabinet des Fées,* the first major anthology of French fairy tales, as volume 5 (Paris and Geneva, 1787), and "Le roi magicien" appears in English as "The Wizard King" in *The Yellow Fairy Book,* ed. Andrew Lang (London and New York: Longmans-Green, 1894).

18. Mailly's tales in fact most resemble Madame d'Aulnoy's; several early eighteenth-century editions of *Les illustres Fées* attributed their authorship to d'Aulnoy. On the resemblance in styles and themes see Lewis C. Seifert, *Fairy Tales, Sexuality, and Gender in France 1690–1715: Nostalgic Utopias* (Cambridge: Cambridge University Press, 1996), 118–23, 156–65.

19. On the discourse of metamorphosis and hermaphrodism in the eighteenth century see Thomas Laqueur, *Making Sex: Body and Gender from the Greeks to Freud* (Cambridge: Harvard University Press, 1990), 61–69.

20. The story "Nadir und Nadine" in *Dchinnistan* is partly adapted without attribution from one of Mailly's strangest stories in *Les illustres Fées,* "Le bienfaisant, ou Quiribirini" (for a précis of the plot, see page 144 of this volume). "Nadir und Nadine" in turn was a source for the libretto of Schikaneder's *Der Stein der Weisen,* a pastiche opera in which one number is attributed to Mozart.

21. Nicholas Till, in *Mozart and the Enlightenment: Truth, Virtue, and Beauty in Mozart's Operas* (London: Faber and Faber, 1992), is clearly uneasy. Such a duet "should—we might think—belong to Tamino and Pamina" (285) and the duet's threat of eros is accordingly defeated. The duet is "childishly naïve" and "like a wide-eyed child" and it is about "spiritual love," not romantic or erotic passion. (285–86).

22. Rose Rosengard Subotnik, "Whose *Magic Flute,*" in *Deconstructive Variations: Music and Reason in Western Society* (Minneapolis: University of Minnesota Press, 1996), 6–7.

23. Christina Zech, " 'Ein Mann muss eure Herzen leiten'. Zum Frauenbild in Mozarts 'Zauberflöte' auf musikalischer und literarischer Ebene," *Archiv für Musikwissenschaft* 52, no. 4 (1995): 277–315.

24. Petra Fischer reviews the reception history of this theory in "Die Rehabilitierung der Sinnlichkeit: Philosophische Implikationen der Figurenkonstellation der Zauberflöte," *Archiv für Musikwissenschaft* 50, no. 1 (1993): 1–25.

25. Dieter Borchmeyer, "Mozarts Opernfiguren: Grosse Herren, rasende Weiber, gefährliche Liebschaften," *Schweizer Theater-Jahrbuch* 52 (1991): 270.

26. Mladen Dolar, "The Object Voice," in *Gaze and Voice as Love Objects*, ed. Renata Salecl and Slavoj Žižek (Durham: Duke University Press, 1996), 17.

27. See Thomas, *Music and the Origins of Language*, 3–9.

28. Sylvia Bovenschen, in *Die imaginierte Weiblichkeit. Exemplarische Untersuchungen zu kulturgeschichtlichen und literarischen Präsentationsformen des Weiblichen* (Frankfurt am Main: Suhrkamp, 1976), 80–149, analyzes the eighteenth-century view of learned women who aspire to a masculine voice, emphasizing the grotesque vocal hyperactivity ascribed to such women, as well as its dismissal as senseless clacking. In *Discourse Networks*, Kittler deals with the other extreme, the romanticized female voice. Styling the female voice as the "voice of the soul" or a perfect mirror for male speech forced its regression into the sigh, in a literary mechanism that obscured both misogyny and an anxious impulse to control female speech, which jointly gave birth to the mechanism in the first place.

29. Edward Dent, *Mozart's Operas: A Critical Study* (London, New York: Oxford University Press, 1947), 225–26, cites a passage from *Sethos* that emphasizes the shrill nonsense talked incessantly in the Queen's court.

30. Jean Paul, "Unterthänigste Vorstellung unser, der sämtlichen Spieler und redenden Damen in Europa entgegen und wider die Einführung der Kempelischen Spiel- und Sprachmaschinen" (ca. 1788), *Sämtliche Werke,* ed. Norbert Miller and Wilhelm Schmidt-Biggemann, vol. 2 (Munich: Carl Hanser Verlag, 1976), 167–85; citation 177, "Aber wir wünschen nur nicht, dass das Elend, das H. v. Kempele über uns durch seine Sprachmaschinen bringt, ihn noch auf seinem Todenbette in Schweis setze, und wir besorgen in der That nichts schlimmers; vielleicht wird ihn sogar in seinen gesunden Tagen, wenn er vor einem Visittenzimmer voll redender Maschinen zufällig vorbeigeht und sie deutlich genug reder höret, der wiederkehrende Gedanke kränken: "ach in dieser grossen Stube könnte auch auf jedem Krüppelstuhl eine lebendige Dame und auf dem Kanapee noch mehrere sitzen, und ihr gewöhliches Gericht, wie ich glaube, halten und überhaupt sich untereinander unbeschreiblich laben, hätt' ich dem Satan widerstanden; aber so schnattern ietz 12 äusserst fatale Maschinen drinnen recht munter, und hören weder auf sich noch ihres gleichen."

31. The various "natures" that birdsong came to represent in philosophy are explored by Matthew Head, "Birdsong and the Origins of Music," *Journal of the Royal Musical Association* 122, no. 1 (spring 1997): 1–23.

32. One *Magic Flute* libretto from ca. 1792 includes an illustration of Papageno as a bird pure and simple, with feathers and sharp talons on hands and feet as well as wings. That this is too much of the chimera for twentieth-century taste to bear is evident in Walther Brauneis's comment that the image is "willfully

wrong." See "Das Frontispiz im Alberti-Libretto von 1791 als Schlüssel zu Mozarts 'Zauberflöte'," *Mitteilungen der internationalen Stiftung Mozarteum* 41, no.
3–4 (November 1993): 49–59, especially 52.

33. This ironic fact was the basis for Chardin's famous painting "La serinette, ou la
dame qui a choisi ses plaisirs," in which a woman plays a mechanical "bird-
organ" to her bird, teaching it to sing in new ways. The bird cannot tell that the
machine is not a real bird, and the woman is pleased with this fact.

34. Julien Offray de La Mettrie, *Machine Man and Other Writings*, ed. and trans. Ann
Thomson (Cambridge: Cambridge University Press, 1996), 33–34.

35. Denis Diderot, *Rameau's Nephew and D'Alembert's Dream*, trans. L. W. Tannock
(London: Penguin, 1966), 160.

36. Ibid., 158.

37. Ibid., 158–59; Daniel Cottom discusses this passage in "The Work of Art in the Age
of Mechanical Digestion," *Representations* 66 (spring 1999): 52–74.

38. As by Daniel Heartz, "The music that [Mozart] wrote, especially that for his
friend Schikaneder as Papageno, outdoes any other from his pen in its folklike
simplicity." See Heartz, *Mozart's Operas*, ed. with contributing essays by
Thomas Bauman (Berkeley: University of California Press, 1990), 256.

39. See Jacob and Wilhelm Grimm, *Deutsches Wörterbuch*, (Leipzig: S. Hirzel, 1897),
2844–45, where the name is described as a specifically Viennese term for the
instrument known elsewhere as a "Strohfiedel." Mozart's indication, "stählnes
Gelächter," in the autograph apparently reflects the decision to translate the
wooden instrument into a metallophone.

40. Ibid., 2845, "Lüstig klingend, ohne Gehalt."

41. The 1793 engravings by Viennese graphic artists Joseph and Peter Schaffer, published in 1795. On the connection to the original production see Friedrich
Dieckmann, *Die Zauberflöte: Max Slevogts Randzeichnungen zu Mozarts Handschrift* (Berlin: Der Morgan, 1984), 181, and 341–42.

42. Subotnik, "Whose Magic Flute," 6.

43. Michel Poizat, *La voix du diable: La jouissance lyrique sacrée* (Paris: Métailié, 1991),
219–26.

44. Ibid., 220.

45. Ibid., 221.

46. Ibid., 220–21.

47. Clément, *Opera*, 73.

48. See Charles Segal, "The Gorgon and the Nightingale," in Dunn and Jones,
Embodied Voices, 17–34, on various classical associations for the flute, including
Marsyas (31). For Segal, who drops briefly in on *Magic Flute*, the "screaming
arpeggios of the vengeful Queen of the Night" are "absorbed and neutralized"
by a "total musical and thematic structure" (33). In much the same way, "something terrible" is absorbed into the flute songs discussed in Greek classical
sources, reflecting the monstrous origins of flute sound (32).

49. Ulybyshev, *Mozarts Leben und Werke*, 4:16.

50. Where Ulybyshev, writing in the 1840s, sees nothing to demonize about this
shift in register, Poizat, writing as a post-Wagnerian, identifies exactly the same

phenomenon yet deplores the descent into any consciousness of performance. See Michel Poizat, *The Angel's Cry: Beyond the Pleasure Principle in Opera*, trans. Arthur Denner (Ithaca: Cornell University Press, 1992), 65–67.

51. Ulybyshev, *Mozarts Leben und Werke*, 4:33.

52. Melanie and Rudolf Heinz see the armor as a tactile reference to the Queen of the Night, "Als solche aber in diesem ihrem virilen Unisono sind sie von dem, was sie ausschliessen, dem Reich der Königin der Nacht, in aller deutlichkeit stigmatisiert; in *schwarzer* Rüstung, mit 'Grubenhelm' ausgestattet, und auch mit der das eigene Kopflicht absorbierenden Rüstung die Geschlechtlichkeit der Körper indifferenzierend. Zwei Männer als die melancholia der ausgeschlossenen Frau." *Silberglöckchen*, 29.

53. Ulybyshev, *Mozarts Leben und Werke*, 4:46.

54. On the musical cues in the original libretto, see Reinhard Wiesend, "Regeianweisung, Werk, Edition—am Beispiel der 'Zauberflöte'," in Manfred Hermann Schmid, ed., *Mozart Studien* 3 (Tutzing: H. Schneider, 1993), 115–36.

55. On K.608 see Annette Richards, "Automatic Genius: Mozart and the Mechanical Sublime," *Music and Letters* 80, no. 3 (1999): 366–89.

56. Terry Castle, *The Female Thermometer: Eighteenth-Century Culture and the Invention of the Uncanny* (New York: Oxford University Press, 1995), 6.

57. Edward Said, *Orientalism* (New York: Vintage, 1979), 118.

Chapter 3

1. Theodor W. Adorno, *In Search of Wagner*, 88.

2. Adorno, "Zur Partitur des *Parsifal*," in *Gesammelte Schriften*, vol. 17, 47–51, citation 48.

3. Adorno, *In Search of Wagner*, 88.

4. Ibid., 88–91.

5. Wagner originally planned to keep the Grail Messenger of acts 1 and 3 and the temptress of act 2 separate characters. On their conflation, see Barry Emslie, "Woman as Image and Narrative in Wagner's *Parsifal*," *Cambridge Opera Journal* 3, no. 2 (1992): 109–24, especially 112–14.

6. Mário Vieira de Carvalho, "*Parsifal* oder der Gegensatz zwischen Theorie und Praxis als Dilemma der herrschenden Klasse," *Beiträge zur Musikwissenschaft* 28, no. 4 (1986): 309–19.

7. Elisabeth Bronfen, "Kundry's Laughter," *New German Critique* 69 (fall 1996): 147–62.

8. Slavoj Žižek, "'The Wound Is Healed Only by the Spear That Smote You': The Operatic Subject and Its Vicissitudes," in Levin, *Opera Through Other Eyes*, 177–214, especially 204.

9. Ibid., 204–5. See also Jean-Jacques Nattiez, *Wagner Androgyne: A Study in Interpretation*, trans. Stewart Spencer (Princeton: Princeton University Press, 1993), 163–72, on Parsifal's androgynous humanity and Wagner's late writings, especially "On the Feminine in the Human," a fragment Wagner worked on immediately before his death (1883).

10. Mann's famous litany appears in "The Sufferings and Greatness of Richard Wagner," in *Essays of Three Decades,* trans. H. T. Lowe-Porter (New York: Knopf, 1947), 336–37.

11. Article in *Gil blas* (6 April 1903). See *Debussy on Music,* ed. François Lesure, trans. Richard Langham Smith (New York: Knopf, 1977), 167.

12. Michael Tanner, "The Total Work of Art," in Peter Burbidge and Richard Sutten, eds., *The Wagner Companion* (Cambridge: Cambridge University Press, 1979), 206.

13. Ibid., 206, 216–17.

14. Ibid., 217.

15. David Levin, *Richard Wagner, Fritz Lang, and the Nibelungen: The Dramaturgy of Disavowal* (Princeton: Princeton University Press, 1998), 4.

16. Ibid.

17. See "R. Wagners Parsifal," originally published as a correspondent's reports from Bayreuth in July 1882, reprinted in *Aus dem Opernleben der Gegenwart,* 4th ed. (Berlin: Allgemeiner Verein für Deutsche Literatur, 1901), 318–20, especially 320, "mir erscheint die ganze Scene [between Kundry and Parsifal] im tiefssten Grunde unwahr, die Musik äusserlich glühend, innerlich Kalt, gebackenes Eis," and 322, "stehen nicht die Verführungsversuche der unwiderstehlichen Kundry fast stief and kühl neben der ähnlichen Scene im *Tannhäuser?*"

18. Tomlinson, *Metaphysical Song,* 133–42.

19. Syberberg's inclusion of this reception history as visual detritus in *Parsifal's* own landscape was one aspect of his film that most irritated certain critics and most amused others. See Nattiez, *Wagner Androgyne,* 290–91.

20. Klaus Umbach, *Richard Wagner: Ein deutsches Ärgernis* (Hamburg: Rowohlt, 1982), 38–40; and Paul Lawrence Rose, *Wagner: Race and Revolution* (London: Faber and Faber, 1992), 158–69.

21. Saul Friedlander, "Hitler und Wagner," in Saul Friedlander and Jörn Rüsen, eds., *Richard Wagner im dritten Reich* (Munich: C. H. Beck, 2000), 165–78, especially 171–73.

22. See Nike Wagner, *Wagner Theater* (Frankfurt: Insel, 1998), 221–34.

23. Adorno, *In Search of Wagner,* 93.

24. This resemblance is discussed by Reinhold Brinkmann, "Tannhausers Lied," in Carl Dahlhaus, ed., *Das Drama Richard Wagners als musikalisches Kunstwerk* (Regensburg: G. Bosse, 1970), 199–211, as a proto-leitmotivic experiment, a musical fragment that transcends the single number and appears in all the acts of the opera.

25. Dieter Borchmeyer refers to this identification (which, he notes, Wagner knew quite well) by calling Holda "das germanische Inkognito der Frau Venus." See *Das Theater Richard Wagners: Idee, Dichtung, Wirkung* (Stuttgart: P. Reclam, 1982), 203–6.

26. See Ernest Newman, *The Life of Richard Wagner,* vol. 1 (New York: Knopf, 1933), 397.

27. Stanley Cavell, *Pursuits of Happiness: The Hollywood Comedy of Remarriage* (Cambridge: Harvard University Press, 1981), 60–61.

28. Cavell writes that because Jean knows the speech to be a repetition, her pretense of interest and absorption as Lady Eve makes this "the most difficult moment of this comedy," at which the pair's "behavior toward one another appears unforgivable." Ibid., 60.

29. In a later movie, *Unfaithfully Yours* (1948), Sturges used the *Tannhäuser* overture again, in a sequence that enlarges this moment from *The Lady Eve*. The movie is about a conductor who suspects his wife of adultery. While conducting a concert, he fantasizes three encounters with his wife; the outcome of each depends on the piece he is playing (the overture to Rossini's *Semiramide*, the *Tannhäuser* overture, and the overture to Zandonai's *Francesca da Rimini*). The Tannhäuser sequence involves a wife who begs forgiveness, and a husband who graciously condescends to pardon. Rossini gets simple murder (husband kills wife), and for Zandonai, the husband surprises the wife and her lover. Sturges knew his Wagner. His mother was a close friend of Isadora Duncan, and Sturges sat on Cosima Wagner's knee at the Bayreuth festival in 1904, when he was six. He played with "a Siegfried Wagner son [sic] who had yellow hair down to his shoulders" with whom he had a mud fight, much to Cosima's dismay. See *Preston Sturges by Preston Sturges*, ed. Sandy Sturges (New York: Simon and Schuster, 1990), 30.

30. Adorno, *In Search of Wagner*, 87–88.

31. Dieter Borchmeyer, *Das Theater Richard Wagners*, 289–94, meticulously sorts out the connections in both their textual and historical aspects; for him, they give rise to a "symbolic magic of associations" between several operas (294).

32. Carl Dahlhaus, *Richard Wagners Musikdramen* (Zurich: Orell Füssli, 1985), 142.

33. Marc A. Weiner, "Reading the Ideal," *New German Critique* 69 (fall 1996): 53–83; and David Levin, "Reading Beckmesser Reading: Antisemitism and Aesthetic Practice in *The Mastersingers of Nuremberg*," *New German Critique* 69 (fall 1996): 127–46.

34. Levin, *Richard Wagner, Fritz Lang*, 85.

35. Philippe Lacoue-Labarthe, *Musica Ficta: Figures of Wagner*, trans. Felicia McCarren (Stanford: Stanford University Press, 1994), xxi–xxii.

36. Levin, *Richard Wagner, Fritz Lang*, 6. See also his "Dramaturgie der Alterität," in Friedlander and Rüsen, *Richard Wagner im dritten Reich*, 92–108.

37. Slavoj Žižek, "'There Is No Sexual Relationship': Wagner as Lacanian," *New German Critique* 69 (fall 1996): 217–18. This essay is expanded and reprinted in Salecl and Žižek, *Gaze and Voice as Love Objects*, 208–249.

38. Goehr, *The Quest for Voice*, 68; "The Art-Work of the Future" is rightly cited here as one theoretical statement of this particular Wagnerian ambition.

39. Kittler, "World-Breath."

40. Thomas S. Grey, *Wagner's Musical Pose: Texts and Contexts* (Cambridge: Cambridge University Press, 1995), 257.

41. Adorno, "Bourgeois Opera," 40.

42. Robert Bailey, "Visual and Musical Symbolism in German Romantic Opera," in *Report of the Twelfth Congress of the International Musicological Society*, ed. Daniel Heartz and Bonnie Wade (Kassel: Bärenreiter; Philadelphia: American Musicological Society, 1981), 436–44. Bailey points out that while it is not unusual in

opera to have some music coming from the stage, and that "the idea is French in origin," the degree to which the technique is extended here makes it "for all its apparent simplicity the most extraordinary scene . . . in the opera" (443).

43. Such suspicion of the word—a tenet of Symbolism—descends to the Symbolists through Wagner's German idealist theories and (according to Lacoue-Labarthe) traumatizes them at the same time. See *Musica Ficta,* 11–17.

44. Adorno, "Zur Partitur des *Parsifals,*" 50; Adorno, *In Search of Wagner,* 88.

45. Cosima Wagner reported in a diary entry of 3 February 1879 that Wagner suddenly came out of his study to tell her that "the entry of the G tympani is the most beautiful thing I have ever composed." She goes on: "I accompanied him downstairs, and he played Parsifal's annointing by Titurel [sic] with the marvelous canon, and Kundry's baptism with the tympani's sound of annihilation [Vernichtungsklang]; R. said 'the annihilation of the entire being, of every earthly desire.'" See *Cosima Wagner: Die Tagebücher,* vol. 2, ed. Martin Gregor–Dellin and Dietrich Mack (Munich: Piper Verlag, 1977), 303.

46. Žižek, "'The Wound Is Healed,'" 209.

47. Dolar, "The Object Voice," 25.

48. Ibid., 25–26. Dolar sets up a history of fictions and philosophical reflections about voice that tell not of the "battle of 'logos' against the [feminine] voice" but of two primal voices—masculine and feminine—against each other. Eventually, however, they realize they are two sides of the same coin.

49. Žižek's excursus, "I Am Going to Talk to You About the Lamella" ("'The Wound Is Healed,'" 192–96), is one of many amusing tutorials on the Lacanian Real.

50. Letter of Hermann Levi to his father, 31 August 1882. See document 240 in Richard Wagner, *Dokumente zur Entstehung und ersten Aufführung des Bühnenweinfestspiels Parsifal,* ed. Martin Geck and Egon Voss, *Sämtliche Werke,* vol. 30 (Mainz: B. Schott's Söhne, 1970), 62.

51. Alfred Lorenz made one of the first arguments about an excluded key when he claimed that act 3 of *Tristan* in its entirely is mystically oriented to the key of E major, a key that appears only briefly, for Tristan's hallucination of Isolde (*Das Geheimnis der Form bei Richard Wagner,* vol. 2 [reprint, Tutzing: Hans Schneider, 1966]). Robert Bailey's analysis of the act 1 prelude to *Tristan* is similar. He points out that the first note (A) could be seen as a "wrong" note, in the sense that the rising minor sixth in the motif it traces (A-F) is elsewhere always a rising major sixth. So there is an absent "right" first note, an A♭, hidden within the note that is there. And the A♭/A dyad crops up again and again in act 1, most obviously in the "Todgeweihtes Haupt" motif. See *The Genesis of Tristan und Isolde and a Study of Wagner's Sketches and Drafts for the First Act* (Ph.D. diss., Princeton University, 1969), 163–64.

52. Such screaming is assumed a priori to belong to the feminine register, and in this, to the same realm before (or after) music that belongs to the maternal. The title of Michel Poizat's first book on opera—*L'opéra ou le cri de l'ange*—says it all. The angel's cry is the *cri aigu,* the high note that morphs into a scream, and it always happens in the octaves above the octave above middle C.

53. Nike Wagner, *Wagner Theater*, 218.
54. Arnold Whittall, "Wagner and Real Life," *Musical Times* 137 (June 1996): 8.
55. See Jeremy Tambling, *Opera and the Culture of Fascism* (Oxford: Clarendon Press, 1996), 45–60, for a discussion of homosexual motifs in the *Parsifal* plot.
56. Nike Wagner, *Wagner Theater*, 218–19.
57. On this point, see Abbate, "Immortal Voices, Mortal Forms," in Craig Ayrey and Mark Everist, eds., *Analytical Strategies and Musical Interpretation: Essays on Nineteenth- and Twentieth-century Music* (Cambridge University Press, 1996), 288–300.
58. Whittall, "Wagner and Real Life," 8: "even that last glimpse into the abyss, the harmony lurching briefly into a remote region as Kundry expires, can be heard as a reminder of dangers that can never be entirely eliminated."
59. Žižek, "'The Wound Is Healed,'" 195–96.
60. What is interesting about Martin Scorsese's *The Last Temptation of Christ* is that, while the crucifixion takes forever, it is shown as fragments, as close-ups of body parts and out of the corner of our eye. But in the film's final seconds, after Christ refuses the temptation that has shown him his human future (depicted in a lengthy flash-forward), we return to "him" and see the crucifixion, shocking, whole, and close-up. This, more than the fantasy that Christ had an alternate happy fate, is the scandal.
61. As Nike Wagner points out, *Wagner Theater*, 217–18.

Chapter 4

1. Jankélévitch, *La musique et l'ineffable*, 172, "s'il est vrai que la 'loquela' . . . est le bruit humain par excellence, le mutisme qui supprime ce bruit sera un silence privilégié. La musique est le silence des paroles; tout comme la poésie est le silence de la prose. La musique, présence sonore, remplit le silence, et pourtant la musique est elle–même une manière de silence . . . et de même il faut faire de la musique pour obtenir le silence."
2. Ibid., 93: "et l'ineffable . . . est inexprimable parce qu'il y a sur lui infiniment, interminablement à dire"; 95: "La musique est donc inexpressive parce qu'elle n'exprime pas tel ou tel paysage privilégié, tel ou tel décor à l'exclusion de tous les autres; la musique est inexpressive en ceci qu'elle implique d'innombrables possibilités d'interprétation, entre lesquelles elle nous laisse choisir."
3. Stefan Jarocinski cites a maxim of Goethe: "The symbol transforms the phenomenon into an idea, and the idea into an image, and does this in such a way that the idea in the image has infinite repercussions, and remains intangible; even when expressed in every language it will always remain unexpressed"; as well as a similar sentiment, dating a century and a half later, from Maurice Blanchot: "[The symbol] merely makes present—by bringing us into its presence—a reality which cannot be grasped in any other way, seeming to emerge suddenly, prodigiously far away, like some strange apparition." See *Debussy: Impressionism and Symbolism*, trans. Rollo Myers (London: Eulenberg, 1976), 23,

24. Without rehearsing the immense bibliography in linguistics, psychology, or philosophy on the nature of the symbol, one can nonetheless point out that twin notions of inexhaustible resonance and distance (entailing an interpretive quest toward an infinitely receding object) recur in most nineteenth- and twentieth-century definitions.

4. Jankélévitch, *La musique et l'ineffable,* 129–30, especially his discussion of Andersen's fairy tale *The Bell.* Jankélévitch sees fictions about unlocatable cities and legendary hidden sites as allegories about music itself, "et de même que l'âme récuse les localisations cérébrales et Dieu les localisations terrestres, ainsi la céleste Kitiège, la Kitiège absente et omniprésente, lointaine et prochaine, qui est la pure musique en elle–même ne figure sur aucune carte . . . échappe à toute topographie" (130). One is reminded inevitably of Hölderlin's most famous aphorism, the opening line of "Patmos": "Nah ist/und schwer zu fassen der Gott."

5. Operatic instances inlude Schreker's *Der ferne Klang,* as well as Ravel's unfinished operatic project *La cloche engloutie,* which was based on Gerhard Hauptmann's *Die versunkene Glocke.*

6. Pierre Schaeffer, *Traité des objets musicaux,* rev. ed. (Paris: Seuil, 1966), 90–99; on disembodiment as a mark of omniscience or divinity see also Nicholas Wolterstorff, *Divine Discourse: Philosophical Reflections on the Way God Speaks* (Cambridge: Cambridge University Press, 1995), 56–58.

7. This paradox is discussed in Abbate, "Ventriloquism," in Irving Lavin, ed., *Meaning in the Visual Arts: Views from Outside* (Princeton: Institute for Advanced Study, 1995), 305–12.

8. Wayne Koestenbaum discusses this phenomenon of "singing with the singer" as one based not primarily on narrative identification with character but on an illusion of bodily identity with the woman performing, in *The Queen's Throat,* 42–43.

9. Michel Chion, *The Voice in Cinema,* trans. Claudia Gorbman (New York: Columbia University Press, 1999), 25–33.

10. Ibid., 21.

11. Ibid., 22–23: "so we are a long way from the theatrical offstage voice, which we concretely perceive at a remove from the stage. Unlike the film frame the theater's stage doesn't make you jump from one angle of vision to another, from closeup to long shot. For the spectator, then, the filmic acousmêtre is 'offscreen,' outside the image, and at the same time *in* the image: the loudspeaker that's actually its source is located behind the image in the movie theater."

12. Chion, *Audio Vision: Sound on Screen,* ed. and trans. Claudia Gorbman (New York: Columbia University Press, 1994), 129–30. *Audio–Vision* is a brief English compendium of previous and newly revised writings by Chion; in it he refreshes various passages on the acousmêtre from *The Voice in Cinema;* see "The Acousmatic," 71–73; "The Invisible Man," 126–28; and "The Acousmêtre," 129–31.

13. Slavoj Žižek, "The Ideological *Sinthome,*" in *Looking Awry: An Introduction to Jacques Lacan Through Popular Culture* (Cambridge: MIT Press, 1991), 124–28, citation 126.

14. This vocal eunuchism is characteristic in certain thrillers. Carol Clover has argued that males with disturbed sexual identities who are sexually ambiguous and possess androgynous voices regularly turn up as villain slashers in horror films, where they are pitted against masculinized female heroines. See *Men, Women, and Chain Saws,* 48–60.

15. Chion, *Audio–Vision,* 131, cites the villain's voice in *Kiss Me Deadly* as an example of a "typical form [of the acousmatic voice] in detective and mystery films, when the 'big boss' who pulls all the strings . . . is finally revealed," and explains that while we constantly see a part of this villain's body (his shoes) the deacousmaticization occurs only when we see his *face.* Thomas Y. Levin notes that fantasies attached to sending one's voice via telephone and then inscribing it via machine view capture of the floating voice by the answering machine (or voice-mail program) as a kind of rematerialization of one's body in another form, as physical traces on the recording medium. See his "Before the Beep: A Short History of Voice Mail," in Annemarie Jonson, ed., *Technophobia: Essays in Sound,* vol. 2 (Darlinghurst, Australia: Contemporary Sound Arts, 1995), 59–67.

16. See Kaja Silverman, *The Acoustic Mirror: The Female Voice in Psychoanalysis and Cinema* (Bloomington: Indiana University Press, 1988), 48: "to the degree that the voice-over preserves its integrity, it also becomes an exclusively male voice"; and 50: "dominant cinema also holds the female subject more fully than the male subject to the unity of sound and image." Silverman also takes up Chion's discussion of disembodied voice, agreeing with the truism that "voice-over is privileged to the degree that it transcends the body. Conversely, it loses power and authority with every corporeal encroachment, from a regional accent or idiosyncratic 'grain' to definitive localization in the image. Synchronization marks the final moment in any such localization, the point of full and complete embodiment" (49). Silverman's "synchronization" corresponds to Chion's "deacousmatization."

17. For a critique of these assumptions about maternal speech, see Donna Stanton, "Difference on Trial: A Critique of the Maternal Metaphor in Cixous, Irigaray and Kristeva," in Nancy Miller, ed., *The Poetics of Gender* (New York, Columbia University Press, 1986), 142–59, and Claire Kahane, "Rethinking the Maternal Voice," *Genders* 3 (fall 1988): 82–91.

18. A challenge to the assumption of operatic music's epistemological certainty, as well as to the ideological component in correspondence between music and text or action, is rare indeed; Adorno's *In Search of Wagner* is one model, and it is significant that this critical skepticism tends to attach itself to Wagner's operas, perhaps because Wagner himself was so suspiciously compensatory in coining words like *"Gesamtkunstwerk."* For instance, Žižek demythicizes Wagnerian *and* film music conceits in terms familiar from Adorno. See chapter 3, note 37, in this volume.

19. As, for example in Susan McClary, "Structures of Identity and Difference in Bizet's *Carmen,"* in Richard Dellamora and Daniel Fischlin, eds., *The Work of*

Opera: Genre, Nationhood, and Sexual Difference (New York: Columbia University Press, 1996), 115–29; and Lawrence Kramer, "Culture and Musical Hermeneutics: The Salome Complex, " *Cambridge Opera Journal* 2, no. 3: 269–94, especially 284–94. For one counterargument, see Abbate, "Opera, or the Envoicing of Women," in Ruth Solie, ed., *Musicology and Difference* (Berkeley: University of California Press, 1993), 225–258.

20. Such assumptions underlie Mary Ann Doane's idea of a "fantasmatic body, " the illusion of unity created by certain elements in film (such as correspondence between sound and image, or continuous music) that work counter to film's fracturing forces (anything from uncertain or group authorship of the "text" to ragged visual cuts). Doane speculates that the viewer/listener, similarly wishing to understand him- or herself as a "unified subject," consumes the illusion and identifies with this "body." See Doane, "The Voice in the Cinema: The Articulation of Body and Space," in *Yale French Studies* 55, no. 1 (1980): 33–50. Adorno and Eisler, as well, famously deflated any presumption of continuity provided by film music that is both fairly continuous and "redundant" in merely reinforcing the emotional or narrative message conveyed by dialogue or action within the visual field. See Theodor W. Adorno and Hanns Eisler, *Composing for the Films* (London: Athlone Press, 1994), 23–24.

21. Hence the title of Claudia Gorbman's *Unheard Melodies: Narrative Film Music* (Bloomington: Indiana University Press, 1987).

22. This music is a classic leitmotif in the Wagnerian sense. It has been associated from the first with menace and eventually is pinned exclusively to the Terminator, accompanying claustrophobic shots of Schwarzenegger and his raptor eyes as he cruises Los Angeles for his victim.

23. Novalis, *Heinrich von Ofterdingen* (Stuttgart: Reclam, 1976), 45–46.

24. See Robert Orledge, *Debussy and the Theater* (Cambridge: Cambridge University Press, 1982), 102–27, for a summary of the project's history.

25. See Edward Lockspeiser, *Debussy et Edgar Poe* (Monaco: Editions du Rocher, 1961), 95: "*Rod:* Tenez, j'ai retrouvé cet antique et curieux bouquin de savoir oublié. Il y ait parlé des anciens satyrs africains et des Aegipans. . . . Pendent des heures, j'ai rêvé sur la musique qui devait accompagner leurs étranges cérémonies. . . . Lisez . . . ici . . . ne croirais t'on pas entendre comme une danse funèbre et passionnée? (*Pendent qu'ils lisent on entend—vaguement—la musique qui imagine R.U.)*". Lockspeiser published in transcription the latest of the various libretto drafts made by Debussy.

26. Orledge, *Debussy and the Theater,* 112–14, argues that an unlabeled sketch page in the Bibliothèque nationale represents this imagined African satyr music from *La Chute de la maison Usher,* citing certain orientalisms in the sketch (tam-tam and cymbal beats).

27. The transcriptions appear in Orledge, ibid., 115–16. There was also a reconstruction-recomposition of this scene in the edition of the opera by Juan Allende-Blin (Paris: Jobert, 1979); the autograph sources are listed in Orledge, *Debussy and the Theater,* 354, note 24.

28. So strong was the association of A with the pastoral mode that minor talents were inspired to exploit the code; in 1922 Gottfried Bohnenblust, an amateur German poet of small literary gifts, published a collection of pastoral poems—including classical forms such as eclogues as well as verses entitled "Siciliane"—under the title *A Dur.*

29. Jankélévitch, *La musique et l'ineffable,* 129: "La réalité musicale est toujours ailleurs, comme les paysages évoqués, chez Gabriel Fauré, après une expression évasive et amphibolique; cette géographie pneumatique où l'alibi estompe et brouille sans cesse le repérage univoque des lieux, elle rend fondante et fuyante toute localisation: ne disions-nous pas que la musique, phénomène temporel, refuse en général toute spatialisation?"

30. This snapping G♮ is also heard within the faded serenade (in the piano part of mm. 35–36, at "[et] leurs molles ombres [bleues]"). The coincidence of this G♮, prefiguring the end stage with the image of "shadows," is perhaps the only overt mapping of word to musical gesture in the song.

31. Cited in Roger Nichols and Richard Langham-Smith, *Claude Debussy: Pelléas et Mélisande* (Cambridge: Cambridge University Press, 1989), 4. Raising the question of sound effects in *Pelléas,* Friedrich Kittler notes that Debussy's music constitutes a new "optics and acoustics" of opera adumbrated in *Tristan,* one in which orchestral sounds become "ambivalent to the extent that a fundamental European distinction between tones and noises, music and nature, becomes blurred." He reads Debussy's musical sound effects for Maeterlinck's play as "gramophonic" and associates them with Debussy's own discussions of sound and cinema technology in the essay "Music in the Open Air." See "Opera in the Light of Technology," in Beate Allert, ed., *Languages of Visuality: Crossings Between Science, Art, Politics, and Literature* (Detroit: Wayne State University Press, 1996), 73–85, especially 80–81.

32. "Mes longs cheveux descendent" was the original text of Mélisande's tower song in Maeterlinck's play, though an alternative text, "Les trois soeurs aveugles" ("The King's Three Blind Daughters," in Jack Mackail's translation), was substituted for the premiere in London. This text was ultimately set in English by Gabriel Fauré for an 1898 London performance, where it was transposed from the Tower scene (act 3 scene 2) to act 3 scene 1, where Mélisande sings while spinning, à la Gretchen. See Jean-Michel Nectoux, "Le *Pelléas* de Fauré," *Revue de Musicologie* 67, no. 2 (1981): 180.

33. *L'éternel retour,* dir. Jean Delannoy, screenplay by Jean Cocteau, music by Georges Auric, starring Jean Marais (Patrice) and Madeleine Sologne (Nathalie).

34. Perhaps there was some element of autobiography in play when Jean Cocteau makes Jean Marais so distinctly an object of desire, a source of beautiful music.

35. Adorno made this claim in 1928 in "Nadelkurven," *Musikblätter des Anbruch* 10 (February 1928): 47–50; "Curves of the Needle," trans. Thomas Y. Levin, *October* 55 (winter 1990): 48–55. The male voice is praised for its ability to survive recording intact, since the male subject is identical to his voice, while the female voice is diminished by subtraction when her body is erased: her voice and body are linked. For consistent treatments of this theme see the essays in

Dunn and Jones, *Embodied Voices,* many of them scholarly offshoots of Silverman's *The Acoustic Mirror.* Silverman analyzes embodiment in both the filmic habit of binding female voice to its visual origins through synchronization, and burdening it with excess acoustic grain (in the form of accents, breathiness, and the like) that reinvokes its physical origins.

36. Maeterlinck's substitute song text, the more formally poetic "Les trois soeurs aveugles" with its multiple verses, suggests the contrary: that Mélisande is simply the medium for a priori text, that she therefore occupies a more conventionally feminine position.

37. Pelléas's singing voice is not a "voice-object": the aesthetic appeal of the beautiful singing voice is in fact a manner of veil, which shields us from anxiety about the voice-object (that is, the voice of the "Other"). See Reinhart Meyer-Kalkus, "Jacques Lacans Lehre von der Stimme als Triebobjeckt," in Wolfgang Raible, ed., *Kulturelle Perspektiven auf Schrift und Schreibprozesse* (Tübingen: Gunter Narr Verlag, 1995), 259–307, especially 304–7.

38. Cited in Jarocinski, *Debussy,* 24.

39. Jankélévitch, *La musique et l'ineffable,* 130.

40. This is what Kittler implies when he writes that "fin de siècle opera is already film theater" ("Opera in the Light of Technology," 81).

41. Christian Metz, *The Imaginary Signifier: Psychoanalysis and the Cinema* (Bloomington: Indiana University Press, 1982), part 1, "The Imaginary Signifier," trans. Ben Brewster, 67.

42. Ibid.

43. Ibid., 66.

44. In Jankélévitch, *Debussy et le mystère;* see preface, note 3.

Chapter 5

1. Luc-Vincent Thiéry, cited in Richard A. Etlin, *The Architecture of Death: The Transformation of the Cemetery in Eighteenth-Century Paris* (Cambridge and London: MIT Press, 1984), 204.

2. See Mark K. Deming, "Le Panthéon révolutionnaire," in *Le Panthéon, symbole des révolutions: De l'église de la nation au temple des grands hommes* (Montreal and Paris: Picard Éditeur, 1989), 142–50.

3. Barry Bergdoll cites a letter to this effect written by the Prince de Clary in 1810 and describes unrealized plans from the early nineteenth century to replace the wooden sarcophagi of both Rousseau and Voltaire with marble tombs ("Le Panthéon/Sainte-Geneviève au XIXe siècle: La Monumentalité à l'épreuve des révolutions idéologiques," in *Le Panthéon,* 188).

4. "Die beiden Sarkophage, in welchen *Rousseau's* und *Voltaire's* Reste ruhen, stehen, in der Mitte der Gewölbe, einander gegenüber. Sie sind von Holz, und mit schlechten Basreliefs getäfelt: künftig werden sie von schwarzem Marmor verfertiget werden. Auf *Rousseau's* Tomba steht die einfach schöne Grabschrift,

von dem Grabe auf der Pappelinsel in Ermenonville: *Ici repose l'homme de la nature et de la vérité.* An den beiden schmalen Seiten des Sarkophag's ragt eine Todtenhand, eine Fackel haltend, wie aus dem Grabe hervor. Es ist eine etwas schwerfällige Versinnlichung der Idee der durch den Philosophen nach seinem Tode gestifteten Aufkärung—welche von dem Dichter gut benutzt werden kann, aber kein Vorwurf für die bildende Kunst ist. Diese Hand aus dem Grabe erregt mehr Grauen, als wohltätige Empfindungen" (Friedrich Johann Lorenz Meyer, *Fragmente aus Paris im IVten Jahr der französischen Revolution* [Hamburg, 1797], 179–80). Meyer uses the word *Sarkophag* interchangeably with *Tomba,* an interesting choice: sarcophagus is a grim word, signifying a tomb made of some substance thought to be capable of consuming the flesh of corpses.

5. Etlin, *Architecture of Death,* 204.

6. Ibid. Etlin summarizes one contemporary report "that in the park at Ermenonville, the person 'to whom France owed the birth of its natural taste in gardens' was given 'not a monument but an eternal tomb.'" The distinction is between a monument as an architectural object, subject to wear and perhaps not physically containing any body, and an Arcadian garden-tomb that, like all things that occupy pastoral spaces, exists in a fictional past, immune to passing time.

7. "Le monument, *monumentum,* offroit aux yeux quelque chose de plus magnifique que le simple sépulchre; c'étoit l'édifice construit pour conserver la mémoire d'une personne, sans aucune solemnité funebre. On pouvoit ériger plusieurs monuments à l'honneur d'une personne; mais on ne pouvoit avoir qu'un seul *tombeau*" (Louis Chevalier de Jaucourt, "Tombeau," in *Encyclopédie ou dictionnaire raisonné des sciences, des arts et des métiers* vol. 16 [Neufchâtel, 1765; facsimile reprint, Stuttgart/Bad Cannstatt: Friedrich Fromann Verlag, 1967], 398).

8. Jacques Dugast, "Avant-propos," in *Tombeaux et monuments,* ed. Jacques Dugast and Michèle Touret (Rennes: Presses de l'Université Rennes, 1992), 8.

9. On the musical tombeau see Michel Brenet, "Les 'Tombeaux' en musique," *La Revue musicale* 3 (1903): 568–75 and 631–38; Charles van den Borren, "Esquisse d'une histoire des 'Tombeaux' musicaux," *Académie royale de Belgique: Bulletin de la classe des beaux-arts* 43 (1961): 253–74; Clemens Goldberg, *Stilisierung als Kunstvermittelnder Prozeß: Die französischen Tombeau-Stücke im 17. Jahrhundert* (Laaber: Laaber-Verlag, 1987); and Marie-Claire Mussat, "Le Tombeau dans la musique du XXIème siècle," in *Tombeaux,* ed. Dugast and Touret, 133–44.

10. Thomas Edison, "The Phonograph and Its Future," *North American Review,* May/June 1878, 527–36.

11. Monique Rollin, "Les Tombeaux de Robert de Visée," *Bulletin de la société d' étude du XVIIième siècle* 34 (March 1957): 76.

12. By 1903, Brenet had already proposed a prehistory for the instrumental tombeau in ancient customs of funerary songs, Klagelieder, threnodies, and works that translate mourning *for* the dead into "the abstract language" of pure music ("Les 'Tombeaux' en musique," 569–71). He also suggested that tombeaux orig-

inated as pieces played during funeral masses, instrumental translations of laments that would have been interdicted by the Council of Trent's prohibition of nonliturgical texts; this explanation is reiterated by Mussat ("Le Tombeau," 133). Van den Borren's "Esquisse d'une histoire" transverses most of Western music history, from medieval laments and "plaintes," to construct a similar vocal music ancestry for baroque instrumental tombeaux.

13. The issue of vocality in French lute tombeaux is discussed by Goldberg, who cites baroque theoretical doctrines of musical rhetoric with their analogies between music and speech (*Stilisierung*, 124–32). For him, the tombeau is a genre in which inert musical material becomes somehow immaterial (hence, immortal), a process he connects to techniques of variation within the conventional forms.

14. Harold Bloom, *A Map of Misreading* (Oxford: Oxford University Press, 1975), 102. Bloom refers to his "revisionary ratio" *apophrades*, the return of precursors, in terms of Freud's mechanism; it seems hardly possible to speak of the tombeau without imagining its place in Bloom's paranoid scheme, since in *The Anxiety of Influence*, published two years earlier, this "ratio" is more dramatically baptized "The Return of the Dead." But tombeaux, as conscious bows to precursors, would be categorically excluded by Bloom's theory, since the influences about which poets become anxious are always unconscious and unacknowledged ones.

15. Denis Gaultier, *La Rhétorique des dieux*, ed. David J. Buch (Madison: A-R Editions, 1990), 19.

16. This motif of tombstones that speak, *saxa loquuntur*, is derived from classical Latin poetry. Its musical implications were noted by psychoanalyst Theodor Reik, who was himself obsessed with music as a form of memory and autobiography. Philippe Lacoue-Labarthe explores Reik's loquacious tombstones in "The Echo of the Subject," in his *Typography*, trans. Christopher Fynsk (Stanford: Stanford University Press), 176–77. Goldberg sees the animated tombstone reenacted in musical tombeaux when musical "material" is transformed into individual "expression" (*Stilisierung*, 117–18).

17. Images of Orpheus are implicit in the choice of the lute as a predominant instrument for early tombeaux, especially given the capacity for translating emotion ascribed to the instrument (Goldberg, *Stilisierung*, 117–18).

18. Gaultier, *La Rhétorique des dieux*, 19.

19. Ibid., 70.

20. Van den Borren, "Esquisse d'une histoire," 273.

21. See Scott Messing, *Neoclassicism in Music: From the Genesis of the Concept through the Schoenberg/Stravinsky Polemic* (Ann Arbor, Mich., and London: UMI Research Press, 1988), and Richard Taruskin, "Back to Whom? Neoclassicism as Ideology," *19th-Century Music* 26 (1993): 290; and the discussion of Ravel's *Tombeau de Couperin* in Martha M. Hyde, "Neoclassic and Anachronistic Impulses in Twentieth-Century Music," *Music Theory Spectrum* 18 (1996): 206–10.

22. See Richard Taruskin, "The Dark Side of Modern Music," *New Republic* 5 (September 1988): 28–34; "Back to Whom?" 286–302; and his review of Kevin

Korsyn's "Towards a New Poetics of Musical Influence" and Joseph N. Straus's *Remaking the Past: Musical Modernism and the Influence of the Tonal Tradition, Journal of the American Musicological Society* 46 (1993): 114–38.

23. Vladimir Jankélévitch, *Ravel* (Paris: Editions du Seuil, 1956), trans. Margaret Crosland (New York and London: John Calder, 1959), 80. All subsequent citations, unless noted, refer to the English translation.

24. Ibid., 156. Quite early on, Ravel was characterized in terms borrowed from the music hall as a prestidigitator whose compositional means seemed invisible; see Roland-Manuel, "Maurice Ravel ou l'esthétique de l'imposture," *La Revue musicale* 6 (April 1925): 16–21.

25. La Mettrie, *Machine Man and Other Writings* (see Chapter 3, note 34).

26. Among commentaries on automata as philosophical and literary phenomena, Joachim Gessinger's *Auge und Ohr: Studien zur Erforschung der Sprachen am Menschen 1700–1850* (Berlin and New York: Walter de Gruyter, 1994) represents a gold standard of exhaustiveness; Gessinger documents the collision of linguistics and automaton mechanics imaginatively and at length.

27. See Béatrice Didier, *La Musique des lumières* (Paris: Presses universitaires de France, 1985), 19–39 and 242–60, on the Encyclopédists' notions of theatrical representation, and 338–75, on Diderot's phenomenology of musical performance, particularly in *Le Neveu de Rameau*.

28. Stanley Cavell, *The Claim of Reason: Wittgenstein, Skepticism, Morality, and Tragedy* (Oxford: Oxford University Press, 1979), 401–11.

29. Liselotte Sauer dates the shift in mood to the later texts of Jean Paul; see *Marionetten, Maschinen, Automaten,* (Bonn: Bouvier Verlag, 1983), 20–26.

30. "Menschen sind Maschinen der Engel," in Jean Paul, *Sämtliche Werke*, pt. 2, 1:1031.

31. "Otez ces professeurs du clavessin, privez-les du papier rayé & de l'usage des notes, & vous en faites des corps sans âme, des êtres inanimés qui ne tiennent à la société que par leur individu. Comme ils tirent tous leurs mouvements de la mesure, il faut ne leur parler que mesure. Lorsque je vis pour la première fois à Venise le célebre Anf. je crus voir un automate, une machine montée sur des fils d'archal. Qu'on imagine un homme d'un autre monde qui ignore ce qui passe dans celui-ci, qui ne dit rien, qui ne fait rien, qui ne connaît rien, qu'on ne peut entretenir sur rien, qui n'a ni expression ni sentimens que ceux qu'il tire des croches, des cromes, & des semicromes. Comme il avait laissé son âme sur le tact de son clavessin, je le priai de la reprendre, c'est à dire d'exécuter une ariette de son composition, afin que je pusse connaître son existence; mais il ne voulut exister, ainsi je ne m'entretiens ce jour là qu'avec son cadavre" (Ange Goudar, *La Brigandage de la musique italienne* [Paris, 1777; facsimile reprint, Geneva: Minkoff, 1972], 84).

32. Hence Alex Ross, disliking Evgeny Kissin, likens him to a machine: "The gestures of the grand style were in place—the left hand coming in just before the right, like antique clockwork—but there was no personality driving them. Kissin reminds me of one of those high-tech reproducing pianos that can summon the approximate ghost of Rachmaninoff from a piano roll" ("The Chosen," *New Yorker*, 29 March 1999: 115).

33. This parallel evolution is beautifully described in Paul Metzner, *Crescendo of the Virtuoso: Spectacle, Skill, and Self-Promotion in Paris During the Age of the Revolution* (Berkeley: University of California Press, 1998), 160–210.

34. G.W.F. Hegel, *Aesthetics: Lectures on Fine Art,* trans. T. M. Knox, vol. 2 (Oxford: Clarendon Press, 1975), 955.

35. Ibid., 956.

36. The prescription for an ideal performance—"obedient" yet not merely "mechanical"—sounds like Gorodish's prescription for the perfect caviar sandwich in Jean Beneix's *Diva* (1981): "The baguette. The knife. Not too thin, but not too broad. And the bread itself. Fresh. But not too fresh."

37. See Richard Taruskin, "Stravinsky Lite (Even *The Rite*)," in *Text and Act,* 360–63.

38. Hegel, *Aesthetics* vol. 2, 956–57.

39. "[É]taient-ils pour cela musiciens? Non: mais des automates en musique, dont tout la mérite est de battre des petits morceaux de bois ou d'ébene qui rendent des sons" (Goudar, *La Brigandage,* 110). Goudar's association of automata with the defects of Italian music continues with his distinction between "la machine harmonieuse" and "l'intelligence harmonique" (115).

40. "Mit Recht vergleicht man Wunderkinder den Kometen. Jedes, das da geboren wird, verstört die musikalische und nicht bloß musikalische Ordnung in ihrem Bewußtsein von Würde, Autonomie, und Freiheit" (Theodor Adorno, "Drehorgel-Stücke" [1934], reprinted in *Gesammelte Schriften,* vol. 18, 43).

41. Annette Richards cites contemporary accounts characterizing the child Mozart as an "automatic genius" and reflecting conventional associations between prodigies and automata. Mozart, she indicates, went somehow beyond the mechanical in his effect, becoming not so much machine as aeolian harp, played (as it were) by divine nature. See "Automatic Genius," 381–82.

42. There is no early-nineteenth-century tradition for hearing the movement this way. Arnold Schering reads Beethoven's next symphony, the Eighth, as a confrontation with various mechanical musical instruments devised by Johann Nepomuk Maelzel, including the Panharmonicon, a form of Orchestrion, and the metronome (*Humor, Heldentum, Tragik bei Beethoven* [Strassbourg and Kehl: Librairie Heitz, 1955], 13–17). The general theme of Beethoven and machines is explored by Ulrich Schmitt, who links speed in performance, abruptness, and a sense of dramatic process to industrial novelties of the early nineteenth century, including steam propulsion, railroads, and the technology of dioramas and panoramas (*Revolution im Konzertsaal: Zur Beethoven-Rezeption im 19. Jahrhundert* [Mainz: Schott, 1990]). Beethoven's steam coffee machine is *the* critical appliance in a new hermeneutics of Beethoven's work.

43. See Heather Hadlock, "Return of the Repressed: The Prima Donna from Hoffmann's *Tales* to Offenbach's *Contes*," *Cambridge Opera Journal* 6 (1994): 221–43.

44. For a response to such critiques see Dolar, "The Object Voice," 7–31.

45. Ibid., 19.

46. C. M. Gabriel, "Machine parlante de M. Faber," *Journal de physique théorique et appliquée* 8 (1879): 274–75. Faber's machine had a vibrating ivory reed mounted in its "throat" to serve as its vocal chords, which suggests less than perfect flex-

ibility (see Henry Seymour, *The Reproduction of Sound* [London: W. B. Tattersall, 1918], 8). By 1918 Faber's machine was mythical; Seymour vaguely dates its creation to 1860. Gessinger cites a report in the *Leipziger Allgemeine Zeitung* of 1847 that refers to singing and is possibly an allusion to Faber's machine: "dasselbe spricht in mehreren Sprachen, flüstert, lacht, und singt" (*Auge und Ohr*, 629). See also Thomas L. Hankins and Robert J. Silverman, *Instruments and the Imagination* (Princeton: Princeton University Press, 1995), 214–16.

47. Seymour, *Reproduction of Sound*, 9.

48. On Chladni's experiments and the prehistory of the phonograph see Thomas Y. Levin, "For the Record: Adorno on Music in the Age of Its Technological Reproducibility," *October*, no. 55 (1990): 38–41.

49. Ibid., 23–47.

50. Levin, "For the Record," 33. Levin connects Adorno's ideas on gramophonic inscription to other modernist notions concerning utopian forms of writing or expression, such as cinema as "universal language." This modernist trope could be set against Enlightenment fascination with alternative "universal" alphabets that looked like the sounds they represented, such as the "écriture organique" proposed by Charles de Brosses in the *Traité de la formation méchanique des langues* (Paris, 1765). De Brosses devised an alphabet that would iconically reproduce articulation and intonation patterns of phonemes. On such alphabets see Gessinger, *Auge und Ohr*, 633–719.

51. Levin, "For the Record," 38.

52. Ibid., 33.

53. Adorno, "Drehorgel-Stücke," 38; on this essay, see Levin, "For the Record," 33–34.

54. In 1925, the year of *L'Enfant et les sortilèges*, Roland-Manuel referred to Vaucanson in discussing *L'Heure espagnol*, where people are given the attributes of marionettes, while automata are ensouled, as by "the great eighteenth-century inventor Vaucanson, who knew how to transform gearboxes into living material." See Roland-Manuel, "L'Esthétique de l'imposture," 20–21. On Vaucanson and his several musical automata, as well as his famous mechanical duck (which could digest food), see Cottom, "The Work of Art," 52–64; and Metzner, *Crescendo of the Virtuoso*, 162–67.

55. The best English description of both automata appears in Alfred Chapuis, *History of the Musical Box and of Mechanical Music*, trans. Joseph E. Roesch (Summit, N.J.: Music Box Society International, 1980), 32–36 and 49–53. See also Gessinger, *Auge und Ohr*, 391–409.

56. Chapuis, *History of the Musical Box*, 33. For an illustration of the mechanism, see Alfred Chapuis and Edmond Droz, *Le Monde des automates: Étude historique et scientifique*, vol. 2 (Paris: E. Gélis, 1928; reprint, Geneva: Slatkine, 1984), 150, reproduced in Gessinger, *Auge und Ohr*, 428.

57. On the shift from androids to boxes see Gessinger, *Auge und Ohr*, 620–31. Singing androids constituted a minor literary theme in nineteenth-century novels, as in Villiers de l'Isle-Adam's *L'Eve future*, whose heroine contains a phonograph. Kittler, *Discourse Networks*, 347–49 analyzes the novel.

58. On the development of the first music boxes both as mechanisms and as objets d'art, see Chapuis, *History of the Musical Box,* 135–245. Musical watches or clocks in the eighteenth century had delicate bells as instruments; manufacture of music boxes with metal combs is dated from 1796. See also Arthur W.S.G. Ord-Hume, *Clockwork Music: An Illustrated History of Mechanical Musical Instruments from the Music Box to the Pianola, from Automaton Lady Virginal Players to Orchestrion* (London: George Allen and Unwin, 1973), 63–102. Ord-Hume reproduces early-nineteenth-century posters for eighteenth-century musical automata, indicating that, as public attractions, such devices remained popular even as the boxes began to compete for attention (see 42–43).

59. Article in the *Teutscher Merkur* of 1784, cited in Gessinger, *Auge und Ohr,* 620.

60. For illustrations see Chapuis and Droz, *Le Monde des automates* vol. 2, 150, 156. Gessinger discusses Mical, von Kempelen, Christian Gottlob Kratzenstein (whose experiments with building an artificial *vox humana* device fed into the prehistory of the speaking machines), a series of other "talking statues" from the Enlightenment, and the nineteenth-century end products of this history (*Auge und Ohr,* 398–434, 537–67, 586–600, and 627–31).

61. See, for instance, the illustrations in Harvey N. Roehl, *The Player Piano Treasury* (Vestal, N.Y.: Vestal Press, 1961), 83–219.

62. Advertisement from 1902 for the Pianola piano-player, reproduced in ibid., 7–8.

63. Ibid., 35–37.

64. Roehl reprints an article from *Scientific American* of November 1927, which marvels how "manifestations of the soul of the artist are being analyzed for mechanical reproduction through the record music roll," and how what seems to be a perfect performance will, "when submitted to the tests of an uncompromising measuring machine," reveal "grossly faulty" playing (ibid., 61–64). Reengineering was common: mistakes could be restenciled, and artists could dictate changes after hearing the unedited roll.

65. Literature on the technology of reproducing pianos is extensive. For a review of the Welte Mignon see Peter Hagmann, *Das Welte-Mignon Klavier, die Welte-Philharmonie-Orgel, und die Anfänge der Reproduktion von Musik* (Bern, Frankfurt am Main, and New York: Peter Lang, 1984); for shorter histories of reproducing pianos, as well as technical details of the inscription process, see the following articles in *The Encyclopedia of Automatic Musical Instruments,* ed. Q. David Bowers (Vestal, N.Y.: Vestal Press, 1972): David L. Saul, "Reproducing Pianos," 273–310; Claes O. Friberg, "Hupfeld Reproducing Pianos," 311–17; David L. Saul, "Understanding the Welte Mignon," 319–23; and Ben M. Hall, "How Is It Possible? The Welte Technique Explained," 327–38.

66. Advertisement for the Welte Mignon from 1928, cited in Bowers, *Encyclopedia,* 71.

67. Cited by Richard C. Simonton, "A Personal Experience with Welte," in Bowers, *Encyclopedia,* 324.

68. Jankélévitch, *Ravel,* 78.

69. Charles Baudelaire, *The Philosophy of Toys,* trans. Paul Keegan (London: Syrens, 1994), 14.

70. Jankélévitch, *Ravel*, 78.

71. Ibid., 79.

72. Ibid.

73. Ibid., 82.

74. Ibid., 80, 81.

75. Ibid.

76. See Mário Vieira de Carvalho, "From Opera to 'Soap Opera': On Civilizing Processes, the Dialectic of Enlightenment and Postmodernity," *Theory, Culture, and Society* 12, no. 2 (1995): 41–61; and Tomlinson, *Metaphysical Song*, 134–42.

77. The transcription was published by Arbie Orenstein ("Some Unpublished Music and Letters by Maurice Ravel," *Music Forum* 3 [1973]: 330–31) and has been discussed by Messing (*Neoclassicism in Music*, 50–52) and Hyde ("Neoclassic and Anachronistic Impulses," 206–11).

78. See Žižek, "Robert Schumann: The Romantic Anti-Humanist," in *The Plague of Fantasies* (London and New York: Verso, 1997), 199.

79. Wilfrid Mellers, *François Couperin and the French Classical Tradition*, rev. ed. (London and Boston: Faber and Faber, 1987), 468–69.

80. Ibid., 471–72.

81. Arthur W.S.G. Ord-Hume, *Barrel Organ: The Story of the Mechanical Organ and Its Repair* (South Brunswick and New York: A. S. Barnes, 1978), 254–61. An illustration of this Musette is found in Bowers, *Encyclopedia*, 769.

82. See Arthur W.S.G. Ord-Hume, *Pianola: The History of the Self-Playing Piano* (London: George Allen and Unwin, 1984), 278 and 319. Plate 148 illustrates a modern player piano manufactured in the 1960s by Aeolian, also named Musette.

83. Jankélévitch, *Ravel*, 133.

84. Jankélévitch calls it a musette (*Ravel*, 127); he also characterizes the scene as a Pastorale (71, 109).

85. Walter Benjamin, "A Glimpse into the World of Children's Books" (1926), reprinted in *Walter Benjamin: Selected Writings,* ed. Marcus Bullock and Michael W. Jennings, trans. Rodney Livingstone (Cambridge: Harvard University Press, 1996), 1:435.

86. Jankélévitch, *Ravel*, 115.

87. Baudelaire, *The Philosophy of Toys*, 24. Possibly, Colette in creating the Child in *L'Enfant et les sortilèges* was drawing on Baudelaire's prose. But perhaps she was simply familiar with the habits of small children.

88. See Charles Rosen, *The Romantic Generation*, 11–12.

89. Žižek, "Robert Schumann," 203–6.

90. Ibid., 207.

91. Ibid., 208.

92. Jankélévitch, *Ravel*, 132.

93. Žižek, "Robert Schumann," 205.

94. Bloom, *A Map of Misreading*, 103.

95. Žižek, "Robert Schumann," 205.

96. Roger Shattuck, *Forbidden Experiment: The Wild Boy of Aveyron* (New York: Farrar, Strauss, Giroux: 1980), 91–119 and 192–207.

97. "Jean de la Porte Napolitain, Auteur d'un Traité de la Magie naturelle, & grand Musicien, dis que c'est par le moyen de la Musique artificielle, qu'on peut apprendre à un muet à parler & à chanter, quoique sourd de naissance, dont il a fait plusieurs experiences, ainsi qu'il l'enseigne, en disant qu'il n'y a, en jouant de quelque Instrument de musique, qu'à en faire mordre la manche à un sourd, & que sur le champ on le voit tressaillir de joye, & on conçoit aisément qu'il entend; il prétend que les sons se portent au cerveau par les deux orifices que nous avons au dessus du palais, & se font entendre; . . . tous ces faits ne paroîtront point surprenans à ceux qui ont quelques notions de l'Art mécanique, puisque, par ces principes, on peut faire chanter des figures inanimées, & faire jouer des Instrumens tout seuls, comme je l'ai déjà dit" (Pierre Bourdelet and Pierre Bonnet, *Histoire de la musique et ses effets* [Paris, 1715; facsimile reprint, Graz: Akademische Druck- und Verlagsanstalt, 1966], 59).

98. Walter Benjamin, "The Work of Art in the Age of Mechanical Reproduction," in *Illuminations*, ed. Hannah Arendt, trans. Harry Zohn (New York: Schocken Books, 1969), 228–34.

∞ SOURCES FOR FIGURES

Figure 1.1. Gustave Moreau, *Orphée*. Reproduced by permission of the Musée d'Orsay, Paris.

Figure 1.2. Frontispiece to Athanasius Kircher, *Phonurgia nova* (1673).

Figure 2.1. "Triumph, du edles Paar." From Max Slevogt, *Die Zauberflöte: Randzeichnungen zu Mozarts Handschrift* (Berlin: Paul Cassirer, 1918).

Figure 2.2. "Die Strahlen der Sonne vertreiben die Nacht." From Slevogt, *Die Zauberflöte.*

Figure 2.3 "The Wizard King," illustration by H. J. Ford. Reproduced from *The Yellow Fairy Book* (London and New York: Longmans, Green, 1894).

Figure 2.4. Ignaz Alberti, portrait of Emmanuel Schikaneder from the original libretto for *The Magic Flute* (1791). Reproduced by permission of the Österreichisches Theatermuseum Vienna.

Figure 2.5. Horace Vernet, *La flûte enchantée*. Lithograph by Gottfried Engelmann, for a frontispiece to *La flûte enchantée*, piano-vocal score (Paris: Schlesinger, 1820).

Figure 5.1. Rousseau's Tomb. Photograph: Lee Mitchell.

Figure 5.2. Title Page, "The Song of Mister Phonograph." New York: G. Schirmer, 1878.

Figure 5.3. The Needham Piano Player. Reproduced from Harvey Roehl, *The Piano Player Treasury* (Vestal N.Y.: Vestal Press, 1961).

Figure 5.4. The Telektra Piano Player. Reproduced from Roehl, *The Piano Player Treasury*.

Figure 5.5. Phantom Hands from a Welte advertisement. Reproduced from Roehl, *The Piano Player Treasury*.

Figure 5.6. André Hellé, watercolor for the frontispiece to *L'Enfant et les sortilèges*. Private collection. Reproduced by permission of the owner.

Figure 5.7. Uncovering Rousseau's Tomb. Reproduced by permission of the Bibliothèque nationale, Paris (collection Estampes).

∞ INDEX